THE
HEAVY
DANCERS

Beyond the Cold War
The Making of the English Working Class
Whigs and Hunters
William Morris: Romantic to Revolutionary
Albion's Fatal Tree

THE HEAVY DANCERS

E. P. THOMPSON

PANTHEON BOOKS
NEW YORK

Library of Congress Cataloging in Publication Data

Thompson, E. P. (Edward Palmer), 1924–
    The heavy dancers.

    1. United States—Foreign relations—Soviet Union—Addresses, essays, lectures. 2. Soviet Union—Foreign relations—United States—Addresses, essays, lectures. 3. Great Britain—Foreign relations—1945-   -Addresses, essays, lectures. I. Title.
E183.8.S65T48 1985 327.73047 84-18978
ISBN 0-394-72895-5 (pbk.)

CONTENTS

ACKNOWLEDGMENTS

My thanks and acknowledgments are due to the journals and publishing houses where some of these materials appeared before (sometimes in slightly different forms): the *Guardian* (London), *Il Manifesto,* the *Nation, New Society, New Statesman,* the *Spectator,* Spokesman Books, Verso/NLB. Some passages of the final sections of 'Double Exposure' have appeared in *END Journal* (October 1984) and in a fuller essay on 'Star Wars' in the *Nation,* 4 March 1985. I cannot begin to list all those who have helped me in this work, including colleagues in the European and American peace movements. But I must thank in particular two helpful and long-suffering publishers, André Schiffrin and Martin Eve; two helpful editors, Victor Navasky and Paul Barker; Dorothy Thompson; Evy King; Cathy Fitzpatrick; W. H. Ferry; and Jan Kavan (and the Palach Press).

E.P.T.

PUBLISHER'S NOTE: The American edition of *The Heavy Dancers* is an amalgam of two separate books published in Great Britain in 1985. The first part of the book consists of the political and historical essays that constitute the first part of the British edition of *The Heavy Dancers*. Excluded are a small number of essays of primarily British interest, and a group of literary essays that Pantheon will publish separately next year. The second part, *Double Exposure*, was published separately in England, as a postscript to *The Heavy Dancers*. We have included this in its entirety in this book, unchanged, and this will explain to the reader the occasional references in it to *The Heavy Dancers* as if it were a separate volume.

PROPHECY

Alas the long sad generations
Of machines!
Bit by bit that dark star
The Pentagon
Is crowded with devices
That speak in unknown tongues.
They take over the conference rooms,
The General's Washroom,
Finally: the Little Chapel
Of the B-52s . . . ,

And now no one knows what they are talking about.
The human concepts given them long ago
Change.
Something happened to the concept of honor
When the oil over-heated;
A bit of dust on a diamond connection
Has wiped out security;
At certain temperatures even the idea of Patriotism
Freezes.

And so it is that this morning the Generals and Bankers
Are discovered, carrying the water,
Carrying fetishes and the colored earth up to the steps
Where now, painted, with feathers stuck in their hair,
They dance heavily: heavily,
Heavily calling out to the Unknown Ones inside.

                                        Thomas McGrath

FOREWORD

The heavy dancers are the image-conscious public persons who crowd the media of the world, summoning up the ancient spirits of the tribe as they prepare us for the ultimate war. I have taken the image, with permission, from the fine poem by my friend, the American poet Thomas McGrath, which is printed on the preceding page. (It will be found in the collection *Passages Toward the Dark*, published by the Copper Canyon Press.)

The more that the heavy dancers condition our minds for war, the more anxious they are to come before the public and assure it that they are devoted to the cause of peace. The peace movement has at least had this effect—it has made them more consummate in their hypocrisy. They command the present, and I send this book to press in despondent mood.

This book is a sequel to the collection published by Pantheon in 1982 as *Beyond the Cold War*. Several of the papers published here were written as contributions to peace campaigning in Britain or West Europe (with the Campaign for Nuclear Disarmament—CND—or with END, European Nuclear Disarmament) or as a guest of different advocates of peaceful American opinion. 'The Defence of Britain' was written in a fit of fury through two nights and one day as a futile attempt to intervene in the media-conducted babble of the British general election of 1983.

Events in the past two years have forced onto the agenda of peace some issues that go beyond the plain demands for the renunciation (or freezing) of nuclear weapons systems. The Western peace movement has had its own problems of diplomacy with the East. Dialogue between citizens across the blocs has been made more difficult by security measures. And the underlying political question of the division of Europe, and indeed of the world itself, can be evaded no longer. At the same time, the continuing Soviet military actions in Afghanistan, and United States support for terrorists in Nicaragua, have demonstrated once more the ways in which the Cold War between the blocs is exported as a hot war into the Third World. It becomes more and more clear that the third way of peace must become a global way, putting together alliances between peaceful opinion in the metropolitan powers, West and East, with forces making for self-realisation in the hungry 'South'.

Hence this book examines political issues more complex than in my earlier writings. When I first set aside my trade as historian five years ago to take my part in the peace movement, we had to labour for a year or more to break through the 'consensual' complacency as to nuclear weapons and their implications. There followed a year or so in which the response (except from the direct apologists of nuclear strategies) was comparatively benign. Some of the Western media found us to be well-intentioned, if misguided, while the Soviet-bloc media found us to be 'men and women of goodwill', even if our arguments were 'incorrect'.

That false spring was blown away as abruptly as was an earlier spring in Prague. Through 1983 and 1984 the peace movements were targeted by Western governments as witting or unwitting agencies of Soviet diplomacy, while those of us who expressed criticisms of Soviet militarism and support for independent peace groups in the East found our arguments suppressed or falsified in the mainline Western media at the same time as we were denounced in the Soviet Union and the Warsaw bloc.

When I came to prepare this collection for the press it occurred to me that some of the matters discussed in these pages conceal a 'hidden narrative' of the non-aligned peace movement in the past five years. This narrative has been hidden simply because the actors have been too busy to write it. It concerns the origins of a part of that movement, especially in West Europe; the increasingly sharp attacks (and calumnies) visited upon it by orthodox Western critics; the difficulties in attempting direct citizen communication between West and East; and the sharp response to these attempts which has come from the official Communist apparatus.

While some part of this record is known to many active members of West European peace movements and to the internationally minded circles in the American movement, only a few hundred people have been centrally involved in these events. It seemed to be time to make the record more public. The longest essay in this book, 'Double Exposure', seeks to do this, and it is an introduction and a key to much that follows.

'Double Exposure' is not offered as an objective narrative of these events. No-one is competent to write that yet, and it would require research into numerous national histories. Yet, since something needed to be written, I decided to write it in a more personal way. Because I have exposed my views often in publication, I have drawn upon myself numerous attacks, some of a quite personal nature. Most have been too trivial or too bigoted to answer; yet replying to some of them has given me a gate-of-entry into general questions of history and of ideology of more public interest.

A writer cannot always (without some auto-suppression) argue out difficult points as a representative of some collectivity: a Campaign or a Committee. Political, moral and philosophical matters raised here are not ones as to which organisations take 'positions'. The positions are my own. And where narrative enters in, I have also drawn directly on my own experience. No doubt in that part of 'Double Exposure' which considers East-West relations, a much fuller (and richer) account could be given by those who have had more direct experience of Soviet, Polish, GDR or Czechoslovak exchanges. But in keeping with the manner of the essay I have confined my examples to matters which came most directly within my observation.

This essay—and other essays in this book—should not be taken as expressing the views of 'the peace movement'. But they could not have been written without its support and its collective experience. I acknowledge this with gratitude.

E.P.T.

Worcester, England
March 1985

THE WAR MOVEMENT

▲ THE HEAVY DANCERS* ▲

We all have opinions. We all agree that other people have a right to their own opinions. We even agree that they can try to change our opinions, and march around with banners in the streets.

But how do ideas and opinions change? How can opinions actually have *effect*—upon politics, upon power?

The innovative area of culture—the area in which opinions change, new ideas and values arise—this is the most sensitive, most delicate, the most significant area of all our public life. If we can't or won't change our ideas—if we blunder on with the habits of the past—then society gets snarled up...Or it begins to die from the head downwards. As British society is doing now.

I'm going to argue that this delicate innovative area of our culture is in some ways more manipulated—more marginal-ised—and more threatened than for a long time. New ideas still do arise, but they are either coopted into a manipulated 'consensus' or they're pushed out into a margin of public life, where people can still march around with banners in their hands—but their hands will never be permitted to touch the levers of power.

There are many ways in which new opinions have arisen in the past. Let's look at only two. I'll call these, first, the

---

* Channel 4 'Opinion', 8 November 1982, and *New Society*, 11 November 1982.

activity of specialist intellectual craftsmen or women; second, the traditions of popular 'dissent'.

By the first I mean all those working in the laboratories of the spirit and the mind, with paint or sermon or pen or with thought and scholarship. I'm thinking of artists and philosophers—of Puritan lecturers and preachers—of satirists, polemicists, dramatists.

These people were never, until recently, out on the edge of the nation's discourse. They took a central part in it. It's true that this discourse was narrow and class-bound, and most of the nation were left to listen outside the windows.

But the means of communication which these intellectual craftsmen used didn't require vast capital to buy a newspaper or else access—by kind permission—to broadcasting media. The small printing-press, the pulpit, the stage—these weren't beyond their reach.

Since these voices were part of the nation's discourse, it follows that this discourse—and especially that part of it which we now define as 'politics'—was a different one from today's. These voices didn't only ask *how* questions: how do we fix the Corn Laws? How do we deal with the poor? They also asked *why* and *where* questions. Why—and how far—should we permit the state to have power over citizens? Where is industrialism leading us?

We're scarcely able to ask these questions, in the central arena of 'politics', today. They may be asked still—but they're kept outside there, on the margins. This is partly a result of our amazing advances in technology. A large part of the popular press is bought, and some part of the public mind is bought with it—by the way, the capitalist press *is* capitalist, as recent deals above the heads of editors, journalists and readers have reminded us. The broadcasting media have different problems.

I'm not here to knock broadcasting. The best British television is good. It's much better than most of what is chucked at the public in the United States. What's generally appalling, on British telly—and on all channels—is not only the prejudicial handling of particular political issues, but also the definition of what 'politics' is, and of who has the right to be in that set of frames.

They go on and on, in these frames, to the point of tedium, with the *how* questions only. How do we get inflation down? How should we cut up the defence budget between Trident and the fleet? A national 'consensus' is assumed—but in fact is manufactured daily within these frames—as to questions of *why* and *where*.

For example, all political discourse must assume that we're agreed on the need for economic growth, and the only problem is to find the party which can best fix it. But across the world people are asking questions of *why* and *where?* Do we have the right to pollute this spinning planet any more? To consume and lay waste resources needed by future generations? Might not nil growth be better, if we could divide up the product more wisely and fairly?

These questions can't be asked in that set of frames. They aren't proper 'political' questions. This is partly because of the insufferable arrogance of the major political parties. Long ago they had the audacity, through parliamentary control of broadcasting, to confiscate this part of the nation's intellectual life to themselves. Politics was defined as party politics, and then it was carved up, unequally, between them.

If John Milton or William Hazlitt were still around, and wanted to break in with a question of *why* or *where*, the managers of all the parties would gang up to keep them off. On every side a producer has to skirt around all these fenced-in estates with their party-political gamekeepers and notices saying 'PRIVATE—TRESPASSERS KEEP OUT'.

So we've got this extraordinary situation. The British people aren't totally stupid. Television acknowledges this with the high quality of certain programmes—in sciences, natural history, the arts. But the central national discourse, as to the ends and purposes of social life—this is sub-adult, managed and inane. *Gardeners' Question Time* is more adult and expert than Sir Robin Day's.

A body-politic without an inquiring spirit to ask *where* and *why* is like a car bumming down a motorway with an accelerator pedal but with no more steering than can just keep the car on the lane. We hurtle onward, faster or slower, but we can't take exits, go somewhere else, nor even stop and turn around.

I've mentioned poets. What a remarkable contribution to our nation's political discourse they've made—think of Langland, Chaucer, Marlowe, Milton, Marvell, Pope, Wordsworth, Blake, Shelley, Byron. . . Their voices weren't some extra condiment, like HP sauce, shaken on the British plate. They weren't interior decorators who made the place more pretty. They were part of what life was about, they asked where society was going.

Yeats's poem, *The Second Coming*, for example, is one of the most necessary, and full-throated, political statements of this century. Yet I couldn't begin to translate it into party-political terms—nor could Yeats himself. The poem measures itself prophetically against our tormented century, the bloodiest century in time. It's not about party-political questions, but it questions the values from which any adult politics should start. If you find any politician, whether of right or middle or left, who can't respond to that poem—then *watch him!* or *her!*

I don't suppose that this programme will be able to summon in poets with poems of that high order. This isn't my point. I'm saying that the broadcasting medium ought to be an open thoroughfare for the nation's opinions, just as the coffee-houses were in Dr Johnson's London or the hustings, pulpit and platform have been. And that the 'Trespassers Keep Out' signs ought to be torn down.

I spoke of another innovatory area from which Trespassers —or new ideas—arise. This is the tradition of popular 'dissent'. I'm thinking of the alternative nation, with its own vibrant but unofficial culture—the true Dissent of John Bunyan, but also the political dissent of Cobbett, the Chartists, women's suffrage pioneers.

There have been times when this tradition didn't lay claim to political influence at all. Bunyan and his fellows were proud of their spiritual apartheid in the 'Valley of Humiliation':

This is a Valley that nobody walks in, but those that love a pilgrim's life. . . Then said Mercy, I think I am as well in this Valley as I have been anywhere in my journey. . . I love to be in such places where there is no rattling with coaches, nor rumbling with wheels; me-thinks, here one may, without much molestation, be thinking what he is, whence he came, what he has done, and to what the King has called him. . .

Some of the most humane innovations in our country's life came in, eventually, from this alternative culture. Its influence was brought to bear on the segregated world of Britain's rulers—campaigns for the vote—for rights of press and opinion—the rights of labour and of women.

But whenever this alternative culture has come to the edge of touching power, it has suffered a crisis of identity. Its very reason for existence has been to *resist* power—to throw back its pretensions and intrusions. And power—or 'the establishment'—has endless resources to flatter, corrupt, or co-opt the occasional dissenter who's allowed a place in power's rituals.

This isn't imaginary. It's happened again and again and it's still happening. So political 'dissent' is caught in a double-bind. It exists to protest, and to campaign in alternative ways. If it accepts a place on the official media, then it falls within the official consensual frames. Worse, by permitting a brief image of 'angry' protest, it may seem to prove that opinion is free in this country—it can give legitimacy to the wholesale murder of free opinion which is going on all around.

You may throw up your hands at this point—*nothing* will satisfy these people! But our case is stronger than you may think. It's not only that the questions normally asked within the official frames prejudge the issues, by only asking *how* questions. It's also that the *how* questions themselves are carefully framed and adjusted: only the proper *how* questions can be asked, in the proper way.

For a century the powers of the British state have enlarged and enlarged. The alternative political culture has never touched these places of power. On the contrary the alter-native political culture is watched *from* these places, by covert agencies like MI5 and the Special Branch. By careful procedures of 'positive vetting', applicants for sensitive civil service posts are screened, and persons of independent views or unconventional lifestyles are kept out. In this way are pre-selected for the senior posts in the state only those persons who are subservient to the reasons of power, and resistant to innovation. It's a sieve designed to make sure that only the unoriginal and the mean-spirited get to the top. This is one reason why our country is dying from the head downwards.

These non-elected and self-vetted persons arrogate to themselves powers which would astonish our ancestors. It's supposed that they alone can determine what is the 'national interest' and invoke the awesome imperative of 'national security'. In this they protract into the present the traditions of an old anti-democratic imperial elite, whose last colony is this island.

So far from being free we are—in relation to these guardians of the 'national interest'—among the least free peoples of the advanced nations of the west. We have no Freedom of Information Act. No safeguards against mail interception and phonetapping. Our press is hedged around with Official Secrets Acts. In recent years our jury system has been fiddled with, our rights of public meeting and demonstration have been curtailed, and a heavy section of chief constables have pressed for heavier, undemocratic powers.

We've forgotten what any 'freeborn Englishman' knew 200 years ago—and what Americans still remember—that the state exists to serve us: we don't exist by permission of the state. Why have we forgotten? Why do we let these people get away with murder?

What they got away with, in 1982, was the Falklands war. It is as if, in normal times, they let the media play around with free opinions, since this flatters the British people's self-image. But in times of 'emergency'—and they alone define what an emergency is—they move in sharply and take over the controls.

In the case of the Falklands war, the lie beamed to us on all channels, from the *Jimmy Young Show* to the mainline news, was that our task-force was acting with the blessing of the UN Security Council, in defence of the rule of law, and in support of Resolution 502:

U.N. Security Council: 3 April: Resolution 502

1. Demands an immediate cessation of hostilities;
2. Demands an immediate withdrawal of all Argentine forces from the Falkland Islands (Islas Malvinas);
3. Calls on the Governments of Argentina and the United Kingdom to seek a diplomatic solution to their differences and to respect fully the purposes and principles of the Charter of the United Nations.

I happen to support this resolution, which was passed just after Galtieri's invasion and before our task-force had been sent on its way. Moreover, world opinion supported it also. This resolution carried with it a quite remarkable weight of international support:

U.N. Security Council: Voting, 3 April

In favour:	France, Guyana, Ireland, Japan, Jordan, Togo, Uganda, United Kingdom, United States, Zaire (10)
Against:	Panama (1)
Abstained:	China, Poland, Soviet Union, Spain (4).

You'll see that despite their hostility to anything smacking of 'colonialism' five Third World nations voted for it. Despite Hispanic kinship with Argentina, Spain abstained. Despite our supposed adversary postures, the Soviet Union and China refrained from using their vetoes. Only Panama sat in the dog-house.

Resolution 502 gave a real basis for an international exercise in enforcing the rule of law: for making the UN actually *work*, for once, through resolute diplomacy and sanctions. Instead, it was seized on by Mrs Thatcher to sanction. . . the rule of war. It was imprinted on British opinion, by every means, that Resolution 502 was a Security Council imperative, demanding instant Argentine withdrawal from the Falklands, and licensing every British military action to bring this about.

But it was nothing of the sort. The resolution had three parts, only one of which was brandished aloft by our government, while the other two were withheld from the British public's view. The relation of these three parts to each other was a question on which world opinion (and lawyers) did not agree, and which should have been referred back to the Security Council.

In the next weeks, while the task-force sailed to the Falklands, our government, with the aid of the United States, did everything in its power to prevent the Security Council from meeting on the issue again. When it finally did so—and called for an immediate ceasefire on the island and the implementation of Resolution 502 in its *'entirety'* and *'of all parts thereof'*, the terms of the voting had dramatically changed:

U.N. Security Council: Voting, 4 June

In favour:	China, Ireland, Japan, Panama, Poland, Soviet Union, Spain, Uganda, Zaire (9)
Against:	United Kingdom (1)
Abstained:	France, Guyana, Jordan, Togo (4)

You'll notice that I haven't put the vote of the United States there. General Haig and Mrs Jeanne Kirkpatrick were having a tiff, and the US vote was cast first with Britain, and then taken back and cast as an abstention. I've estimated its total value as nil.

You'll also notice that it is Britain this time, and not Panama, in the dog-house. That's quite remarkable. It was Mrs Thatcher's extraordinary achievement, in only two months, to run through all that credit of international goodwill and to have run up an equivalent debt of world censure. At the height of the Falklands 'victory' Britain stood alone in the Security Council, condemned or snubbed by every nation, just as Begin's Israel stands today.

But did you know that? Neither the media nor Mrs Thatcher went out of their way to tell you. That UN vote was passed over in silence. But to receive the world's censure is a serious thing. If the world is to survive, then every nation's citizens must develop an internationalist conscience, and attend to such censure as a matter of utmost gravity.

I'll be tougher. You perhaps suppose that during the Falklands war you weighed up the pros and cons for yourself and formed your own opinions. But many of you did *not*. You sucked in your opinions at the pap of an authoritarian state. The managers of our state moved in and did a job on the public mind. They issued us with public lies: refused us necessary information: and—do you remember?—when *Panorama* attempted a mild debate, there was a hullabaloo from the Tory benches.

If they could do this three months ago, then they can do it again tomorrow. Whenever they want they can manufacture 'public opinion' and then tell us it is our own. They are doing this still today.

I've gone into this, not to defend Galtieri's invasion (I don't). My own opinion is that if we'd honoured Resolution 502—in all its parts—world opinion might have enforced a negotiated solution less bloody to both parties, less painful to the islanders—but also less intoxicating and less politically advantageous to Mrs Thatcher. By resorting instead to the archaic and barbaric rule of war, we rocked an already-dangerous world, sank our country's reputation in the eyes of the world with the sinking of the *General Belgrano*, and gave a cue to Mr Begin for his own exercises in 'self-defence'.

Behind this lie more sensitive questions. What *is* the true security of our nation? Who decides? What claims can the nation-state rightly make on the loyalties of citizens? Might it be possible that the threat to our security today comes from outmoded notions of national interest? From the so-called security services? If the world is to go on—and it may well not—may it not be necessary for citizens in every country to develop international—or non-national—codes-of-honour, which may on occasion refuse the claims of their own nation-state? Should we always obey the Official Secrets Acts even when we stumble across evidence which threatens the liberties of the people or world peace? Just as Lollards or religious reformers in the old days put the Bible or their own consciences above the dogmas of the church, should we stand now on our consciences against the armed state?

We are living in abnormal times. Never has civilisation been nearer to the end of the line, with so much banked-up destructive power, such scattered and confused spiritual defences. Remember how Yeats's poem begins, with an image from falconry. The hawk of violence has been loosed from the wrist—perhaps from our own wrists of bigotry and apathy. . .

> Turning and turning in the widening gyre,
> The falcon cannot hear the falconer. . .

Next it will stoop—on us and our world.

It has been loosed from the wrists of normal people. The most dangerous people of all are those who would have us believe that everything is *normal*—that we need only to go on as we are and trust them to manage things—the people who would rock us to sleep in a cradle called 'deterrence'.

It's often true, in history, that the 'normality' of one time turns out—a few decades later—to have been absurd. The comfortable and powerful, who thought that they were actors, were only puppets whose arms and heads were moved by other strings.

If we could make a true national discourse again, an opinion open to questions of *why* and *where*, we might be astonished to find, behind the rituals of 'normality', the absurdity of the rituals of our own time. I'm thinking of a poem by one of my oldest friends, an American and a life-long 'dissenter', Thomas McGrath. As you read it, put your own features on the heavy dancers of our time. I can see them now—the party-political pundits, the heavy chief constables, the chat-show conductors, the paid defence 'experts', the Falklands liars—all of them now, going about their normal business—with painted faces, feathers in their hair, moving heavily in their primitive dance—summoning up the ancient spirits of the tribe as they prepare us for the ultimate war. The poem, called *Prophecy,* appears on page ix as the epigraph of this edition.

▲ THE SOVIET 'PEACE OFFENSIVE'* ▲

Neither moralism nor fellow-travelling sentimentalism can be of service in guiding the peace movement in its difficult relations with Communist states. We are dealing, just as we are with the NATO states, with immensely powerful entrenched military interests and with leaders who seek to advance their own objectives.

The problem with the Communist rulers is that they are the ideological look-alikes of their opposite numbers in the West, thinking in the same terms of 'balance' and of security through 'strength'.

The Soviet rulers may have no aggressive plans, but 'the deterrent' remains immensely serviceable to them in freezing the *status quo* in Europe and in holding together their increasingly-restive client states. At any time from 1980 to 1982 they could have halted the build-up of the SS-20s, just as they could commence direct reductions now. It is as painful to them as it is to Mrs Thatcher to lose a single missile.

At a recent Prague summit meeting of the Warsaw Pact powers (January 5th, 1983) a package of proposals was issued which takes up several of the themes raised in the Western peace movements in the past three years: nuclear-free zones in Europe, the prohibition of nuclear tests, a zone of peace in the Mediterranean, a nuclear-free belt (taking up

---

* From the *Guardian*, 21 February 1983, and *The Nation*, 26 February 1983.

and extending the proposals of the Palme Commission)
running through Central Europe.

What could possibly be wrong with this plethora of Soviet
peace proposals? In many cases the proposals are good, they
offer advantage to both sides, and they deserve vigorous
support. What is wrong is what the proposals do *not* offer
(or what they close off from discussion) and their manipulation of European domestic politics to the advantage of the
Soviet Union.

What the Soviet proposals close off from discussion are
the most sensitive and troubling questions in the relations
between the two blocs. The aim of Soviet diplomacy is to
encourage Western European nations to edge from beneath
American hegemony at the same time as Soviet hegemony
is reinforced over Poland and the rest of the Eastern bloc.
At the same Prague summit a secret session was held on 'the
need to re-establish the leading role of the Party'. While a
peace offensive is being directed towards the West, the
East is being placed under quarantine lest the infection of
peace should spread.

If Soviet policy were to bring some measures of disarmament closer, then it might be possible to put up with it.
But it will not. It envisions that in 1983 Soviet diplomacy,
aided by the Western peace movement, will succeed in
dramatically reversing the post-war balance of political
relations. The Russians count on public opinion, direct
action and elections blocking or dislodging cruise and
Pershing missiles from one Western state after another, and
uncoupling Europe from US strategies. Thus NATO
modernization will be thwarted by the actions of West
European peoples, the seat will be knocked from under the
American negotiators at Geneva, and the Soviet Union will
regard with a benevolent eye the wreckage of NATO.

I am not filled with alarm at such an outcome, nor would
CND back away because it would give to our opponents, for
the ten millionth time, opportunity to accuse us of being
'one-sided disarmers' and Soviet dupes. Since this is a
potential Cuba crisis in reverse, there would be no harm if it
was, this time, the West that was outfaced and forced to back

down, even at the cost of leaving the Soviet Union with some notional 'superiority' in a category of weapons that is itself notional. This might, in a single episode redress the Russians' historical inferiority-complex (in nuclear matters) and NATO's assumption of the prerogative of superiority.

Yet this is not what is going to happen. In serious political terms it is unrealistic to expect that such a (welcome) loosening up of NATO could take place alongside a *hardening* of the Warsaw bloc. Established power, drawing upon immense reserves of ideology and of wealth, will rally to the defence of the old Cold War 'West', while at the same time repression in the East would sap the very springs of action of the Western peace movement.

The force generated by this movement in the past three years has always had a particular political accent: impatience at the domination of Europe by *both* superpowers; a desire to set nations free from their client status, to open frontiers and resume a flow of ideas and people between East and West. These desires are an integral part of peace conscious-ness, not an 'extra' which might be added to nuclear dis-armament. They go along with disarmament, both as pre-condition and as consequence. They were clearly stated in the original END Appeal of April 1980.

The Western peace movement derives its strength precisely from its political independence, its 'unacceptable' demands upon both blocs. If it should sleepwalk into dependency within a Soviet games-plan, its support could fall away as rapidly as it arose. The movement could be painted by its opponents into an unpopular pro-Soviet corner. We could come to the end of 1983 with Chancellor Kohl reinstalled in power and even (God forbid!) Mrs Thatcher.

The Soviet peace offensive is strictly for export. It goes along with a worsening climate of Cold War at home. Trials of Solidarity leaders continue in Poland. Arrests of independ-ent peace workers are reported in the GDR. On the same day as the Prague summit a leading spokesperson of Charter 77 in Czechoslovakia, Ladislav Lis, was arrested: among 'in-criminating' documents seized by the security police were drafts of his messages to the Western peace movement. In

Moscow the distinguished historian, Roy Medvedev—an early signatory (in 1980) of the Appeal for European Nuclear Disarmament—has been given, for the first time for some years, an official warning under the catch-all ('anti-Soviet activities') clause, Article 70.

For months hostility has been visited upon the small group of scientists, doctors and academics who formed last June in Moscow the Group to Establish Trust. Visitors from the Western peace movement have recently had long talks with the Group. They are convinced of their bona fides and are humbled by their dedication in the face of a record of persecution which far outdoes what happened to the Quakers in the 'Sufferings' in England in the late 17th century.

Sergei Batovrin, the young artist who founded the group, had eighty-eight of his antiwar paintings confiscated at an exhibit the group sponsored on Hiroshima Day, August 6. He was confined for some weeks in a psychiatric hospital and was placed under house arrest five times in November; his apartment has been repeatedly searched by the KGB.

Other members of the group have been temporarily detained on trumped-up charges, interrogated and sacked from their jobs; their telephones have been cut off and KGB cars have been stationed outside their apartments. Oleg Radzinsky, a young teacher, was arrested at the end of October; he was recently transferred from the Lefortovo Prison to the Serbsky psychiatric institute. Reports that he is in poor health are causing concern among his friends. Two supporters of the group in Siberia were arrested last July for collecting signatures on a peace petition from workers in a sawmill; they too are now in a psychiatric institute.

The group has sent urgent signals to sympathisers in the West that it expects the arrest of all of its members any day. A case is being prepared against them, and they have been accused in *Literaturnaya Gazeta* of being 'dying carrion-crows' and (absurdly) of supporting the massacre of Palestinian children. In a letter in the current *END Journal*, Prof. Yuri Medvedkov, a distinguished geographer, writes: 'We risk our liberty and even our lives every day but to be outside the peace movement is impossible to us. It's the point of honour, the point of being humans.' And Batovrin concludes a recent interview:

> We are not just talking of the persecution of a small group of people. . . The fate of the world depends upon whether each person understands that a peaceful future requires a peaceful defence of the right to struggle for peace.

It dismays and astounds me that there should be any hesitation in the Western peace movement about coming to the group's defence. Genuine peace movements have always defended one another's rights: the right to communicate, the right to opt for alternatives to military service, the right just to exist. END is aiding, with a little success, members of the Turkish Peace Association now on trial. Support for these groups surely should not require discussion.

Yet a clatter has gone up, rather widely, that suggests that 'human rights' have 'nothing to do with' our only proper concern: disarmament. The unavowed premise underlying this clatter is the mirror image of standard Western apologetics, now transferred to the East: the Soviet Union is only 'responding' to the Western weapons buildup; unlike Western nukes, Soviet nukes are only for 'defence'.

But nuclear weapons are no nicer when they are wrapped up, on that side as on this, with professions of peaceable intent. It is helpful to be reminded (as we often are) of the prodigious Soviet losses in World War II. Those losses fostered a historical consciousness that contrasts with that of the United States, where there are still popular notions that war is always for export; it never visits the American home. That callow, boastful and menacing voice is not heard in the Soviet Union; there is no appetite there for a war of conquest or expansion.

History's legacy to Russia is paranoia, a tetchy sensitivity to any 'instability' near its borders, a readiness to see in any foreign ideas—even in a flight of doves—the conspiracies of Western imperialist agents. Those weeping Soviet grandmothers who still deck with flowers the graves of the last war have dry eyes for Afghanistan, as they had, in 1968, for

Czechoslovakia. The Soviet people will support their rulers
in preparations for any war that is 'in defence of peace'.

I am sorry to rehearse these plain truths, which I will be
told are 'anti-Soviet'. But it is time for the peace movement
to wash the sleep from its eyes. If we are entering into
political relations with the Communist states, then we must
do so as actors and not as the acted upon. If the Soviet
leaders are in earnest about some measures of disarmament,
and if they need the force of Western peace opinion to
achieve their objectives, then we must insert our own transcontinental demands into the negotiations.

The Western peace movement has never been just about
particular missiles. It has been about human neighbourhood,
communication, survival: the hope for what Ian McEwen
has called 'womanly times'. It has refused to adopt the
abstracted logic of the two great adversary blocs. The
Western peace movement is expressive of a political and
cultural sea-change which touches sensitive places in our
consciousness, subverts the pat certainties of thirty-five years
of Cold War, questions the game-plans of the old alliances.
It is in one sense an opening to the East: not to the East of
armed states but to the East of our fellow creatures.

The peace movement is a phenomenon analagous to the
'thaw' in the East after the death of Stalin. One reason the
thaw came to an abrupt end was that the clever statesmen of
NATO saw in it only Soviet 'weakness' to be exploited for
their own advantage; there was no corresponding thaw in the
West. If the Soviet leaders make the same error in 1983, and
seek to exploit what they perceive as 'weakness' and disarray
in the West to their own advantage, then not only NATO but
the human story itself may be finally screwed up.

This is the moment for the Western peace movement not
to fall in behind this or that makeshift of arms control but
to enlarge our demands upon both parties to the maximum
possible—and perhaps impossible. The opportunity that we
have now may never be repeated. We must strike directly at
the structures of the Cold War itself. A freeze on weapons
will not be enough. At the same time we must work for a
general and simultaneous thaw in both blocs.

The time to induce this mutual thaw is now, when Western peace consciousness (which *is* the thaw) is still growing, and when the Soviet leadership (which wants desperately to halt NATO modernisation) is bidding for the Western peace movement's favours. We must make it clear that we find it intolerable that independent voices in the East are harassed or silenced; that we will not scurry around to conferences in Moscow or assemblies in Prague so long as that repression continues; that we intend to act as free citizens of a healed world and that we do not require permits from Zhukov or one of his clerks to talk with citizens on the other side, and that, if it has to come to that, it is as easy to sit down in front of the Soviet Embassy as on Greenham Common.

I am not proposing some Cold War 'linkage' between disarmament and human rights. Our refusal of nuclear weapons has always been unconditional: this demand is dependent on no prior condition whatsoever. Rather we must press, in the same moment as we refuse weapons, for an opening of frontiers and prisons. Neither the cause of peace nor that of liberty can wait upon the other: it is natural that they go forward together. A genuine thaw in the East will make the cause of peace in the West unstoppable. Renewed repression in the East will feed the roots of a renewed Cold War.

There is a marvellous peroration in the declaration of the Prague summit about 'the broadest possible intercourse' between East and West. It calls for 'the extension of the mutual spiritual enrichment of the European peoples, propagation of truthful and honest information, and cultivation of sentiments of mutual friendliness and respect'.

Amen to all that. But what has this got to do with negotiations between statesmen? (Whoever heard a statesman propagate 'truthful and honest information'?) This is work for free citizens, not for arms controllers. We already have the work in hand. If the Warsaw Pact leaders really want a general and reciprocal thaw in the relations between peoples, then they need do very little. They can start now. They could open some frontiers; they could open the doors of some prisons and psychiatric institutes. They could call off the KGB surveillance of members of the Group to Establish

Trust, equip the security men with thermal underwear and send them off to watch an SS-20 site.

If we are to seize this last chance of putting Europe back together, the best thing we can ask of the current set of statesmen, East and West, is to get out of the way.

▲ THE WISDOM OF SOLOMON* ▲

If you board a flying machine at Kennedy or Logan Airport and turn right at Greenland, you will reach the European continent, an old place where in every state they speak a different language.

Across that continent, from the Baltic Sea to the Black Sea, there is an artificial line. One major city is even cut in two by a wall. On each side of this line are large and growing nuclear and conventional military establishments; there are also continuous ideological hostilities and skirmishes between rival security services. Two world wars have broken out in Europe, and, next to the Middle East, Europe is as likely a starting point for World War III as any.

Europe also is doing its best to screw up the Third World. The arms trade is one of the few vigorous parts of the slack Western European economy, and socialist France is especially mercenary and amoral in its salesmanship. The Soviet Union, whose most important production centres are in Europe, is the United States' leading competitor-colleague in this dirty trade.

When President Carter halted arms exports to certain Latin

---

* My article, 'The Soviet "Peace Offensive",' caused offence among some peace workers in both Britain and the United States. On April 16th, 1983, *The Nation* published a polemic against my views by Norman Solomon, in which I was accused of confusing the issues of disarmament and human rights. My reply was published in the same issue of *The Nation* and in part in *New Society*, 2 June 1983.

American tyrannies because of human rights violations, Britain, West Germany, France and Israel were only too eager to step into the market. To be sure, the implicit understanding was that these arms were to be used only by one Latin American country against another, or by their military dictators to slaughter their own poor. But the war in the Falklands, as a testing ground for advanced European military technologies, was a stupendous production from the studios of Nemesis Inc.

It may be overdue that we Europeans should become more Eurocentric in our political concerns: that is, should consult one another and try to resolve some of our own problems. If we could set matters right in our own backyards, we might be less of a danger to the world.

For the past three years the Western European peace movement has been signalling its unequivocal refusal of NATO's modernized weapons: cruise and Pershing 2 missiles. Unequivocal and unqualified: we are not interested in discussing any compromise. There has to come a point at which the nuclear arms race stops—whatever arguments of 'balance' are employed—and we in Western Europe are committed to stopping it here, at Greenham Common and at Comiso. We are even chided sometimes, by friends in the American freeze movement, for our 'unilateralism'.

I don't say that we will succeed. I say only that this is where we are and we can do no other.

Nor do we stand in particular need of lessons from Yuri Zhukov, the president of the Soviet Peace Committee. Yet we have been receiving from him, and from several official sources in the Soviet Union and Eastern Europe, rather a lot of instruction in the past few months. Zhukov, who is a *Pravda* editorialist and a very big Soviet noise, is displeased because we are not acting according to his script. We have not confined ourselves to refusing NATO weapons but have criticised Soviet nuclear weapons as well; and we have refused to align ourselves with Soviet policies in Poland and Afghanistan. We have also voiced our solidarity with independent peace groups in his country.

For these reasons we are now being unmasked by Soviet ideologists as 'anti-Soviet', Cold War and even 'pro-Reagan' elements—'infiltrated' into a movement which, in its recent incarnation, we happened to start ourselves! And Zhukov and his friends in the World Peace Council are trying, in an old-fashioned, 1950-ish way, to split our movement and bring it under Soviet hegemony. There are selective conferences in Moscow, pressing messages to us from several embassies, a great 'Peace Assembly' to be held in Prague in June 1983—and much more. We find this politically inept and morally offensive.

Our perception is this. For three years we have set every-ting else aside to campaign against NATO's new weapons. And in three years we have not extracted one real concession from the East. There are, it is true, some admirable proposals on paper from the Soviet Union and the Warsaw Pact powers, just as there are a few (rather less admirable) proposals on paper from NATO. But in terms of action, nothing. The two concessions we have explicitly pressed for have not been made.

First, we have asked—on two occasions, in April 1980 and in August 1981—for the Soviet Union to stop building up the number of its SS-20s. No answer; until a total was reached in 1982 clearly in excess of the corresponding Western weapon-ry. Second, we have asked them to stop harassing and im-prisoning independent peace workers on their side. The answer to this has been worse than no: repression is being tightened.

The SS-20s may not bother North Americans, since their range does not extend across the Atlantic. We argue that the cruises and Pershings would gravely disturb the strategic equilibrium, and that the terms 'intermediate' and 'theatre' weapons are misnomers. They are in fact forward-based US strategic systems, operated by US personnel, which can reach deep into Soviet territory. I think I was the first polemicist to say that they would set up 'a Cuba crisis in reverse'.

But the SS-20s are highly visible to Western Europeans, and a never-ending barrage of NATO propaganda ensures

that this is so. They are targetted now on Bonn and London
and Rome. If Europeans find that disquieting, it is, no
.doubt, a regrettable Eurocentric failing on their part. Norman
Solomon reassures us that the presence of these weapons can
be explained by the Russians' 'self-perceived defensive needs'.
But I do not think that Soviet self-perceptions will limit the
SS-20s' destructive power.

Solomon apologises further for these peacekeeping weapons
by making several fallback references to an essay by Roy and
Zhores Medvedev. The conclusion of the Medvedevs' historical
discussion of the leading role the United States has played in
the nuclear arms race is that this has created 'a pervasive
inferiority complex' in Soviet military circles. It ought not to
be treasonable to suppose that there could be circumstances
in which an inferiority complex (armed with nukes) could be
as dangerous to life on this planet as the technological ego-
tripping that characterises US weapons deployment.

I have not allocated 'greater blame' or even 'equal blame'
to the Soviet Union for the nuclear arms race. Historical
blame is beside the point: both sets of weapons are a present
danger and both must be stopped.

The stopping of them is a political problem. In the West
there must be a massive mobilisation of public opinion.
There is a world of difference between the leaders of NATO
(who are determined to deploy their infernal new weapons)
demanding one-sided cuts from the Soviet Union and the
Western peace movement (which is not only expressing but
acting out its unqualified refusal of those weapons) calling
on the Russians to make concessions in advance of the new
weapons' arrival.

The object of the request is to prevent the weapons from
ever coming. A direct Soviet concession of this order, in
response to the peace movement, would so augment the
force of Western peace opinion that we could sweep the
weapons off the future's board.

Please remember that no European nation, East or West
(the Soviet Union excepted) is represented at the Geneva
negotiations. Yet the negotiators there are bargaining about
intermediate-range weapons, the possible instruments of a

'limited' nuclear war in the 'theatre' of Europe. Western European nations can take part in the bargaining in only one way: by refusing to allow their national territories to be used as sites for the missiles. This refusal requires an act of political will, supported by powerful, aroused public opinion. The deployment of an unnecessarily large number of SS-20s is the best argument our domestic political opponents have, and it is one which is employed, day and night, in every newspaper and on every TV station. Some reciprocation by the Russians—not endless futuristic paper proposals to be fed into the labyrinth of superpower negotiations, but direct concessions to Western peace opinion—would begin to draw our opponents' poison.

I am not wedded to this course. I am ready to defer to the wisdom of Solomon—and, no doubt, to the wisdom of Yuri Andropov also. Soviet politicians and military leaders are 'realists'. What can our scruffy, undisciplined and argumentative millions—our idealistic and ill-marshalled demonstrators, our peace campers untutored in protocol, our pathetic declarations of nuclear-free zones in towns and counties, our movers of resolutions at party conferences and church synods—really promise to deliver?

To the Russians, we are background music only, and music not even loud enough to swing a German election. Andropov and his colleagues will take no more notice of us than an occasional glance at an opinion poll. They will attend to the *real* music—the rantings of Margaret Thatcher in Westminster, England, and of President Reagan in Orlando, Florida—to form their assessments of the true intentions of the ruling groups of the imperialist West. They do not have much reason to trust in Western democracy, nor any experience with its procedures. They have already ordered their own cruise missiles.

Our problems have been made worse in recent months by inept Soviet interventions in Western political life (including the peace movements), accompanied by continued repression in the East. Solomon is indignant that I even raise these matters, and I quote his comments since I have been looking at them for several days with growing despair:

> The Russians' essential perfidy is repeatedly alluded to by Thompson
> in references to repression in satellite countries like Hungary, Czecho-
> slovakia and Poland. We are encouraged to think that what happens
> in Eastern Europe is an index of the Kremlin's sincerity about
> wanting a halt to the nuclear arms race. But if we talk about Buda-
> pest, Prague and Warsaw, let us also talk about Santo Domingo,
> Santiago, and the countrysides of El Salvador and Guatemala [where
> the United States has been helping to finance an extermination drive
> against the Maya Indians].

This passage is so innocent of political analysis that I don't
know where to begin. I will start with an anecdote about a
recent conversation between a Norwegian peace activist and a
Soviet official. 'The European peace movement built up to a
"hot autumn" in 1981,' my Norwegian friend said. 'Why do
you suppose it was not followed, in 1982, by an even hotter
spring?' The Soviet official was puzzled and searched in vain
for a reply.

What my Norwegian friend was referring to were the unprecedented demonstrations—totalling more than 2 million
people—in Western European capitals in October and
November 1981. (We have been told that these rallies helped
breathe new morale into the American peace movement.)
And why were there not 3 million or 4 million demonstrating in spring and summer of 1982? The answer is martial
law in Poland and the repression of Solidarity. A hope that
had been growing, a hope of healing our split continent by
the convergence of popular movements, was abruptly ended.

It is nonsense to try to extract something called 'the
nuclear arms race' from the ideological and political context
of which it is an integral part. In Europe we live in visible
contact with one another (whether antagonism or reciprocation); but, even if it is less visible, the United States and the
Soviet Union are tied into the same political context. Martial
law in Poland threw whole sections of the Western European
peace movement—notably the Eurocommunist masses in
Italy—onto a lame, defensive leg. In my view, the recent West
German elections were lost to the cause of peace in part

because of the clumsiness of Soviet interventions. And West German voters might have had reason to feel uncertain about the Kremlin's 'sincerity' at a time when peace activists were being harassed in East Germany and the 'Swords into Plough-shares' badges were forbidden on their arms.

It is of course true that US intervention in the West German elections was more foul and more flagrant than the Russians'. The point is that NATO's interventions and solicitations were effective, and the Russians' were *counter-effective*. NATO's were effective because they exposed and exploited the nasty ideological sores on the other side. It helps neither analysis nor political action to apologise for those sores or to pretend they don't exist.

Nor should we join in the old propaganda game in which human rights and human wrongs are turned up one by one like cards in the game of 'Snap'. This game is played by the ideologists of both superpowers for the delectation of the readers of *Commentary* and *Literaturnaya Gazeta*. It is a game of distraction, a grand confuse-a-citizen or confuse-a-comrade show. It is a game we should expose as one of the mental chains that hold humanity down. Let us never, for the shadow of one moment, engage in arguments that excuse offences against life or liberty on one side because similar or worse offences can be pointed to on the other. These remain two offences, there is no way in which one cancels out the other. The point is to end them both.

We are driven, of course, to take part in this game of swapping human wrongs by the barefaced hypocrisy of our own rulers. When President Reagan and Prime Minister Thatcher have the gall to claim their side is the protector of human rights, and to use the claim as Cold War propaganda and as legitimation for the preparations of the ultimate human wrong of nuclear war, how can we do other than throw that claim back in their guilty faces? Turkey has the worst human rights record of any European country; it is a partner in NATO, and a partner currently being nudged by certain US operators to flex its military muscle threateningly to destabilise Papandreou's Greece. And if we cast an eye across the globe, it is probable we would find that the most savage offences against human rights are now being committed in Latin America, often under US license and with US aid; the United States supports and condones these barbarities—some of which arise from indigenous contexts—by pleading the irrelevant categories of the Cold War.

But if we agree that the United States (or the West) is the greatest sinner against human rights, we solve no problems by simply crossing the floor of the Cold War and adopting the perceptions of the other side. We must situate ourselves in an alternative position and develop a 'third' perception, one which could bring into a single coalition the forces of peace and democracy in the First, Second and Third Worlds.

The political issue raised by my article was not the matter of human rights in general but the integral relationship between the ideological and security structures of the two opposing blocs and the nuclear arms race. In this context, certain human rights are highly sensitive and visible questions, which impinge emphatically upon the problem of disarmament.

My argument is that there is unlikely to be any permanent disarmament—or any disarmament at all—unless there is a reciprocal thaw in both blocs, an opening of direct communication and exchange between citizens, and that renewed repression in the East, in particular of independent peace voices, will weaken Western peace movements and could—if they do not take precautions—paint them into an ineffectual 'pro-Soviet' corner.

Solomon ignores this argument, and I am persuaded that he does not understand it. It may be less obvious to Americans than to Europeans. But I doubt whether he means to understand it, since he resorts to the strategy of leaving the argument unexamined and smearing it with the imputation of racism. 'It is worth pondering,' he writes, 'that Thompson devotes rigorous attention to Soviet-sponsored repression in client states primarily populated by white Europeans, but ignores brutal repression in US client states populated largely by nonwhites.' And he goes on:

For English-speaking whites in the West, it is all too easy to presume that the twinned international efforts for peace and freedom are more undermined by the jailing of a dissident in Prague or Moscow than by the execution of political prisoners in Guatemala or the Philippines, though a nuclear superpower is responsible in each instance.

And I and the European peace movement stand condemned for our 'Eurocentric fixation'.

This is a predictable form of argumentation by people who suppose themselves to be advanced radicals, and it consists of strewing the ground with tripwires of guilt ('English-speaking whites in the West', 'Eurocentric', etc.). In seeking to circumvent these tripwires we are forced to skirt the most relevant political problems also.

By all means let us talk about the situation in Guatemala and El Salvador when it is relevant, as it now very urgently is. Let us also ('Snap!') talk about Afghanistan. If Solomon comes to Europe he will find that much talking about them is going on, although it is not always easy to know what we can do. But what is happening in those countries has rather little to do with nuclear weapons, and it does not even need a superpower to do it, although that helps. It is as old as, and older than, the Maxim gun. Insofar as the violence of the superpower confrontation is being worked out in these peripheral client states, one way of aiding the victims is to challenge the Cold War itself—in its central military and ideological emplacements—and to strengthen the links between nonaligned movements and nations. This is what we are trying to do.

What Solomon fails to consider is any policy by which the peace movement might break down the confrontation of blocs; nor does he consider the mechanics of twinning the nonaligned peace work on both sides.

Just one example: we are being urged by the World Peace Council (a Soviet-oriented body) to send representatives to the Assembly of Peace to be held in June 1983 in Prague. We are not, as it happens, being simultaneously urged by the Atlantic Council (a private group which promotes co-operation between Europe and the United States) to send representatives to an officially sponsored peace assembly in, say, Guatemala City, to protest against Soviet SS-20s, so we cannot get out of both (or into both) by playing Snap.

Here are a few of the difficulties we have with the invitation to attend the peace assembly in Prague: (1) Czechoslovakia is a Soviet client state, although the Czechoslovak people supposed themselves to be sovereign until August 1968, when (2) the intervention of Warsaw Pact forces taught them better. This intervention was provoked by (3) a reform movement within the country's ruling Communist Party, not by any Western imperialist provocation. (4) The forces that entered Czechoslovakia in 1968 remain in occupation to this day, although it was claimed then that their stay would be temporary. (5) In 1977, after the signing of the Helsinki Accords, a Czechoslovak civil rights organisation, Charter 77, was set up, in which some former Communists of 1968 were prominent, to press for the observance of those accords. It has been consistently harassed, and members imprisoned. (6) Last year the spokespersons for Charter 77 addressed several messages to Western peace groups, suggesting that the movements in the East and West recognise and support one another and work for peace, for true detente and for the observance of civil rights. (7) This January one of the people who signed those letters, Ladislav Lis, was arrested, and he remains in prison. Parenthetically, in 1968 Czechoslovakia's government-sponsored Peace Committee had the temerity to protest at the Warsaw Pact invasion—perhaps the only recorded case of an official peace committee in the Soviet bloc protesting against an action of the Warsaw Pact. The committee was promptly disbanded and a new, compliant peace committee was appointed. And (8) this body will be the host organisation of the great Assembly for Peace. To raise money for the assembly, the government has 'invited' working people to pay a 'peace tax' from their wages—for example, to sign over their pay for one Saturday morning shift—which payments will be voluntary, of course, but the refusal of which may call down upon the recalcitrant ones unwelcome attention.

Many Europeans find this whole scene to be a can of

worms. But what can we do about it? To refuse to go to the conference might be seen as a refusal to 'talk with the other side', which everyone now wants to do. To go might be seen as a condonation of the Soviet occupation of Czechoslovakia (a legitimate demand on any European disarmament agenda is the withdrawal of those forces) as well as an acceptance of the repression of civil rights workers who have been trying to open a dialogue with the Western peace movement. This question has put us at sixes and sevens and divided us more than any propaganda ploy by President Reagan could do. In the end, some European peace workers will refuse to go, on one principle or another; others will go with open eyes to see if anything can be done, and others will sleepwalk through the whole affair in an exalted peace-loving trance. The media in the West will expose us all, without discrimination, as Soviet stooges. The event will do only harm to the cause of peace and will alienate democrats in the East from Western peace forces. Many of those democrats are patriots claiming to be exercising their constitutional rights, and they do not thank us in the West for writing them off as 'dissidents'.*

It is only by attending to such details that we can see the emptiness of the wisdom of Solomon. According to any universal scale of human rights and wrongs, the execution of Maya Indians in Guatemala, the raping of women and the burning of villages is certainly more foul than the 'jailing of a dissident in Prague or Moscow'. But in the complex politics of peace, the major adversaries are NATO and the Warsaw Pact, and the lines of antagonism and reconciliation run not through the countrysides of Guatemala and El Salvador but through Berlin, Warsaw and Prague. The future of the world depends, in the end, on the peoples of the Soviet Union and the United States finding some mode of mutual reconciliation (and disarmament); and the people of Europe could be either a prize of war or a hyphen bringing them together.

I have to reply to Solomon that the twinned international

---

* CND's National Council, after a full and fair discussion, decided to send two observers to Prague. While at the Assembly the observers also had meetings with members of Charter 77.

efforts of peace and freedom *are* more undermined by the jailing of a dissident in Prague or Moscow than by the sack of a Guatemalan village. This is not because the first is worse than the second; it certainly is not. It is because the first may be more sensitively situated within the delicate and complicated politics of peace. If not just any 'dissident', but, say, Ladislav Lis of Charter 77 or Oleg Radzinsky of the Moscow Group to Establish Trust Between the USSR and USA is thrown into prison, it is a defeat for communication between citizens of East and West and a serious reversal for the cause of peace. It signals that the Communist authorities are not yet willing to reciprocate our efforts with the least thaw of their own.

The making of an honest political discourse between East and West is an extraordinarily complex business, with misrecognitions on all sides and with the security agencies of both blocs doing all they can to screw up the dialogue. It is not enough to rush across to the other side with an outstretched hand. The Kremlin may be sincere in wishing to see a halt in the nuclear arms race, but it is equally sincere in taking measures to insure that the infection of the peace movement is halted at its borders. Yet if we are steady and nonprovocative, I do not think these measures will be able to stop it. And, as I have said, if there is no mutual thaw, I doubt if we will succeed in stopping nuclear arms.

I am glad to learn that many US peace organisations have come to the defence of the Moscow Group to Establish Trust and its kindred groups in Leningrad, Novosibirsk and Odessa. It is not that these beleaguered handfuls of independent-minded citizens—who may be worn down into silence by incessant harrassment—are the only Soviet citizens concerned with peace. They symbolise the principle of trust and direct citizens' detente, and hence of internationalism against state power. If that principle is abandoned, the poison of compromise with power will enter all our work.

I had almost forgotten Norman Solomon. I find his tone offensive and unfraternal, and I object to his accusations of treason and racism, but I don't hold him an enemy to the cause of peace. If he wishes to be useful to that cause in his writing, however, there are certain habits he should kick.

One habit is that of using human rights as the coin of propaganda, as if a debit on one side can be scored as a credit to the other. This habit, which is widespread on both sides of the Atlantic, reveals how far we are from truly endorsing the consciousness of nonalignment. We remain in bondage to the schema of the Cold War, exchanging one ideology for its mirror image.

Another habit is that of setting up tripwires of guilt as an alternative to arguing. This strategy of discourse is very much of our time, among radicals and conservatives alike. It is sad to see it at work in the peace movement also: it is a kind of competitiveness, in which those who were once eager to prove themselves more revolutionary-than-thou (more anti-racist, more antisexist, etc.) must now prove themselves more antinuclear-than-thou.

The temptation to adopt that strategy grows as the confrontation becomes sharper. High moral commitment, the willingness to fast or to enter prison, is necessary and valuable in our movement, but I am bothered when guilt and a sense of emergency are allowed to displace political analysis, and even to license a flight from rationality.

Norman Solomon is too eager to take upon his white Western English-speaking nuclear terrorist back every one of the world's sins. I will allow him, and the United States, many of those sins; but it is indecently greedy to claim them all. There are plenty of European operators—and not all of them in the West—who have helped screw the world up, and keep the Cold War gelid. The present rulers of Britain are a reminder that Europeans have lost neither the inclination nor the power to multiply the world's human wrongs. And it is not even true that every person oppressed south of the Mexican border is oppressed at the sole behest of US imperialism. There are ruling families there, descendants of conquistadors, who would not thank us for implying that they are not 'white', and who are vigorous and self-motivated oppressors. And, although it is not quite decent to say so, if one scans the globe with care one may even detect a black rogue or two.

To take upon one's shoulders all the guilt of the world is itself a sort of patronage of lesser sinners and a default on internationalism. It is to say that only The Worstest, the US of A, can do evil in earnest; the rest of us are evildoers only as American clients and proxies. But if the United States were blown away tomorrow, I dare say the world could go on doing wrong.

It puzzles us Europeans, this new image of American radicals as a group of self-flagellants bent to the ground by the weight of their sins. For it does not correspond with our experience. We find that Americans are often struck from a very different mould, and draw upon different and honourable American traditions. If they were blown away tomorrow, we would gravely miss them.

What Solomon has obscured is that I was not calling for less but for *more*. I was summoning support for an assault, not only upon certain weapons-systems but upon the structures of the Cold War itself, from which those systems continually arise. And I was calling on the peace movement to exert whatever influence it has to impose a thaw upon both East and West.

To attempt this extraordinary (but essential) overthrow of ideologies and power, the European and American movements must act together. We are not different kinds of people but the same kind of people working in different places for the same ends. Even Normon Solomon and myself. Now that we have had our fun at the expense of each other, I dare say that we will both turn back to the same kind of work.

▲ AMERICA AND THE WAR MOVEMENT * ▲

There are two ways into the disarmament argument. One is from the globe itself: the threat to the species, the ecological imperative of survival. The other is from the injury done to people by the deformations, whether economic or cultural, of their own war-directed societies. And the problem is this: both arguments are being won, yet none of the structures of power have been shifted an inch by the argument, and not one missile has yet been stopped in its tracks.

The dangers to the biosphere posed by nuclear war are discussed in *The Aftermath*,† an expert collection of studies originally published as a special issue of *Ambio*, the journal of the Royal Swedish Academy of Sciences. The papers set forth the consequences of nuclear war in epidemiological terms, its effects on the ozone layer, on global food supplies and fresh water, on ocean ecosystems and on much else.

The message has been delivered before, though rarely with such authority. No serious attempt can be made to refute it. There can no longer be any doubt that the procurers of nuclear weapons threaten the human species and most mammalian species besides. Yet the procurers continue with their business, and simply enlarge their public relations staffs to handle meddlesome scientists, bishops, doctors and peace movements. Where we had only an arms race five years ago, we have an apologetics race today as well.

---

* From *The Nation*, 24 September 1983.
† *The Aftermath*, ed. J. Peterson (Pantheon Books, New York), 1983.

*Beyond Survival*** is towards the other end of the spectrum. It is a collection commissioned in the euphoric aftermath of the vast Manhattan demonstration of June 12th, 1982, and the editors and contributors suppose that they are addressing politics. And so, in some part, and helpfully, they often are. But the politics which they address are less those of power—its reasons and its irrationalisms—than those of building the alliances and coalitions which make up the disarmament movement.

Hence *Beyond Survival* appears at times to be introversial to an outsider like myself: the movement is placed upon a couch and undergoes analysis. Most of the analysts are competent, and all recommend new ways of bringing into a single coalition the constituencies of the poor (although they do not often use this term), the blacks, the feminists, the Hispanics, the labour unions, the gays, the environmental lobbies, and any other groups around which might have occasion to protest.

All this is offered cogently enough to help on the vigorous discussions already going on within the multiform American disarmament movement. And the emphasis upon the urgent need to enlarge the goal of the movement to take in opposition to US military interventions (whether nuclear or not)—that is, to transform the disarmament movement into a peace movement—is welcome, and is forcefully presented in an essay by Noam Chomsky.

My reservations concern the absence of a different kind of 'politics', by which I mean the objective analysis of power: its strategies, structures and controls: and the strategies (national or international) for contesting that power. The politics of most of these essays is deduced from subjective inferences. We explore the self-image and grievances of disadvantaged constituencies, and deduce that all of these would be less powerless if they could only meld their protests into a common movement—an ever bigger June 12th movement going in more revolutionary directions. 'Will we cling

---

** *Beyond Survival: New Directions for the Disarmament Movement*, edited by Michael Albert and David Dellinger (South End Press, Boston, USA, £8.00).

to divisive prejudices,' asks David Dellinger, 'and deny connections between the approaching War to End War and the abuse of millions because of their race, sex, sexual preference, or age in a society dominated by the blindnesses of class arrogance?' And the movement itself then comes to be its own self-sufficient goal. It appears as a kind of therapy: 'take up thy couch and walk!'

Race, gender, sexual preference, ageing and class are all thrown together there as if they were all occasioned by the same forces of oppression (by capitalism? patriarchy? imperialism?) and all to be resolved by the same forms of resistance. It would take me too long to sort that set out: yet some of the grievances indicated (offence to the aged) are beyond mortal repair but might be softened by reform of manners and sensibility, others might be mended by reforms of law and institutions, and yet others (class) may require more revolutionary remedy.

Mass movements may be therapeutic (they often are) but this cannot determine their strategies and goals. The peace movement is engaged in a long rolling contest with the strongest establishments of armed power in the history of the world—and the strongest of all in the United States—and it cannot afford to lose the contest. It might even be thought to be patronising to tell blacks (or women or Hispanics or gays) that they should support the disarmament movement because they are oppressed or disadvantaged and therefore it is in their self-interest to. . . etc. etc. These constituencies are made up also of citizens, who are open to the same rational arguments and appeals to solidarity as any other.

I am arguing the case for a more objective mode of political analysis than is now current, and for a plainer vocabulary of international bonding and solidarity. The politics of individual ego-fulfilment have had a long run, and they have made some real gains—and power has looked down upon it all with benign self-assurance. Indeed, power has opened its portals a crack and has allowed the winners to come in. Among the small advance party of United States officers trained to launch cruise missiles which arrived several weeks ago at Greenham Common in my own country, it was announced (with self-congratulation) that there was one woman. I confess that I read of this example of affirmative action with confusion and shock. What kind of 'individual rights' ideology is it which affirms the right of every person to exploit or to exterminate their fellows?

It is a marginal point, and most of all in Mrs Thatcher's England. The larger point is that, if the survival of human civilisation is truly threatened (and I suppose that it is), then the politics of self-expression and self-fulfilment of particular interests must be placed under some political self-control: they cannot be pressed always to the point of dissension and inner division. And the political self-control must arise, not from subjective inferences, but from a shared perception of the objective crisis which threatens all interests alike, and hence from shared strategies and shared goals.

Since the crisis is now global, then the shared perception and the strategies of resistance must increasingly become international. This is where the American peace movement (whose work is crucial to civilisation's survival) faces quite exceptional difficulties. *Inside* the United States many persons feel themselves to be most bruised and restricted by the structures of racism, sexism, etc.; and of course they must and will contest these oppressions. But *outside* the United States, in Central America and increasingly in West Europe, it appears that it is arrogant American hegemonic nationalism which is most threatening (and which may even descend in the shape of a black F-111 pilot or a female cruise missile launch-officer). American military personnel are now, after all, *everywhere:* in El Salvador, in the Sudan, in the Lebanon, in England and West Germany, in Turkey and in Greece, in Diego Garcia and South Korea and Honduras and around the Persian Gulf. What are they doing there? And by what right? It is to ask us un-Americans to show superhuman exercises of self-restraint if we are not to pray, at times, for a reversion to good old-fashioned Middle American isolationism. There is nothing wrong with authentic American nationalism, if it is concerned with America's own cultural and historical traditions: but will it please go home and stay indoors?

I have written 'hegemonic nationalism' and not 'imperialism'. Of course United States imperial interests and strategies palpably exist (albeit with some inner contradictions). Yet the naming of power in the United States simply as 'imperialism' may make the whole problem seem too tidy. For it suggests that the problem may be easily isolated, as a powerful group of interests somewhere over there—the Pentagon, the multinational corporations—whereas what must be confronted is a whole hegemonic 'official' national ideology, which permeates not only the state and its organs but also many 'liberal' critics of the state (in the Democratic Party), which saturates the media, and which even confuses opposition groups within the society.

People in vast regions of Middle America know almost nothing of the world across the waters (where their fellow countrymen are being rapidly deployed) except the fragmentary ideological fictions offered in their local media. Yet it is this ideologically-confected national self-image—the herded self-identification with the goals (any goals) of the nation-state, the media-induced hysterias during the Iranian hostages crisis and in the Falklands/Malvinas War, the manipulation of the minds of vast publics as to the benign motives of their rulers in invading Afghanistan or the Lebanon or in intruding into Central America in support of 'national interests'—which constitutes, quite as much as weaponry, the threat to survival.

The most dangerous and expansionist nationalist ideologies are those which disguise themselves as missions on behalf of human universals. Such ideologies build upon the generous, as well as the self-interested, impulses of the evangelising nation. (Middle America believes that US militarism is about the export of 'freedom'). This was true of the French in Napoleonic times and even of the British at the zenith of empire (the 'civilising mission', the 'white man's burden'). These ideologies have now shrunk back (almost) within their own historical and cultural frontiers, and are (almost) content to be simple nationalisms once more, celebrating unique historical experiences and cultural identities.

Today they are the Soviet and the American nationalist ideologies which have become expansionist, and which walk the world in the disguise of universals: the victory of World Socialism or the Triumph of the Free World. And of the two it is the American which is the most confusing. Because the United States population is made up of so many heterogeneous in-migrations, it is possible to fall into the illusion that America is a reservoir of every human universal, rather than a peculiar, local, time-bound civilisation, marked by unusual social mobility, competitiveness and individualism, and with its own particular problems, needs and expectations.

Because of the youth and rapid growth of America, nationalist ideology is more artificially-confected there than in any other nation. It did not grow from experiential and cultural roots, fertilised and watered by a watchful imperial ruling-class, as in Britain. It was, like other artefacts of the New World, a conscious ideological construction, in the work of which ruling powers in the state, the media and the educational system all combined. The ideology consists, not in the assertion of the superior virtues of the (German/ British/Japanese) race, but in the pretence that America is not a race or nation at all but is the universal Future. It lays arrogant claim to a universalism of virtues—an incantation of freedoms and rights—and asserts in this name a prerogative to blast in at every door and base itself in any part of the globe in the commission of these virtues. As it is doing in Central America now.

Characteristically, in the going rhetoric which still engulfs this nation, 'human rights' require no more definition than that these are goods which Americans enjoy (to a superlative degree) and which other guys don't have. This truth is held to be self-evident. It is a cause of immense self-congratulation: and a means of internal bonding, ideological and social control, vote-soliciting, and even attributed identity. If an Other is required, as foil to all this glittering virtue, then this is provided by Communism. But anti-Communism is necessary, less because Communism exists, than because there is an internal need within the ideology to define the approved national self-image against the boundary of an antagonist.

I rehearse all this because I wish to define the size of the problem facing the peace forces in the United States. I do so with respect: our forces in Britain were in no way strong enough to throw back a similar gust of ideology (more local but also more intense) during the Falklands War. We know the consequences. President Carter's helicopter operation to rescue the hostages in Iran was a fiasco, and he was turned out of power. Margaret Thatcher's helicopter (and task force) operation to rescue her hostages in the Falklands was a triumphant success: and she has now been returned to power in triumph.

The American peace movement—if it is to have any hope of success—must perforce challenge not only the military-industrial complex (or imperialist interests) but the hegemonic ruling ideology of the nation. It must strive to deconstruct this ideologically-confected national self-image, which now gives a very dangerous popular licence to expansion and aggression, and to disclose in its place an authentic self-identity. I will leave it to Americans—to poets and to historians—to say what this self-respecting self-image should be.

When I said that we un-Americans pray for a reversion to isolationism I was of course in jest. What we pray for—and what we can now recognize with delight—is the rebirth of American internationalism: but an authentic internationalism, which conducts its relations with equals, and which conducts them with like-minded popular movements and not with client states or with servile parasitic élites.

It is only the positive of internationalism which will be strong enough to contest and drive out the reigning national (or supra-national) ideology. There is a concern and generosity in American radical, labour, religious and intellectual traditions within which this internationalism has long been nourished, although sometimes as a threatened minority tradition. The greatest achievement of the American disarmament movement of the past two years has not been in winning this vote or that, but in raising peace consciousness throughout the continent, in questioning the self-congratulatory official image of America, and in providing a nation-wide network of groups within which the level of international discourse and information is continually rising.

Yet this still must rise a little further. The foundation-
stone of internationalism cannot be guilt: it must be
solidarity. We need, in some new form, a 'Wobbly' vocabulary
of mutual aid and of plain duty to each other in the face of
power. And we need to hammer out together our international strategies, in which the American movement clearly
sees itself and *feels* itself to be part of a whole 'International'
of self-liberating impulses from imperialisms and war.

Let us take the example of the *Iowa* task-force, which New
York and New Jersey officials and representatives (many of
them supporters of the Freeze when it seemed a vote-winner)
have invited into New York harbour. Maybe the citizens are
already stirring a little, and are realising the incredible folly
of basing a fleet of eight warships armed with nuclear-tipped
cruise missiles, nuclear depth charges, ASROC missles (some
nuclear-tipped) in the densest population centre in the world,
and making New York thereby a prime counterforce target
(and candidate for nuclear accidents such as collision and
fire).

What few have yet understood is the political strategy
behind this operation. All the fuss about the 'Euromissile'
crisis is about 572 cruise and Pershing II missiles—forward-
based US strategic missiles to be sited on European territory.
But quietly behind these are now coming the 4,000 plus
sea- and air-launched cruise missiles. There are two clear
political functions for the *Iowa* task-force. The first is as an
'insurance policy' in case the European peace movements
should succeed in chasing cruise and Pershing off their
territory. The fall-back will then be onto sea-launchers for
cruise: if necessary over 300 missiles could be placed on
World War II battleships (like *Iowa*), so that two ships
could carry more missiles than the entire allocation to
Europe.

This launcher (or launchers) could then lurk about off the
coast of West Europe, in the North Atlantic, or could move
into the Mediterranean. They would be more mobile than
ground-launched missiles but also *less politically visible*. No-
one could sit down in front of them; they would draw no

demonstrations. They would get European NATO leaders off the political hook. If the missiles were thrown out of Comiso and Greenham Common, they would reappear, anchored off Staten Island.

The second function of the *Iowa* task-force (like similar task-forces, also armed with cruise missiles, based on California and Hawaii) will be as mobile intervention fleets: that is, as nuclear pirate fleets. The *Iowa* force could dodge from Iceland to the Indian Ocean: could appear menacingly off the coast of Lebanon or Libya, supporting the Rapid Deployment Force; or 'quarantine' some part of Africa.

Whichever way the 'Euromissile' crisis is resolved the shadows will advance across the Atlantic to your coasts. If cruise and Pershing go down in Europe, then the Soviet military may well 'reply' by increasing the number of their forward-based missile submarines, to bring American prime targets (of which New York must now be one) within comparable flight-time (some eight minutes) of the Pershing II to Soviet targets.

The European peace movements do not wish to export Europe's troubles to America. If things get worse for you, nothing will get better for us. We are living the same problem: we must live it together: and re-learn all that lost vocabulary of solidarity.

We shall also require solidarity in the face of power. It has been apparent that (at least since January) there has been an orchestrated NATO strategy of rolling back the peace movement, on both sides of the Atlantic, by the most careful employment of public relations, media management, the provocation of dissension, and, very probably, the infiltration of agents and provocateurs. The old NATO élites feel more threatened by their domestic peace movements than they do by their purported adversary (the Warsaw bloc); they fear that a whole way of managing the world, and of controlling publics and clients, may be slipping away into some dangerous and unstable unknown. (The Warsaw power leaders are suffering similar anxieties.) In that sense, the most important thing of all to them is not to be forced into defeat by their own domestic opposition. The MX is pointed, not at

Russia, but at the Freeze; the cruise missiles at Greenham will be pointed at CND.

This is to say that our peace movements are engaged in one of the sharpest confrontations of our national political lives. We must disabuse our supporters if they suppose that they are confronting certain weapons only—'the bomb'. The peace movements cannot opt whether to be more 'political' or not. They have challenged 'the bomb'—and behind it they have found the full power of the State. If they are to reach 'the bomb' they must now take on also a whole State-manipulated and media-endorsed ideology.

It is ideology, even more than military-industrial pressures, which is the driving-motor of Cold War II. What occasions alarm is the very irrationality—the rising hysteria—of the drive, when it is measured against the 'objective' economic or political interests of ruling groups or forces. It is as if—as in the last climax of European imperialisms which led on into World War One, or as in the moment when Nazism triumphed in Germany—ideology has broken free from the existential socio-economic matrix within which it was nurtured and is no longer subject to any controls of rational self-interest. Cold War II is a replay of Cold War I, but this time as a deadly farce: the content of real interest-conflict between the two superpowers is low, but the content of ideological rancour and 'face' is dangerously high.

If history eventuated according to the notional rational self-interest of states or of classes, then we could calm our fears of nuclear war. It is scarcely in the interest of any ruling-class or state to burn up its resources, its labour-force, its markets, and then itself. But ideology masks out such interferences from an outer rational world. Just at the moment when the adversary posture of the two blocs is becoming increasingly pointless—and when a cease-fire in the Cold War would be greatly to the advantage of both parties—ideology assumes command and drives towards its own obsessional goals.

We may call this ideology 'imperialist' if we wish (and on both sides). But in naming it as 'imperialism' we should avoid the reduction of the problem to simplistic preconceptions (for example, Leninist) of what imperialism is. No two imperialisms have ever been the same—each has been a unique formation. And none can be reduced to a mono-causal analysis: for example, the pursuit of markets and profits, guided by some all-knowing committee of a ruling-class. Even in Europe's imperialist zenith (which culminated in the direct occupation and exploitation of subjected territories) a wide configuration of motivations were always at play: markets, missions, military bases, naval and trade routes, competition between imperial powers, ideological zeal, the vacancy left by the dissolution of previous power-structures (the Moghul empire), populist electoral hysteria, the definition of frontiers, imperial interest-groups, the expectation of revenue or gold or oil (which sometimes was not fulfilled).

American and Soviet 'imperialism' are also unique formations, and of the two it is Soviet which is most threatened and insecure, and American which is most expansionist. The American formation is a whole configuration of interests: financial, commercial (or 'corporatist') and extractive (the search for reserves of fossil fuels, uranium and scarce minerals): military (the alarming thrust of the arms trade, with its crazily insecure financial underwriting, which, in its turn, must be underwritten by military guarantees); political (the establishment of hegemony not by direct occupation but through the proxies of parasitic ruling élites in the client nations): and ideological. This formation is plainly beyond the control of any all-wise committee of a ruling-class: the White House is simply rolled around every-which-way as the eddying interests break upon its doors. Now one interest, now another, penetrates into the Oval Office.

In this messy, indecisive formation it is clearly ideology which—in the person of the President and his closest advisors —binds the whole configuration together and gives to it whatever erratic direction it takes. The rhetoric of the Cold War legitimates the whole operation, and therefore the Cold War is necessary to power's own continuance: the Cold War's ideological premises must continually be recycled and its visible instruments of terror must be 'modernised'. But since this direction increasingly defies the self-interest of any of the participants, ideology itself becomes more hysteric: it combines into one mish-mash the voices of militant Zionism, born-again fundamentalists, traumatised emigrés from Communist repression, careerist academics and bureaucrats, Western 'intelligence officers' and the soothsayers of the *New York Times*.

There is now (in this sense) a 'war movement' in Washington and in London. It is made up of (a) particular military-industrial interest groups—searching for bases, fossil fuels, new weapons, markets for arms; (b) New Right ideologues and publicists, and (c) the confrontational rhetoric and policies of populist politicians of the right. The climate thus engendered is sheltering nakedly militarist adventures and interventions, legitimated within the cant of Cold War apologetics.

But the military confrontation between the blocs has less and less rational strategic function: nuclear missiles are now becoming symbolic counters of political 'posture' or 'blackmail', negotiations are about political 'face'. Both SS-20s and Euromissiles are superfluous to any sane armoury. And the cruise and Pershing missiles have got to come because they are symbols of US hegemony over its own clients, and their acceptance is demanded as proof of NATO's 'unity'. They must be put down in noxious nests in England, Germany and Sicily, in order to hold the old decaying structures of life-threatening power together. The rising military appropriations are all for glue to paste over the places where the postwar political settlement ('Yalta') is beginning to come apart.

Nuclear weapons are not designed for the continuation of politics by other means: they are already the *suppression* of politics, the *arrest* of all political process within the frigid stasis of 'deterrence', and the *substitution* of the threat of annihilation for the negotiated resolution of differences. And within this degenerative process, the simulated threat of the Other becomes functional to the tenure of power of the rulers of the rival blocs: it legitimates their appropriation of taxes and resources, it serves to discipline unruly client states, it affords an apologia for acts of intervention, and it is a convenient resource for internal social and intellectual control. Increasingly the symbolism of State terror is employed to menace domestic opposition within each bloc. Like a curving ram's horn, the Cold War is now growing inwards into the warriors' own brains.

The war movement in the West encourages—according to the Cold War's 'law of reciprocity' (whether missiles or ideology) —an answering ideological response in the East. In Moscow as in Washington and London the tattered scripts of the early 1950s are dug out of the drawers and the lines are rehearsed. (Some of the old actors are still around.) The *New York Times* and *Pravda* recite the old crap: 'KGB agents', 'agents of Western imperialism', 'un-American activities' and 'peace-loving forces'. . . indeed, some of the malodorous agents (of both sides) are actually sent in. But the true adversaries which power fears, and seeks to hem in within the old ideological controls, are now not without but *within* their own blocs and spheres of influence: the real enemies of United States and NATO politicians are Central American insurgency, European 'neutralism', and domestic peace and radical movements: the real enemies of the Soviet power-élite are Solidarnosc, Afghan insurgents, and the growing desire of East European peoples for greater autonomy.

There could be two ways back from the precipice to which a threatened and dying ideology is conducting us. One would simply be a reassertion within the power-élites of the United States and the Soviet Union of the claims of rational self-interest. What is the point of burning up the world when, with a little loss of rhetoric, it could be managed and exploited to their mutual advantage? If this way is taken, then the élites will back away from war: they will come to some agreement (above the peace movements' heads): go back into arms control and SALT: and draw up a new 'Yalta' for the entire globe, dividing it up between them according to agreed rules: Afghanistan and Poland for you, El Salvador and Nicaragua for me.

This way is so much preferable to nuclear war that it seems churlish to call it in question. Indeed, it has some support in the United States, among élite groups which are now getting into discourse with their Soviet analogues, and who give some backing to the Freeze. Yet the trouble with this superpower settlement, this Orwellian 'Yalta 1984', is that it could never be more than a brief interim arrangement: it might last for five or ten years. For the superpowers can no longer command that the rest of the world—that Poland and Nicaragua, Europe and Latin America—stand still. It is indeed a question as to how much longer the élites can command their own domestic publics.

So that, even if the élites of both superpowers snuggle up together and attempt to take this first way back from nuclear suicide, it can only afford a brief interval before the second way to human survival is resumed. This is the way of the 'International' of peace movements, of non-aligned nations, and movements for civil rights and for liberation, working out—through many complexities—common strategies of mutual support and solidarity. Their common aims will be the enlargement of spaces for national autonomy, the peaceful break-up or melding of the blocs, and the refusal of every syllable of the vocabulary of nuclear arms. No-one can draw an accurate map of this way and show where it leads. We must find out together as we go along.

▲ QUESTIONS TO CASPAR WEINBERGER* ▲

Mr. President. Ladies and Gentlemen. I also wish to express my pleasure that Mr Weinberger is here. I think that this is a recognition not only of the standing of this society but a recognition also of the depth of concern in Europe and in this country on the issues of peace. And I welcome it also as

---

* On February 27th, 1984, I debated at the Oxford Union with Caspar Weinberger, the United States Secretary for Defense, the motion 'That there is no moral difference between the foreign policies of the US and the USSR.' The debate had been originally scheduled for May 27th, 1983, but Mr Heseltine intervened to prevent the debate (long before the date of the general election had been announced to the British Parliament) on the grounds that 'such a debate in a year that might see a general election might not be advisable'. (*New York Times*, 20 April 1983.) Since Heseltine was then planning his electoral strategy—in which the peace movement, the Labour Party, and several other parties were to be lampooned with every resource of the Tory Party and most of the media as uncritically and one-sidedly pro-Soviet—it was clearly against the interests of his party that a public debate of this kind should take place just before the election. His intervention was a wholly improper and unconstitutional interference in public life and in the affairs of the Oxford Union Society.

Mr Weinberger and his side 'won' the debate by 271–232 votes. However, Mr Laurence Grafstein (a past-president of the Union who was one of the speakers on Mr Weinberger's side) has candidly noted (in the *New Republic*) that 'it was the presence of about a hundred Americans in the debating chamber which proved decisive'. Some of these voters had been specially flown across the Atlantic for the occasion!

I am grateful to BBC 2 (Special Projects) and to Mr Elwyn Parry Jones for sending me a transcript of my speech. I have corrected it for clarity and made a few cuts, but made no changes of substance.

one of those signs of the openness to debate of the American
system: an openness which I have myself often benefited
from. I have been able to say in the United States what I
wanted to say on behalf of the British or the European peace
movement. I have been welcomed at the National Press Club
in Washington, at campuses and churches in the United States,
and I know very well that I would not be able to speak
openly in the same way in the Soviet Union.

Without this tradition and vitality of openness in American
intellectual life, humanity would not now know the perils in
which it is placed. If it had not been for the tradition of the
United States scientists, of 'whistleblowers' like Daniel
Ellsberg, or of arms controllers who have come out and made
the most radical criticism of their own state policy—if it had
not been for publications like the *Bulletin of the Atomic
Scientists*, we would not even know about the nuclear winter
that would follow even a medium exchange of weapons. We
would not know this through Soviet sources, and we would
not know it from British sources which are obsessed with
'official secrecy'.

This emphasises that we are tonight not discussing the
relative merits of the two political systems. We are not
discussing whether we would prefer to live in the Soviet
Union or in the United States. There is scarcely any room for
choice in this for any serious intellectual worker who needs
the tools of his trade, who needs to be able to consult the
libraries or to publish without censorship.

We are discussing tonight the foreign policies, not the
internal social systems, the foreign policies of the United
States and the USSR and the moral differences between them.
And I can find none. Today the world is dominated by two
towering superpowers, locked in each others' nuclear arms,
aggravating each other, inciting each other in their ideological
postures, rendering and reducing to client status their lesser
allies.

Mr Weinberger will find some Europeans and many British
in an ill-humour today. And he shouldn't be surprised. He is
himself something of a philosopher, a rigorous thinker on
questions of deterrence. In his *Defense Report* for the Fiscal

Year of 1984 he wrote out some of his reflections. Deterrence, he said is 'a dynamic effort', not a static one, and he
set out a view of an entire 'continuum' over which deterrence
had to be not only effective but constantly modernised and
enhanced, linking the highest level of conventional arms to
the lowest threshold of nuclear weapons: a continuum in
regions, a continuum in ranges of missiles, a continuum in
time itself, envisaging the possibility of an extended nuclear
war. And this was a philosophy of 'enhanced deterrence'.
Now enhanced deterrence is not a stable state, it is a radically
unstable state. It has, in the worst-case analysis of the
planners, an in-built accelerator, and these two systems are
now acclerating towards each other at a growing pace towards
a terminal collision.

We in Europe were found by some clever philosophers in
NATO several years ago to be in a weak point in this
'continuum'. And for three years negotiations have been
going on over our heads about a matter which could scarcely
concern Europeans more: that is, the nuclear weapons sited
on our own territory and which might be used in a European
'theatre of war'.

By no means all the blame for the enhancement of deterrence in Europe lies with the United States. Our own political
leaders have been throughout consenting adults in the
corruption and subordination of this nation to the hegemony
of United States' military policy. Now the first flight of these
missiles, owned and operated by the United States, are here
on our territory and they are supposed to be for our greater
security. Do we really feel more secure because cruise and
Pershing have come? No-one feels more secure: neither
Europeans nor the Soviet people nor the people of the
United States.

We believe first of all that the military scenario has always
been absurd. We have these serpents' eggs and more are
coming. (By the way, perhaps we could ask Mr Weinberger
when the next flight will come?) But I would like (since he is
our guest) to warn Mr Weinberger before he replies that we
have an engine in Britain known as the Official Secrets Act.
And although he might be able to give this information to the

United States Congress—or even to the Soviet Ambassador—
if he gave it to the British people it might be an offence
against the Official Secrets Act since these are Acts to
prevent the British people from being informed about matters
deeply of their concern. We have the case now of a young
woman in the Foreign Office who is accused of a terrible
offence against 'official secrets'. And Miss Sarah Tisdall,
who is accused of this offence, is accused of having leaked to
an extreme revolutionary newspaper called the *Guardian* a
memorandum sent by our Defence Secretary Mr Heseltine to
Mrs Thatcher and others in which he explained how he
intended to con the British people and manage opinion at
the moment of the arrival of cruise. So that Mr Weinberger
must be cautious as to what he says about these matters in
this country.

All the serpents' eggs are now clutched on a site in Britain
whose location, thanks to the action of some of my fellow
countrywomen and their friends from North America and
Europe and elsewhere, has been rather well advertised. Even
the British people know where the cruise missiles are. I think
probably the Soviet Union knows where they are. And if the
'evil emperor' is anxious to make a pre-emptive strike (as we
are told by some people) than all the eggs could be smashed
in one basket in a perfect 'Pearl Harbour'. So no-one can
really be expecting this pre-emptive strike to come.

No, the missiles must move out first from the base. But
while these missiles are themselves so small that verification
is extremely difficult—and therefore arms control agreements
are being cast in jeopardy by cruise missiles coming—the
convoys which take them out to their firing-places in the
country are very well open to satellite observation. So it is
insane. The first sign of those convoys moving out would be
a signal to satellite observation that our govenment (or the
United States Government rather, because they are owned
and operated by the United States) was planning a strike; and
this would be an incitement to the Soviet military to make a
pre-emptive strike before their own missiles were struck. This
is insane. Although I would reassure Mr Weinberger that the
situation isn't quite as bad as that. We have got a fence

around these missiles, in fact we have got quite a tall fence. We have now got three fences and we have got them pretty well encircled by soldiers and by police and best of all by the Greenham Common women, and then outside by the peace movement of the nation. All we have to do now to make the missiles completely safe is to get the police to turn around and face the other way.

The second reason that we do not feel more secure lies in the predicted consequences of this action. The blocs have closed against each other. The counter-deployment is going on of SS21's, 22's or 23's, including deployment in Czechoslovakia and East Germany (which have hitherto been only very lightly, if at all, occupied by nuclear weapons). We have been saying up and down Europe for two years that the dragons' teeth sown in Comiso and Greenham Common would spring up as missiles on the other side. And so it has taken place. Any child could see that. Any child. Why can eminent statespersons not understand what Auden wrote in agony at the commencement of World War II?

> I and the public know
> What all schoolchildren learn:
> Those to whom evil is done
> Do evil in return.

The missiles are futile, of course. The Dutch women's peace movement have told me they have found out that the cruise missiles are actually cartons full of washing powder. It doesn't matter what they are: they are symbols and they are symbols of menace, of 'posture', of clientage and subordination in the recipient nations, of NATO or Warsaw Pact 'unity'.

But they are not only symbols. Nor are they all that there is. We know what is coming on behind them. Thanks to the openness of the American system we know much more about what is coming on on the United States' side. MX, BI, Trident (there and here), the Iowa task force with its load of sea-launched cruise missiles, the air-launched cruise missiles: 1,300 are in production now and in the fiscal year '85. And

beyond that the vista of space weapons and space scenarios
for war. And there are other little bits of things in Mr Weinberger's latest 1985 Fiscal Year *Report;* I think that there
are five new short-range nuclear systems now being brought
forward and two new chemical systems. There are (perhaps
he will tell us?) plans for siting new ground-launched anti-
ship missiles in the Western Isles and in Scotland.

I say that this is a condition of barbarism. And I put
forward two documents, essential to my case. These are both
part of the propaganda that led us to this disastrous situation.
One is called *Soviet Military Power* and it has a foreword by
Mr Weinberger. It is a 'Sears–Roebuck' catalogue of all the
deadly military equipment, whether naval or air or on the
ground, possessed by the Soviet Union. And the other, which
was produced in answer to it by the Soviet propagandists, is
called *Whence the Threat to Peace?* This also is a catalogue—
rather better illustrated, because they could get the illustra-
tions more easily from the United States' press—of all the
marvellous military equipment being developed in the United
States. They have even copied each other in maps. Here is a
power projection in the United States catalogue, with a *huge*
Soviet Union, with arrows going in every direction around
the world. And in the Soviet catalogue, the Soviet Union is
rather smaller and all the arrows are spreading out from the
United States towards the five continents of the world.

The usual half-lies and propaganda statements are made in
both these books. But the tragedy is that *both* these books
are largely *true.* William Hazlitt said about a philosophical
radical, the Rev Fawcett, in the 1790's that he had Thomas
Paine's *Rights of Man* and Edmund Burke's *Reflections on
the French Revolution* bound together in the same covers,
and he said that, taken together, they made a very good book.
But bind these two together and they make the most evil
book known in the whole human record. They are a
catalogue, an inventory of the matched evils of this accelera-
ting system, a confession of absolute human failure. What
moral difference is there between these two catalogues?
What language of 'ought' can be found there? Is this the
product of our most advanced civilisation? 'Was it for this

the clay grew tall?'

The globe has shrunk now to a little gourd. It is controlled by two vast, mutually-exacerbating military structures at the summit of which there is extraordinary centralised power in the functions of the President of the Union States and the First Secretary of the Soviet Communist Party. We know now that throughout last autumn this power lay in the hands of two elderly men, one of whom was on a kidney-machine and half-dead from the neck down, and the other of whom (in the view of his critics) was on an autocue-machine and half-dead from the neck up.

The trouble with the statesmen and military leaders of both blocs is that they talk the same language. They both burn our taxes and our resources before the nostrils of the great Sacred Cow called the 'balance' or 'parity'. We haven't, on this side in this debate, played the game of 'snap'. We haven't tried to list the offences on one side and trade them against the offences on the other. Vietnam—Afghanistan; Central Europe—Central America, the joint competition in the foul trade in arms. If anything, I would say, looking over the last 30 years, that the Gulag has been shrinking over on that side, and is tending to enlarge in the area of dependency on this side, the client or proxy states of the Western powers. There is now a formidable United States presence everywhere: Oman, Turkey, Iceland, South Korea, Egypt, Diego Garcia—what are you doing in Diego Garcia?—Somalia—what are you doing there?

We have seen this process by which the Brezhnev doctrine was extended from Eastern and Central Europe to Afghanistan; while the Truman doctrine (taking over from Britain in 1947) proclaimed an area of special United States interest, first in Greece, Turkey, and the Near East, and was then extended by President Carter to the Persian Gulf. We see now before our eyes today an extraordinary notion of 'peace-keeping', in the Caribbean, around Nicaragua, or off the coast of Lebanon, where the *New Jersey* battleship is just steaming up and down lobbing half-ton shells into the villages in the hills above Beirut—lobbing half-ton shells—what is this? Congress doesn't understand, the American people cannot understand.

(By the way, it was reported in the *Washington Post* in July
that there are eight Tomahawk cruise missiles in deployment
on the *New Jersey*. It would reassure us very much to know
that these missiles, with a range of 1,500 miles, do not have
nuclear warheads. Because if they do have nuclear warheads
they can reach deeply into Asia.)

What 'moral interest' is here? If anything I would say that,
of the two, the United States administration under President
Reagan has been more threatening in its military posture,
while the Soviet Union has been more responsible for the
ideological and security blockages which prevent any healing-
process in the world to begin. But no micrometer can find a
moral difference in the mutual postures of hostility. And I
want to ask Mr Weinberger: what is this quarrel about? It is
an irrational condition. It consists in itself. The superpowers
feel threatened because they *are* threats to each other and
have historically become so. It is an acquired inertia. It is a
self-reproducing system.

When, at a certain historical moment at the end of World
War Two, the armies met and caused a divide like a geological
fault across the centre of our continent, we then had as a
product of those particular historical circumstances and
contingencies the origin of the Cold War. You can look back
there for moral differences, but now, after 35 years, there is
no more morality. This division has outlasted its historical
tenure, the moment of its origin. Struck by the permafrost
of deterrence occasioned by nuclear weapons arriving at that
moment of division, there commenced a self-reproducing
process in which the hawks feed the hawks of the other side.

Each side pretends to moral superiority. The Soviet Union
pretends to be a socialist heartland but it fears most of all
democratic socialist impulses; hence the crushing of the
'Prague Spring' in '68, hence the crushing of the self-activating
working-class movement of Solidarnosc in Poland. And the
threatening military posture of the West repeatedly gives to
the old post-Stalinist rulers an extended historical tenure. It
is the 'evil empire' claptrap, the 'sworn enemies' claptrap
which Mrs Thatcher was using only last year, which causes
prison doors to close on the other side, which leads to the

tightening of security systems, which gives a justification and legitimacy to the post-Stalinist leadership which has outlasted. . .

Lawrence Grafstein (interrupting): With the greatest respect, sir, do you really believe that Mrs Thatcher's voice or Mr Reagan's voice, shrill as we all agree they are, is responsible for the closing of prison doors in the Eastern bloc or in the Soviet Union?. . . I can't see how you could hold someone's words responsible for someone else's deeds?

E.P. Thompson: I thank you for this correction. I said 'accomplices'. I hope that I said 'accomplices'.* This is a reciprocal process. Each time the West adopts a threatening and menacing posture there is an instant response from the other side which makes the position of the doves weaker and the position of the hawks stronger, which induces the enhancement of the security system and which makes more difficult the communication which our peace movement has been with great difficulty developing over the last three years.

We see this logic at work all the time. I want to give you one example of this. We now know that Mr Andropov was dying through the three months during which the NATO missile deployment was coming to fulfilment. There was then the makings of a succession-crisis, and the succession has now been decided. If we suppose that there are divisions (as many experts say) in the Soviet leadership, between the doves and the hawks, do you really think that the doves were being strengthened and encouraged as Pershing and cruise came into Europe? NATO acted precisely in such a way as to induce a response of fear and insecurity in the Soviet Union and to bring about the opposite result. And then the leaders of the Western world go to Moscow and proclaim that they want to have a 'dialogue'. . . with a coffin!

On this side we have the Western ideological use of 'human rights'. The cause is just but the employment of it is again and again the most odious hypocrisy. I need not remind you of the blind eye to offences in our own back-yard. I would

---

* I didn't!—E.P.T.

refer you to Amnesty International's report on *Political Killings by Governments:* You won't find that it says that political killings take place on that side of the world but not in the 'free world's' area of influence. It's a very much more jumbled picture than that and one which leads to a much more complex reading. And secondly there is the double-talk that goes on: the enthusiasm of President Reagan for workers' control in Poland when the American air controllers were put in irons; or of Mrs Thatcher for Solidarnosc, when by a stroke of the pen seven or eight thousand British trade unionists at GCHQ, Cheltenham, are suddenly told that they have the same trade-union rights as Poles. I only want to say this. The strategy of a Cold War ideological linkage between human rights and Cold War is deeply counter-productive. No one is ever going to get any human rights in Czechoslovakia or Poland because a cruise missile or Pershing is pointed at them.

Let me end by being constructive. Am I speaking for 'neutralism'? Am I saying 'a plague on both your houses!'? Yes. But we—that is Europe—are also pretty plaguey. We are a source of the plague, we were the source of World War One and World War Two. And what we owe to ourselves, but also to the American and the Soviet people, is a more active strategy than mere neutrality. Neutrality isn't going to save us from the nuclear winter if the superpowers engage. We need to make a space between the two superpowers: a more tranquil space, maybe by nuclear-free zones in the Baltic and Balkans, a corridor in central Europe; by commencing a healing-process of citizens, of scholars, of doctors, of churches, a healing-process underneath the level of the states.

The European peace movement in the last three years has not just been about certain categories of missile. Underneath there has been a huge subterranean political-geological up-heaval, the demand for greater autonomy both as individual nations and of Europe as a whole. I think Americans will understand when I say that we are on the edge of a moment that they might remember from their own history. We are in a place like 1771 or 1772. Europe is meditating now a declaration of independence.

I want to ask Mr Weinberger what his solution is, beyond all the build-up of these missiles. What solution does he offer? I suggest that what we need is an 'Austrian solution' for Europe, and then for the world. Yes, the problem as Mr Shultz has said, is in effect 'Yalta'. But 'Yalta' has got two sides: one side is the Soviet presence in Eastern and Central Europe, and the other side is the heavy American military hegemony in western and southern Europe. And you will never reach a settlement on one side without a settlement on the other. That is the strategy we have to look for. I am making no moral apologies for the presence of Soviet troops in Czechoslovakia or in Hungary, but as realists we must know that they will not withdraw unless there is some concession in the West and especially in West Germany. While West Germany is stashed with military forces will there be a withdrawal on the other side?

Americans should reflect how this situation came about. There has not been in this century any major war on American territory and forever may this continue. But if, some 40 years ago, invading armies had come by way of Canada into New England, had sacked Boston, Providence, New Haven, Albany, Rochester, Buffalo—had gone as far west as Detroit—had invested New York, so that New Yorkers died by one-third of the population—ate shoe-leather, burnt their books and their floor-boards, as the Leningrad people did—had got to the borders of Washington, as Hitler's armies got to Moscow—had then fought block by block right into the heart of Chicago, as happened in Stalingrad—had left 20 million dead—then the United States might have made, after that, a client buffer zone of Canada. That would not have been a 'moral' action. I'm making no apology for it. It would have been a consequence of history, a matter of state interest.

But those who served in World War Two would not have believed it, they would have been amazed if they had been told that 39 years after the end of World War Two there would still be Soviet forces in East Europe and United States forces in West Europe. At that time we had a vision, and that vision extended also to the United States and the Soviet Union, of a socialist and democratic world. We have now to re-trace our steps back down to the point where 'Yalta' was fixed and try and unscramble it.

When friends come to help us its fine for them to stay in the house for three or four days, but when they stay for three weeks we get a little bit restive. After 39 years enough is enough. So it's now our duty to start this healing-process and its yours, Mr Weinberger, to assist us to this new object-ive whose end must be the withdrawal of these forces from both sides. This is not anti-Americanism—it is not anti-Sovietism. We'll send you home with flowers and we will welcome you back to our universities or to our countries as visitors with flowers once more. But it is in the interests of the people of both sides to be rid of the burden, the anguish, and the danger involved in this European connect-ion.

The first moral difference that will appear will be when either superpower makes an actual *act* of disarmament. Then we can start to talk about morality. Until that happens I rest my case on these two odious books and I ask Oxford to support this motion in the name of a universalism at its very foundation in the Middle Ages: a universalism of scholarship which owed its duty to the skills of communica-tion and learning and not to those of the armed state. As William Blake wrote:

> The strongest poison ever known
> Came from Caesar's laurel crown.

I support this motion in the confidence that this house will reject the poison of Caesar.

BRITAIN
CRUISES ON

▲ CARELESS TALK COSTS LIVES* ▲

There is something quixotic in this—for a post-imperial island nation, with an ailing economy, to send out on three days' notice 26,000 men and a vast armada to the opposite end of the oceans in defence of a few hundreds of its own nationals threatened by an invading tyranny.

It is in defiance of all calculations of interest. There is no realism about it. And it is this which has caught, for a moment, the heart of half the nation. Those who suppose the British to be a nation of shop-keepers are riding for a fall. The British can also be a nation of romantics. They like to argue their politics, not in terms of interests, but in terms of oughts. This is true of the British Labour movement also. Inside every shop steward there is a Don Quixote struggling to get out.

The British are also a rather old seafaring nation, the island anchorage of the greatest naval imperialism ever known to the world. For 500 years the ships have set out, from the Thames and Medway, from Plymouth, Portsmouth, the Clyde, to quarter the globe and to accumulate that extraordinary empire by acts of aggression a great deal less decorous and less bloodless than the invasion with which the Falklands War commenced. It is odd that we should be so moralistic today about other nations' faults. We expect them to grow up instantly to our own senescent sanctity

---

* *Guardian*, 31 May 1982.

without passing through our own adolescent sins.

The whole British people had a part in this naval empire. It was not just a preserve of the ruling class. They were the common people who built and manned the ships and whose families awaited their return. Naval victories were a staple of popular ballad and broadsheet. Drake and Nelson were genuine national heroes, not invented from above.

There is a long resonance in this, and an old resource for Tory Populism. Naval officers have been the most competent cadre of the British ruling class—as seamen, navigators, administrators. Some even, through shared hardships and loyalties, became democrats or 'Friends of the People'.

And there is another ancient resonance, which one can sense to be vibrating now. The English nation came of age with the defeat of the Armada. The naval battles which first secured our empire were mainly with Hispanic peoples. Our privateers scoured the oceans, robbing the King of Spain of his treasure and singeing his beard.

The European maritime nations exported their rivalries and fought them out before astonished native audiences at the furthest ends of the earth. 'We did maik them such a breakfast as I do verielie think was neyther in the way of curttesy or unkindnesses well accepted.' So wrote Captain Thomas Best in a despatch of 1612 recounting the Battle of Swally Hole—one of those sharp engagements in which the English gained dominance over the Portuguese in the contest for ports in India.

'The Dragon, being ahead, steered from one to another, and gave them such banges as maid ther verie sides crack; for we neyther of us never shott butt were so neere we could nott misse.' The fight took place 'in the sight of all the army of the Muslim Governor who stood so thick upon the hills beholdinge of us that they covered the ground.'

Manners have changed today. We do not have to wait for Captain Best's despatch to come to us by sail around the Cape. We are told about it all—or we are told as much as some official thinks it proper that we should know—the next day by Mr Ian MacDonald. There has been some loss in the vigour of the language, as well as in veracity. But that is a small price to pay for progress.

And progress has made other gains. This is an electronic war, a war of top technicians. Our men-of-war no longer steer between the enemy and crack their sides. Torpedoes and missiles are launched at ranges of twenty or more miles. All that opponents may ever see of each other is a radar blip.

And there is no astonished army of the Muslim Governor now viewing the Battle of Falkland Sound. The audience, thick on the hills, are not only the sheep—or such of the sheep as have not already been changed, by the opposing forces, into mutton. It is also that of the arms traders and war gamesmen—the 'experts' of the whole world.

These are rapt in attention. Shares are rising and falling. Sea Harriers are up but aluminium frigates are down. Since the *Sheffield* was sunk the makers of the Exocet have already received new orders for sixteen hundred (or was it sixteen thousand?) missiles. Full order books for that. And 'lessons' are being learned. United States naval strategy is already undergoing a major review. Too late for us, of course. Progress is going on, and we are the price.

We can see, more clearly than we could two weeks ago, the features of World War III. It is not only that the Falklands War is being fought with nuclear-age technologies in which only the nuclear-tipped warheads are missing. It is also that the consequences of the militarisation of the entire globe have become transparent.

This is not just a matter of the export of sophisticated weaponry from the advanced to the Third World: sales to Argentina of the Exocet, of Skyhawks, of Sea Wolf and Sea Dart, Type 42 destroyers (sister ships to the *Sheffield*) and the rest. No doubt our forces in the Falklands are already reflecting upon that, and in due course the British public may give it a thought also.

It is also that, with the weapons, the advanced world is exporting—directly or indirectly—military juntas. Look where you will, the pressure is that way: Chile, Guatemala, El Salvador, Argentina, Poland, Afghanistan. If we want to crusade against fascist juntas, we need only scan the list of our own best customers for arms. Our loyal NATO ally,

Turkey, is a junta of that kind, with above 30,000 political prisoners in its jails and with the executive Committee of the Turkish Peace Association at this moment on trial. This year the United States has increased its hand-outs to Turkey of military aid.

The peace movement has been warning of this for years, but our government has noticed only when a junta blew up in its own face. It is not as if our governments (Labour or Conservative) were given no warning. In 1978, to his credit, President Carter cut off military sales to the Argentine on the issue of human rights. France, Britain, Israel and Germany eagerly stepped in to take up the slack. If (which God forbid!) one of our nuclear submarines should be sunk, causing a major reactor disaster in the South Atlantic, it would perhaps have been located by a Lynx helicopter (Westland Aircraft Ltd) equipped with Ferranti Seaspray radar and Decca electronic supports.

Helicopters in the Argentine have had other uses. It is said that some of the thousands of 'Disappeared Ones'—oppositionists seized by the junta's security arm—were simply dumped from the bellies of helicopters into the South Atlantic. An American business man recently over-heard Argentine officers jesting about 'the flying nuns'—two French disappeared nuns who were dealt with in that way. It is a clean and convenient means of disposal.

That is an odious regime. Yet there is something a little odious also about the hypocrisy of our own politicians. We are now, very suddenly, in a war to the death with a fascist regime. Yet our government has no interest in liberating the Argentine people, or in strengthening the democratic opposition to General Galtieri. On the contrary, by taking recourse to military measures, instead of diplomatic and economic sanctions, it has strengthened the junta and given it a surge of populist nationalist support.

To be honest, I do not think that Mrs Thatcher—and still less President Reagan—want to see the fall of the Argentine junta. They would like to humiliate it, to be sure, and to see it reshuffled into more accommodating forms. But they will not wish to threaten *juntadom*, whether there or in Chile.

For if the junta fell under pressure from its own people, something far 'worse'—an Argentine Allende or Castro might come to power.

If the West had wished to destabilise the junta it had the means at hand. The Argentine is one of the most indebted nations in the world. And why? Because Western banks have loaned to Argentina the wherewithal to buy expensive Western weapons-systems. If Western banks had been willing to pull the plug and default the junta, in a few months unrest might have overwhelmed and overturned the military rulers.

But this would have been a desperate remedy with an uncertain outcome. It would have caused pain in the ledgers of the Western banking system. It was better to settle the matter in traditional ways, by the loss of blood rather than the risk of money. It was better to send out a task-force.

And do we realise—does *anyone* yet realise—what we—or our betters on the front benches of all the major parties—have done? In that quixotic moment of injured national pride and historical reminiscence, we have sent 26,000 men 8,000 miles away, without adequate air cover, to confront some of the most advanced weaponry yet devised.

The politicians squint at us complacently from the screens, one eye on the cameras, the other on the opinion polls. They are confident that they—or at least those poor bastards out there in the South Atlantic—will pull it off. Yet romanticism married to that kind of calculation of political advantage is a poor guide to reality.

Careless talk costs lives. It is costing lives now. Talk of paramountcy, sovereignty, flags, unconditional surrender; careless talk on the Jimmy Young Show and at the Scottish Tory Party conference; the careless roar of the House of Commons at feeding-time. Now they have got their meat.

It is impossible to write a line on the possible outcome of the Falklands War without hazard. To write is like rolling marbles on the deck of a ship in a storm. I write this now on Friday. What will we learn when it appears on Monday? Will Port Stanley have fallen to British marines? Will one of our capital ships have been sunk? Will a cease-fire have been enforced by world opinion?

I wish only to say this: we have done a dreadful and un-thinking thing. We have allowed a desperate gamble to take place with human life, in preference to a longer course of diplomatic and economic attrition. The gamble may pay off (and greatly to Mrs Thatcher's political advantage), owing to the immense resources, experience and skill of the British forces.

But it is not inevitable that it will, and it is necessary that someone should incur the odium of saying so. Our task-force is now at risk. Its air defences, always inadequate, depend upon two carriers. If the *Hermes*, instead of the *Atlantic Conveyor*, had been sunk, then the terms of battle would have tilted dangerously against us.

And what would happen then? Will 500 years of imperial naval history end in a tragic encounter in Falkland Sound? And how will the land forces be rescued and brought back? How, across those 8,000 miles, can we mount another Dunkirk?

Our politicians and much of our popular media have been guilty of appalling levity. The sinking of the *Belgrano* and the *Sheffield* ought to have enforced a change of tone, an interval of reflection. I would have been opposed to the sending of the task-force even if I had known that it would bring a quick, and almost bloodless, victory. Our proper course was always pursuance of the full terms of UN Resolution 502, in *all* its parts, and with the endorsement of world opinion. Our resort to force has already endangered the peace of the world by weakening the authority of the United Nations, which, ineffectual as it is—and as we have made it—is yet the only institution which points forward to an international rule of law.

But we are now, as I write, brought to a desperate situation. A major British defeat could have appalling conse-quences within our culture: it could turn us into something much like a junta ourselves. Already the authoritarians of every hue are having their festival. After the careless talk has ended, the really ugly talk begins.

That is why the peace movement must now go out into those storms outside and rescue what is sane and pacific in our culture. If the first thoughts of all of us are with our brave lads in the South Atlantic—as it is obligatory for every politic speech to commence these days—then our second thoughts ought to be how to get them out of that cold and hostile place.

I can see no way in which CND's demonstration in Hyde Park on June 6th can not also be a demonstration to halt and to pass back into the hands of United Nations negotiations the outcome of the Falklands War. I know that there are some notable critics of our resort to force in the Falklands who are not nuclear disarmers; and I know that there are some nuclear disarmers who think that the Falklands War is not a proper issue to concern CND.

But I think that we must all, calmly and in good order and in the greatest possible numbers, go to the Park together. This is a crisis of historic dimensions, a crisis in our culture and our polity, and an ideological confrontation which we refuse at our peril. And, even more than this, it is our urgent duty both to our kin and also to their Argentinian fellow-sufferers in the South Atlantic.

We never know anything of the truth of wars until a few years have passed. It will all trickle out later—the crises of supplies, the official lies, the troops sickening in the ships, the equipment bogged down on the islands. We may also learn of episodes of skill and courage which we can celebrate with a whole heart—above all the extraordinary rescue operations (on both sides) of the hundreds who have already been tipped into those seas.

But now this is a war which must be stopped. Even if—as with the Peruvian or the Secretary-General's formulae—with a little loss of Mrs Thatcher's face. That is in the true interests of all parties, including the Falkland Islanders.

It is also in the interests of a threatened world. The peace movement did not deserve this tragic diversion. Militarisation is now global and the defences against militarist passions must be global also. There can be no gaps in that line.

I have heard it said that the British peace movement is finished, knocked sideways by the Falklands War. It was a fair-weather movement only—a peace movement which fainted at the sight of a real war. I ask you to walk out quietly and without provocation into that opposition, and to answer it with your numbers.

▲ THE DEFENCE OF BRITAIN* ▲

This is the most important general election to be fought in Britain in this century. Yet I am already weary of it, after only ten days, and I find that my neighbours and acquaintances are weary also.

The British people must take a decision on June 9th which will affect, in the most literal sense, their lives, and the lives of their children and of their children's children, if these are to have any lives at all. Yet we are not being serious about it.

The matter which we must decide concerns the defence of Britain and how this may be best conducted. When I consult the dictionary I find that 'defence' means 'protection' or 'means of resisting attack'. I take it that we all regard this as an important matter.

---

* A pamphlet written (and published by Merlin Press), in the middle of the 1983 General Election.

We would wish to protect this island against a foreign invasion or occupation. There may be a few things wrong with this country—in fact we are coming to realise that there are a great many things wrong in this country, with its economy and its social life—but we none of us suppose that they will be made any better by having Russians or Americans ruling over us.

'Defence' also makes us think of various good things, like our 'liberties' and our 'traditions' and our 'way of life', although I find that people are becoming more and more uncertain as to what their liberties and traditions are, and whose way of life (that of the security services or that of the unemployed?) is to be defended?

Yet whatever doubts we have, we all can think of things in the British way of life which we like, and we would want to protect these against attack. I would think, for example, of our jury system and of our free press.

But the strange thing here is that when we think of the things that are worth defending, it often turns out that the attack is coming, not from without our society, but from within. The Russians have not been tampering with our jury system—it is something which we might hope to export to them if times become happier—but this has been done by British police commissioners, judges, attorney-generals and the present Lord Chancellor. And a large part of our free press has been bought, over our heads, by money (some of it foreign money), making it more and more inaccessible to the common voice of our people.

So that the 'defence of our way of life' turns out to be something which cannot be done by paying over large taxes to a Ministry of Defence (which used to be called a Ministry of War) to buy more and more deadly nuclear missiles. A cruise missile cannot do anything at all to protect British liberties, any more than it can do anything to export liberties to people who live 'under the yoke of Communist totalitarianism'. No-one has even tried to explain how nuking other people will make them more free.

The 'protection' of our liberties against 'attack' has, for the greater part of our history, only rarely come to the issue of battles and weaponry. It has been done by means of law and pamphlet and sermon and the formation of democratic organisations—parties and chapels and trade unions—and by debates within the nation, and even (for this has not yet been bought over our heads by the property developers) by means of the vote.

This vote itself was a liberty which had to be fought for, won, and defended, by Radicals, Chartists and Suffragettes. It was never handed down on a plate from on high. But the 'fighting' was never a matter of buying bigger and more deadly weapons. It was done by acts of the mind and the spirit, by the persuasion of peaceful numbers, as at Peterloo, or the witness of supporters—in fact by such means as the peace movement still uses today.

The nuke and the vote belong to two distinct and opposed human technologies: mechanical brute force or the skills of civilised human life. They can buy the first (out of our own public revenue) but I hope that they cannot yet buy the second. The true defence of our liberties today requires defending these against the insatiable appetite of 'Defence'.

I must now explain to readers a certain difficulty about this pamphlet which they are reading. Over three years ago I wrote a small pamphlet called *Protest and Survive*. It made a little stir at the time, sold a good many copies, became adopted as a slogan, was republished in a Penguin book of the same title, and altogether it was the most ill-advised action of my life, for which I have been kicking myself ever since.

For I passed, with its publication, from being a private citizen and a free-lance writer and historian into being a famous (or infamous) Public Person, 'Professor' (which I am not) E.P. Thompson, on call at any hour of the day and sometimes night for the service of a huge, untidy, sometimes quarrelsome but always high-spirited and dedicated movement arising in every part of the globe which is called 'the peace movement'.

I did not call this movement into being. It happened of itself and I was happened by it. It was a necessary event. If, after 38 years of gathering nuclear threat, and the insatiable

and growing appetites of the nuclear armourers, some people
had not stood up and started waving banners to each other
across the globe, then one could properly have assumed that
the human spirit had rolled over on its back and given up
the ghost.

But I had myself become, with a few strokes of the pen, a
prisoner of this peace movement. After all, one cannot come
forward before the public and inform it that there is an
extreme and immediate danger that civilisation is moving
into a terminal stage—that everything we know of as civilisation may be at an end in some twenty or thirty years unless
this process is reversed—that whatever enfeebled populations
survive us amidst civilisation's radio-active ruins will carry all
the infirmities of genetic damage—one cannot utter a mouthful like that and then say: 'Thank you, I am now going back
to look after my garden.'

No way. I had said that if we hoped, in this island, to
survive, then we must protest. And it follows that I must be
seen to be protesting with the protestors, or else I must eat
my words. If I could have seen a way to eat my words,
perhaps I would have done so, even though some of them
were large and unappetising. They were not nice orotund,
facile words, such as the 'True Peace-Keepers' use ('deterrence', 'security', 'negotiating from strength') which the
Great British Public is invited to swallow three times a day,
and which leave it burping contentedly before the telly.
Some of my words were too acid to swallow, and others
(like 'exterminism') would have taken an awful lot
of chewing.

I could not eat my words because I still consider them to
be true. I still consider civlisations's condition to be near-
terminal. I still think that we must protest if we are to
survive. Indeed, one or two of the more sombre predictions
which I made over three years ago have already come to
pass. The nuclear arms race has become very much worse.
The hawks of one side continue to feed and to fatten the
hawks of the other. The East and the West are hardening
the lines of ideological combat against each other. New areas
of the globe (Central America, the Middle East) are being

sucked up into the Cold War confrontation. Newcomers are expected daily to enter the nuclear club: perhaps, very soon, Argentina. As the Cold War confrontation hardens, so the security state is visibly strengthened on that side and on this, and a shadow is thrown upon civil liberties here in our 'free' world as well as in the Communist world.

So I must, for a little longer—either until the forces of peace win some little victory (and we have won no victories yet) or until the sky becomes so dark that it is too late for anything to matter—continue as a prisoner of the peace movement.

There could be worse forms of captivity. For this work has, in the past three years, brought me the friendship and companionship of thousands of people—people whose resourcefulness remind me of the best moments in our nation's history, and even make me wonder, in incautious moments, whether our people are really as dead and deluded as our media and our rulers seem to intend them to be?

And there has been another compensation also. For I have seen, in the past three years, a great many more places and vastly more people in the world than I ever expected to see. For the peace movement is a happening which is going on now across all Europe and across the Atlantic and it has somehow got down under into Australia and it has always (since Hiroshima) been there in Japan.

Martin Eve, my friend and publisher, has just phoned up to say that I can have 32 pages instead of 24. So in order to fill up this page I will mention the foreign places where I have been. These have been Holland, Czechoslovakia, West Germany, Norway, Finland, Belgium, the United States, Iceland, Ireland, Switzerland, Italy, France, Denmark, Austria, Hungary, Sweden, and the Isle of Wight.

Everywhere I have met with the same rising peace consciousness, the same gestures and assurances of international solidarity. I have met with extraordinary goodwill, extended not so much to me as to fellow peace workers in Britain. And this goodwill I now pass on to you.

I have peered through the fence at the cruise missile installations at Comiso, the base in Sicily which is the twin

to Greenham Common. I have listened to leading musicians
perform at a great peace rally in Iceland, whose ancient saga
legends of the doom of the gods and the overthrow of
civilisation chime in with the dark forebodings of our own
days. I have spoken to a packed meeting in Derry (or
Londonderry) where people from that deeply-divided community, Protestant and Catholic, came together to work for
peace. And I have spoken at an 'unofficial' meeting in a
private apartment in Budapest, where over 100 young people
crowded the floor and the adjoining rooms to testify their
desire for honest 'dialogue' between East and West.

All that is heartening, and it keeps one going. It is part of
what the peace movement is about. The 'peace movement'
is very much larger than those who join organisations or who
wear its badges—it is also a mood, a happening, a raising of
consciousness. It is not just—as some people suppose—a
'no' movement, no to nuclear weapons: it is also a 'yes'
movement, yes to real exchanges and friendship between
peoples.

But I was explaining about a certain difficulty with this
pamphlet, and I also mentioned a visit to the Isle of Wight.
There is a connection between these things. As I have said,
three years ago I wrote *Protest and Survive* and it made a
little stir. On May 1st of this year I was invited by the very
vigorous branch of CND on the Isle of Wight to speak at a
meeting, and, since I had never visited the island, my wife
and I decided to take a day off walking on the downs.

It was a beautiful day, and the Island was spared some of
the drenching weather the rest of us have been having. What
came into my mind, as we walked the downs, was what an
extraordinarily favoured part of this planet we have the
good fortune to live upon, and also how favoured this planet
itself is in a universe which is mostly made up of emptiness
and fire and gas and dust.

It is a fit which is falling upon me more frequently, in the
intervals of 'grass-roots activism', and I suppose it is a pre-
monition of something: perhaps senility. It came upon me
again, three days ago, when I drove across from Worcester to

a rally of Christian CND in Carmarthen in South-West Wales. Mile upon mile a garden unfolded itself before me, with lush grass and with huge trees with late-opening leaves and lilacs in bloom; the wet spring had left these counties as the greenest place in the whole universe, the place with the strongest grass-roots of anywhere in the globe. It seemed to be a pity to leave this place in the knowledge that, in a few decades or so, it would be burned up.

I think that we are favoured, and that we owe a duty, not only to ourselves, but also to our ancestors who attended to the culture both of our fields and of our laws and institutions —who made them kempt and yet not too tidy nor too disciplined—and a duty also to hand on the place to the future. Despite the worst that agro-businesses and multinationals can do, despite the avarice of developers, despite the blasting of our inner cities, and despite the growing invasion of an arrogant state upon our rights, there is still enough here—not just to preserve but carry us forward—to bring us through to a humane commonwealth.

That sort of mood fell upon me also in the downs on the Isle of Wight. We are not well-fitted by our history to be the kind of people who just lie down and give up the ghost. There is something here that is still worth defending. Even if there is little opportunity for livelihood now in our shattered inner cities, there are people there who still inherit a culture which enables them to resist. And I thought of a pamphlet which I might write, as my contribution to the coming election next October. It would be a sequel to *Protest and Survive*, and it would be about the defence of all this—of our lives and of our liberties. It would be called *The Defence of Britain*.

In the next few days I mentioned the idea to a few friends, and also on my telephone. This was a great mistake. For someone who keeps my activities under surveillance must have carried the news post-haste to Mrs Thatcher, and she, hearing that I was about to write another pamphlet, with a great whirring of wings, like a pheasant trying to get lift-off into the air for fear of a fox, rushed across to the Palace and instructed the Queen to call an instant election.

She supposed that in this way she had put an end to my pamphlet, and, indeed, she and Mr Heseltine borrowed its title for their own election manifesto (a matter of plagiarism which I may not discuss here since it has still to be argued before the courts). And I supposed much the same. But the conduct of this election, in its first week, was so disgraceful and the treatment of the issues placed before the nation has been so trivial, and I have been made by this so generally angry, that the idea of a pamphlet came into my head once more.

I must explain my meaning more clearly. It is not that all the political parties have policies, on the questions which affect the nation in critical ways, which are equally meaningless and awful. That has been the usual situation in the past thirty years, but this time it is different. On the question upon which all other questions hang, that of nuclear weapons, several of the contending parties have very good policies: and the parties have been influenced in making these policies by the arguments of the peace movement over the past three years. In particular, the Labour Party, Plaid Cymru, and the Scottish National Party, as well as several lesser parties such as the Ecology Party, have admirable stated policies and I commend them warmly.

The members of the Liberal Party also have an admirable policy, and the Party itself *ought* to do so also, but in fact it does not. Instead it has a sort of shifty hole, called 'Don't Know', on the crucial question of cruise missiles. This is because of a successful exercise in a well-known British tactical ploy called moving the goal-posts.

What happened was this. The Liberal Party Conference met at Llandudno in the late summer of 1981 and debated the issue of cruise missiles very thoroughly. As it happens, both I and my friend Bruce Kent (whom the Papal Pro-Nuncio Monsignor Bruno Heims—a Swiss gentleman who usually occupies himself entertaining prominent Conservative Catholic laymen to dinner, and making the sauces with his own hand—has recently described as a 'useful idiot', but whom the British people, if they survive, will come to remember as the most useful Englishman of this decade)—

both I and Bruce were invited by the Liberal delegates to speak at the Conference at fringe meetings.

I will only say that this fringe meeting was one of the most searching and thoughtful discussions of the whole issue of nuclear weapons, and of the international questions attending upon this issue, that I have been privileged to take part in in the last three years.

Bruce Kent came back to spend the night with us in North Wales, and the next morning we walked down the mountain at mid-day to the pub. We had a radio with us and switched on the 1 o'clock news, when the first item was that the Liberal Party at Llandudno had, after full debate and by a firm majority, declared itself against cruise missiles. And I beheld the spectacle of Monsignor Kent, on a Welsh mountain-side, whooping and dancing a jig.

It seemed like a victory for democracy. The constituency workers had argued: they had done their research: they had selected their delegates: they had marshalled their forces: they had carried the ball down the field, and, POW! they had driven it directly into the goal. But what we had not allowed for was the cunning of Mr David Steel and the Parliamentary Liberal Party.

For these MPs (or the majority of them) simply strolled onto the field and carried the goal-posts away. I do not know where they put them, for they have not yet been found. (Last year's Liberal Party Conference was not even allowed to discuss 'Defence'). It turned out that the active Liberal Party workers, in their annual Conference, by no means had the right to determine such significant matters as party policy. This was, it transpired, a matter for their betters. Labour Party constituency workers will sympathise, since they have themselves often been through this goal-post-moving routine at the hands of the Parliamentary Labour Party in the past thirty years.

What was going on behind the scenes was this. The leaders of the Liberal Party, who have long been in the wilderness and who have long had a wholly unjust share of parliament-ary representation in relation to their electoral support, were interested at that moment less in their own constituency

activists than in a very large and somewhat tuneless cuckoo
which had just fallen out of the Labour Party nest, and
which called itself the Social-Democratic Party. In short,
they had scented a chance to get back into serious political
business again, and they were negotiating that odd two-
headed political creature which is now beckoning us to the
polls, under the name of the Dalliance.

Now the Liberal head of the Dalliance is against cruise
missiles, or it ought to be if the decision of its own delegates
is respected, but the other, SDP, head of the Dalliance is
looking in the opposite direction. This makes it difficult to
go anywhere in a straight line, rather like a three-legged race
in which both parties are tied back-to-back. It therefore
seemed advisable that, on the matter of cruise missiles, the
Dalliance should have no policy at all and should just have
a hole.

I do not explain all this out of disrespect for the Liberal
Party, but simply out of disrespect for politics. I dare say
that the Liberal Party's leaders have a good many second
and third thoughts about cruise missiles, but they are obliged
to keep these private to themselves for fear of being bitten by
the other head of the Dalliance. It should be noted that our
media, which have spent much of this election trying to get
their fingers into a hairline crack between Mr Foot and
Mr Healey, on the matter of Polaris, have left this huge
fracture on defence policy within the Dalliance strictly
alone.

A great many Liberal Party members have continued, with
sadder hearts, to play a significant part in the work of the
peace movement, including the work of CND. Many Liberal
candidates remain true to the democratic decision of their
own party conference and they deserve support accordingly.
This is also true of some members and supporters of the
SDP, who are more serious and well-informed upon international questions than one might suppose from the pro-
nouncements of their leaders upon 'Defence'. It is probable
that there are candidates of the SDP who are deserving of
the peace movement's support—if they will answer its
questions clearly and give the necessary assurances.

But I fear that I cannot offer the same references for Dr David Owen, whose statements on 'Defence' in the current election are intended to wean away the sucking Tory voter from the dugs of Mr Heseltine, and which fill me with dismay. One must add by the way—although the poor fellow cannot be held responsible for his image, since that is made up for him by his media advisors—that Dr Owen, when he pronounces frowningly on 'Defence' with all the pomp and pretentiousness of a self-assumed 'statesman', resembles nothing so much as that ferryman, Charon, whom the ancient Roman poets said would carry us across the river of Styx, a river which divides the world of the living from the underworld of the dead.

I have now conducted you on a brief tour of the British General Election of 1983, although I should add that there is another party offering itself at the polls. This is the Conservative Party. While some of its members, and more of its supporters, and perhaps even some of its MPs, are seriously concerned about matters of peace, the policy of its leaders on 'Defence' are ferocious and it has no policy at all on disarmament. It is not a party which can be returned to government without risk to our lives. I shall come back to this matter anon.

I must return now, however, to explaining a certain difficulty about this pamphlet. I left off at the point where I said that the conduct of this election, in its first week, was so disgraceful that the question of a pamphlet came back into my head once more.

The conduct of this election is disgraceful, not because the candidates or the party election workers are behaving disgracefully, but because the election has been confiscated by the media and is played according to its rules.

The first of these rules, with the television and radio, is that instantly an election is proclaimed the shutters are closed upon all opinions in the nation's head except those which are authorised by the Two Main Political Parties and the Dalliance. Nothing is allowed to be thought or said unless it is an authorised party-political thought, or unless it is said by some media Presenter like Sir Robin Day or Mr Brian Walden who have some special license to interfere with the national mind. Anything else which might be in our minds is extinguished until the polls are declared.

The second rule is that the media themselves decide what are the 'election issues', and they do this by blowing up whatever is trivial, searching out 'colour' and 'Personalities', and by trying to stir up little episodes of dissension within the parties (but especially within the Labour Party) by picking at old scabs and inspecting the sores underneath.

The third rule is to bludgeon us day after day with meaningless opinion-polls, shoddily put together, and based on illiterate or irrelevant 'yes/no' questions which refuse electors the chance to express alternatives, complexities, hesitations or doubts.

The result of all this is to side-track every serious issue into by-ways, and to present the nation's political life as if it was no more than a collection of comic actors slipping about on banana skins and hitting each other over the head with bags of flour. I do not know that any of the politicians are particularly responsible for this treatment, although at this moment the trivialisation is very much to the advantage of Mrs Thatcher who is handled with a special awe.

Mr Michael Foot is managing to survive this exercise remarkably well, and despite the worst efforts of the media he is coming through as a fallible human being, with sincere convictions, in the midst of a whole Tussaud's gallery of infallible self-important image-conscious 'talking heads'. Mr Foot does not come across as a 'strong' or cunning candidate for Prime Minister, but simply as a man whose appetite for power, for power's own sake, is now exhausted, and who is ready to act according to principle and according to his conscience—in short, in the view of the media, an unfit politician.

Mr Foot apart—one watches this telly-carnival with astonishment. Some of the 'debate' is about 'Defence', and it was we, in the peace movement, who forced this upon the political agenda. Yet, in the very moment that the agenda is declared open, the arguments which we have rehearsed throughout the country for three years have been hidden from sight or forgotten; secondary issues are blown up to immense proportions; false scent is laid across the track (how many jobs in 'defence' industries might be at risk?); and our case is presented to the people in a wholly distorted form like a grotesque cartoon.

Well, that is it. Three years of our labour is swilling away down the media drains. And there is no way, no way at all, in which the peace movement can get into this political 'debate'. For by these same media rules our voice is eliminated. Only 'party-political' spokespersons are allowed a place in the great revolving media wheel, and even then there may be only three spokes. Every other voice is excluded as marginal to the nation's political life.

What is strange about this is that (a few thousand devoted constituency workers of the various parties apart) the people who in the past three years have taken the most serious and committed part in the political life of the nation, and who have shown the deepest concern for the nation's destiny, are the members of the peace movement.

Week after week they have carried the argument to the people. They have held public meetings. They have discussed within chapels and churches and within political parties, trade unions and universities. They have gathered from every part of Britain to demonstrate in the streets. They have canvassed the housing-estates. They have raised money, in great part out of their own pockets, and they have conferred with fellow peace workers throughout Europe.

Some of them have done more than this. The women at the peace camp at Greenham Common, and the campers of both sexes at Molesworth, Upper Heyford, Faslane and other places, have testified to the seriousness of their political convictions in a way that makes the whole carnival of media politics look shoddy.

They endured, with caravans and makeshift shelters, one of the coldest winters of this century, in 1981-2, and although last winter was more kind, they have now been enduring the wettest spring in our records. And some of them have been willing to suffer for their convictions fines and imprisonments.

I know that some part of the public have been persuaded (by the media) that the 'Greenham Women' are an odd set of people and a general pain. Maybe one or two odd things have been done, and maybe some of them have endured so much that they have got a bit bossy and have come to think of themselves as *the* only true peace movement, with the rest of the nation, who have not been out there in the frost camping with them, left nowhere.

But since (if we except a few Queens and Duchesses) men have bossed this nation about for nearly all of its history, and have stirred up a good many wars in the process, it may not be a bad thing that some of the women are getting uppish just now. And if the media are really anxious to go after a bossy woman, they do not have to make the long trek from the pubs of Fleet Street down to Greenham Common. They need only go to their own front pages, where they will find our Governess seated like Britannia on the backside of the old pee, a Trident in her hand and the helmet of Deterrence squashed upon her head.

It is true that one or two things that the 'women for life on earth' have done, with a multitude of supporters, have been so odd that, although I am by profession a historian of the social movements of our people, I cannot think of any actions quite like them. And most of all I think of that astonishing day, December 12th, 1982, when, as if from nowhere, 30,000 women gathered quietly and without any sense that they were doing anything more dramatic than taking in the washing from the yard or popping up to the corner-shop, and formed that immense and life-affirming ring around the nine hostile miles of the fence of Greenham Common military base.

I was fortunate in being an observer on December 12th, not because the women had any need of me but because a car was in need of a driver. And I walked half way around the perimeter fence as the women quietly assembled, and as flowers and children's drawings and photos and poems and baby-clothes were pinned upon the wire. It was an extraordinary sight, and it was also strangely down-beat and self-conscious in a characteristic British way. To tell the truth, they did not do it with any great *éclat* or sense of theatre at all. No-one was quite sure exactly what was supposed to happen, nor even the exact moment when the miraculous linking was finally achieved. Some of the linked women were facing into the base, but at another part of the perimeter they had turned their backs upon the base and were looking outwards into the world. At one part there was a chant of 'Peace and Freedom!' and at another part some snatches of song.

It was a very untidy, low-key, British sort of do. Women had come from all parts of the country, and some had driven through the night. They came, they embraced the base and they greeted their sisters, they showed their presence, and then they drifted back home. (Some stayed, of course, to blockade the gates the next day.) But undoubtedly Other Nations would have done the whole thing better, and produced the whole drama with greater effect.

Yet the fact is that the women of Other Nations, who have done many ingenious and courageous things, have never mounted any action for peace with this particular quality of life-affirming symbolism nor on such a massive scale. It was an extraordinary event, which will very certainly be remembered in our history, and which carried a message outwards into the world which could not be misunderstood. It carried a quiet, unassertive, welcoming symbolism of a novel kind, unlike any other demonstration which I have ever witnessed. It did not only symbolise but it actually *was*, for a moment, an expression of international sisterhood, peace and love.

I have gone down a side-turning once again. I was explaining the ways in which the media's rules confiscate to 'party-political' routines the most serious political voices in this country. The peace movement has conducted the major political argument in this country over the past three years. Yet now that an election has come—and 'election' means a process of *choosing*—it finds that it must wait anxiously in the margin of events, while others who understand the arguments only imperfectly rehearse the debate, and adjust

or devalue our priorities to meet the contingencies of a
party-political yes-you-did-no-I-didn't sort of campaign.

And the rules of the electoral game are even odder than
this. For it was decided some time ago, under the pressure
of democratic opinion, that the amount of money permitted
to be spent by any candidate in his or her constituency must
be strictly limited and carefully accounted to the returning
officer. And that any external intervention in election
campaigning in a constituency which might be held to
favour one particular candidate over another should be
chargeable to the favoured candidate's expenses (which must
come within the permitted limit); or, if such intervention
can be shown to have been made without the candidate's
authority, such actions may be found *illegal*, with dire and
dreadful consequences to all concerned.

Those who know the American electoral system, where
vast quantities of dollars are expended upon lobbying for
votes, some of the money coming from hidden and disreputable sources (such as the arms industries) and most of
it being spent on foul and libellous smear campaigns directed
against progressive candidates, will appreciate the motives
behind our own electoral rule.

Yet a gaping hole was left at the top of this law, by which
the national expenditure of political parties is totally un-
limited. Hence we have the position today, where the Conservative Party has raked in a huge quantity of money (most
of it from businesses which will in due course pass the cost
on to us by raising the price of their products), a sum which
has been estimated in the press at various figures from four
to twenty million pounds.

The Tories in fact have got so much money to spend upon
buying the mind of the British people that they have not the
least idea what to do with it, but are swilling it around all
over the place, like one of those car-washes with huge
rotating brushes. For example, they have been buying double
pages of adverts in the daily papers, printed in outsize type
so large that the reader crawls around inside it like an ant.
Since I have not yet been able to get hold of a reducing-
glass powerful enough to bring down this display to a read-

able type-face I don't yet know what these spendthrift advertisements say.

These are some of the reasons why I became angry and began to think once again of writing a pamphlet. It is too late, of course, to get it around the country. But at least the writing of it will relieve my spleen. The democracy of Britain finds itself once more, as it has done so often in the past, with a whole set of rules and laws like locked doors between it and full access to the democratic process, and with money like water-hoses playing with full force against its face. And CND finds itself, as George Cruikshank's 'Freeborn Englishman' found himself in 1820, with a padlock through its mouth.

I thought about this first on Sunday the 22nd of May. And I rang up Martin Eve to sound out his opinion. The project (he thought) was just feasible, although made more difficult by the fact that Monday May 30th has been styled as 'Whit-Monday' bank holiday, and is a day when not only bankers

but also printers close down their whole premises and have
a Revel.

If I was to write it (he said) then I must write it at once,
and complete it within three days. The whole thing would
put all my friends to great inconvenience and exertions, and
all for the purpose of easing a pain in my spleen. Yet as my
publisher and friend of many years, he was willing to
humour me in my dotage.

I have now almost completed my explanation of the
difficulties attending the production of this pamphlet. As
it happened I was unable to allocate the lavish space of
three whole days to the writing of it, since on Monday
May 23rd (as no doubt Mr Heseltine has been informed
already), my wife and I had to make a very quick and private
day-trip to Vienna to consult with Soviet friends. What with
this and that, the writing could not commence until 4 p.m.
on Tuesday, May 24th and the copy is to be delivered in
36 hours' time.

The difficulty, then, is that this thing is being written a
damned sight too fast, and through one day and two nights.
This has in no way eased my spleen, and that is no doubt
why the house has suddenly fallen empty of all inhabitants
save the dog which is cowering in the hall and my cat, who
normally sits on my shoulder to offer editorial advice, but
who on this occasion has fled to the kitchen. And that is
why this thing is coming out pell-mell and hugger-mugger
out of my unconscious, with Greenham here and the Liberal
Party at Llandudno there and the Isle of Wight somewhere
else. I have no time to ferret facts out of my files or to
deploy quotations or take breath for meditation, as I had
when writing, in thirty days rather than thirty hours, *Protest
and Survive.*

I have now completed the introduction to this pamphlet and
I believe that there are still a few pages left for the argument.
Fortunately we shall not need much space for this, since the
major part of this argument has, in the past three years,
already been conducted and won.

In *Protest and Survive*, three years ago, it was still necessary to explain with care what a nuclear war would entail, and to show why the proposed exercises in 'civil defence' were futile and could be interpreted only as efforts to tranquillise the public mind. That argument is settled now, and its settlement has been signalled by those numerous local authorities (as well as by the whole nation of Wales) which have declared themselves to be nuclear-free zones, and which have saved the ratepayers' money for more useful purposes.

So we have moved forward a little, and everyone in Britain who cares to know, now knows that a nuclear war would be an unthinkable disaster to this island, and scarcely a voice can be heard (as a few voices may still be heard in the USA) to suggest that such a war could be 'winnable'.

Indeed, most people are now persuaded by our arguments that cruise missiles on our territory, owned and operated by United States' personnel, so far from contributing to this nation's 'defence' or 'security' will actually increase its insecurity, by making these bases targets for attack and by placing the finger of a United States President firmly upon our own trigger. And even most of those who cannot yet see why these missiles must be refused, would accept them in this island with the greatest reluctance.

The evidence of this can be seen in the growing concern among Conservative voters, and some Tory back-benchers, over the question of a 'double key'. In fact cruise missiles are not operated by a key at all, but by a code; but no doubt some double-code could be devised.

We have been assured repeatedly that we ought not to concern ourselves about this matter, since the missiles can never be fired without a 'joint decision' of the President and the Prime Minister, and that an agreement to this effect was worked out many years ago which has had the assent of successive governments of both major political parties.

The peculiar thing is that this agreement, which concerns the sovereignty of the British people, has never been published nor set before parliament. And recent research in the archives has suggested that Winston Churchill (that is, the *real* Winston Churchill, who was once a person of some note, as older people may remember) was gravely dissatisfied with it, because it laid down conditions, not for 'joint decision' but for 'joint consultation'. And I have little doubt that if the real Winston Churchill had ever authorised the basing of a fearful new generation of foreign-owned and foreign-operated weaponry upon our territory—and I have some doubts whether he would, once he had taken a steady look at President Reagan and his advisers and formed an opinion as to their stability—then he would very certainly have ordered a double key, and he would have worn that key on his own watch-chain.

A few months ago Mrs Thatcher chose a new Defence Minister to succeed Sir John Nott; and she chose him with delay and care, not to defend Britain against the Russians but to defend her administration against CND. Mr Heseltine is a good sort of knockabout party-political busker, who cannot read deeply into things, who enjoys stamping about on the hustings, and who does not care very much what he says, nor whether it is true or not.

One of his first one-acters was to put on a contractor's helmet, invite the media into Greenham base, and show them around. It was clear that the bad press the government was getting about the 'double key' was bothering him, and, with the telly cameras whirring, he was asked a planted question by a deferential journalist. 'Aha!' came back Mr Heseltine's comforting response. The matter of the double key was no problem, no problem at all. In fact no key was needed. For we British had a recourse already. Every time a cruise launch-convoy sallies out of Greenham, it will be accompanied by a sturdy platoon of the RAF Regiment. And if our lads should notice that the Yanks were up to any unauthorised hanky-panky, then they would simply bonk them on their heads and place the whole convoy in jankers.

This tale was strictly for the British viewer and no efforts were made to convey it to America. In March I was invited to address the National Press Club in Washington on the question of Euromissiles, and the members received me with courtesy and straight faces. But when I told them this story about Heseltine I had them rolling in the aisles. And again and again, in the United States, it was made clear to me that many Americans cannot understand what has come over the British and why we put up with it. I am not referring to members of the huge and growing American peace movement, but to the professional reporters of the Fourth Estate. They do, after all, remember a time when it became necessary for their own people to make a Declaration of Independence.

I am now going to make a prediction, and by the time that this pamphlet is off the press you will know whether it is true. When Mrs Thatcher returns from the Williamsburg Summit she will bring back with her a 'key', a key specially presented to her by President Reagan himself, large enough to unlock the door to her second term in office.

It may not be a *real* key, of course. It may be a great big fulsome Presidential Promise, cut out in the shape of a key: that never, ever, will he blow this place up without telling her about it first. Mrs Thatcher will have this key placed in her hand, like one of those huge 21-year-old birthday cards, and she will be told that Britain has at last attained to its nuclear majority. And she will come tripping down out of the Concorde, waving the key in the air like Neville Chamberlain just back from Munich, and singing to the electorate in its last somnolent week—

> I've got the key of the door,
> Never been twenty-one before!*

---

* STOP PRESS. DOUBLE KEY. PREDICTION VINDICATED. 'Britain "will have Cruise firing veto",' according to the *Daily Telegraph*, 27 May. President Reagan said in an interview with television networks from nations attending the Williamsburg Summit that the issue of who would be in control of the firing of cruise missiles. 'I don't think either of us will do anything independent of the other. This constitutes a sort of veto power', he said. It is reported that this 'sort of veto power' was made up into an iced lolly shaped like a key and was pressed into the Prime Minister's hand on her arrival at Williamsburg. The ceremony was *private*, lest the German Chancellor might want an iced lolly also. In case Mrs Thatcher's lolly might *melt* before the election, the President's aides put another nougat key into her handbag, which will be produced if the opinion polls start to turn against her.

Enough of this show-biz. For if that is to happen, it will only be the beginning of it. The British public will then have to start puzzling out how to get a double-key to Mrs Thatcher, and to whoever might follow her (Good Gracious, perhaps Mr Heseltine!).

It would be better, of course, if cruise missiles were never to come at all. The majority of the British people have realised this. But some are still held back by real objections. And of these we will look at two. First, there are those who are distrustful of any act of 'one-sided disarmament', since they suppose that this would make it easier for the other side to go on arming without restraint. Second, there are those (often the same persons) who deeply fear and distrust 'the Russians'. We will discuss these two questions in order.

The first argument treats of missiles ('which of course *we* would never use') as if they were negotiating chips. They are—well, er, yes, they *are* missiles, but what they are *really* is a means of getting back at a new level into the balance game so as to get a position of purchase from which to negotiate downwards, multilaterally, with the Russians.

One trouble with this argument is that exactly the same argument is being used by the armourers on the other side. Their weapons, also, are only for 'defence', and *they* would never use them. They have to hang onto their SS-20s because they are negotiating chips. Another trouble—but I am bored out of my mind with this—is that all the counting of numbers and of balance, on both sides, is partisan and is skewed.

But Mrs Thatcher has some special troubles of her own. It is possible to argue, with honesty, that NATO should go on threatening to bring in cruise, as a bargaining-chip, provided that at the same time one is working earnestly and with good-will to find some urgent and fair settlement at Geneva. I think it is a bad argument, but it is not dishonest, and there are glimpses of honesty of this kind in the SDP's policies on the question.

This is sometimes called (with much self-congratulation) 'the multilateral approach'. It is a difficult approach to sustain, since its British advocates have got no-one to be multilateral with. The British have not been invited to the

Geneva negotiations, so that all that they can do is to wait anxiously outside the door. Since it is becoming abundantly clear that neither the Americans nor the Russians are going to give enough ground for an agreement, the waiting British multilateralists will at length have to lie down and die, with a good conscience, in a multilateral ditch.

But Mrs Thatcher just possibly could not only *sound* multilateral but *be* multilateral. For she has been offered a multilateral partner. Mr Andropov in some recent proposals suggested that he might bring down the number of SS-20s targetted upon Europe until they matched the sum of the British and French 'independent deterrents'. At that stage (he proposed) the Russian and Western missiles could be negotiated downwards and perhaps phased out together. He was offering Mrs Thatcher his arm, for a waltz on the multilateral ballroom floor.

One would have supposed that Mrs Thatcher would have accepted Mr Andropov's proposal with squeals of delight. For here she has been, throughout all her term in office, pining like a wallflower and dreaming of the day when she might find a partner to be multilateral with. And now that *handsome* Mr Andropov glides over the floor and selects her as his chosen partner!

But this was not her reaction. When it comes to questions of disarmament Mrs Thatcher is *very* hard to suit. She is most particular. Mr Andropov had suggested that he might introduce his SS-20s to her Polarises. This did not accord at all with Mrs Thatcher's strict sense of Victorian propriety. The Polaris, she said, was only a weapon 'of last resort', whereas the SS-20 (one supposes) is an ill-bred sort of weapon which might resort at any time and place.

For crying out loud, *what* does the woman mean? What *is* a 'last resort'? God preserve us, in that event, from the first and second resorts! Are we to shell out cruise missiles, and are the Russians to shell out SS-20s, as the small coinage of a nuclear war? And is Polaris to be preserved, deep on the sea-bed, only for the ultimate dark deed, the final passage of this island across the River Styx, where those scowling ferrymen (all of Mr Brian Walden's 'experts') are patiently waiting? Or has she worked out some secret suicide pact with Ronald Reagan, so that when, in 'the last resort', it is time to go she may go with him?

I cannot stand the multilateral homilies which come out of that woman's lips. When she croons in her husky way: '*We* are the *trooo* disarmers' I cannot even admire her gall. Prime Minister, when have you ever made *any* proposal, in good faith, to disarm *anything* (except, of course, the Russians)? You have ordered every weapon that has come your way. You have without hesitation welcomed into our island the cruise missiles. You have been willing to beggar the country to buy Trident. You have ordered the Tornado fighter-bomber. You have turned down each and every proposal from the other side, sometimes before it was even received and read. Your administration has, in the United Nations, voted against a resolution for a bi-lateral nuclear weapons freeze. You have opposed 'no first use'. You have fought, with unseemly gusto and with an eye for political self-advertisement, the unhappy Falklands War.

I said, many pages back, that the Conservative Party has no policy for disarmament. Mrs Thatcher certainly has none. She is, quite simply, a one-sided armer. It has never been clear to me why it is supposed that it is always right for every nation to *add* to its armaments by unilateral measures. Yet if any unilateral measure of *dis*armament— any initiative to get the log-jam on the move—is brought into public discussion there are at once cries of 'foul!' and even of 'treason!'

It is the use of the word 'multilateralism' by such persons as our Prime Minister which has brought it into disrepute. For it has become, with her sort of person, nothing but a hypocritical cover underneath which one-sided arming can go on. As for effective measures of multilateral and reciprocal disarmament, this has always been the objective of the peace movement. Unilateral measures by this country are, exactly, what may at last get this whole multilateral process going. We have said this again and again and I will not waste any more time on the point.

But how do we know (for this is the second question of

our honest objector) that if we do anything the Russians are going to respond? The plain fact is that we do *not* know that the Russians will do so, and we do not know that the Americans or the French or the Israelis or (perhaps next year) the Argentinians will respond either. How on earth can we be expected to make such a promise?

If one looks at that list, it seems just a little more likely that the Russians might respond than anyone else. For our weapons are pointed at them, and Mr Andropov is already there, on the ballroom floor, inviting our multilateral partnership. The Soviet Union, in the past year or two, has made quite a number of multilateral proposals—they have said they are in favour of a nuclear weapons 'freeze' and of 'no first use'—and while no doubt their statesmen will (just like the statesmen of the West) try to twist any agreement to their own advantage, at the moment they look a good deal more likely to be willing to come to some sort of agreement than does President Reagan, who has a quite insatiable appetite for new armaments and whose eyes are fixed now upon the star wars of the twenty-first century. In any case, looked at in terms of mere political calculation, Soviet statesmen would be incredibly foolish—and would lose the propaganda battle of the century—if Britain were to commence to disarm and if they were to find no way to respond.

I am not, now, in this pamphlet going to take in the whole 'Russian Question', since the pages are running out and since I must take this copy to be set into print in some three hours time. I have already written a good deal about this matter, as have other people in the peace movement who are more expert than myself. And there would be no harm if some of our opponents actually *read* some of the things which we have written before they started libelling us as being 'soft on Russia' and the rest.

For example, they might read my book, *Zero Option*, in which, among many choice articles, they will find a lecture, 'Beyond the Cold War'. They will find there that I am not a misty-eyed optimist but a pessimist about the Soviet Union: that is, I am deeply pessimistic about it so long as the Cold War and the armaments race continues. I sketch out there a process, which has now been going on for more than thirty years, by which the hawks of the West and the East keep on strengthening and feeding each other.

Every upward movement in arms on one side meets with an upward movement on the other, and this is true not only of arms but also of ideological hostilities. When President Reagan, speaking at Orlando, Florida, rants on about the Soviet Union being 'an evil empire' he is actually helping it on in that direction, since the Soviet rulers respond by tightening up their security system and by putting their military preparations into repair.

It is true that I do not regard the Soviet Union as an aggressive, expansionist empire but as a vast sprawling empire, perhaps already in decline, facing all kinds of internal stress and economic difficulty, unable to feed its own people with grain, and over-ripe for modernisation and (if things should go well) democratic changes.

If it is an expansionist power, then it is not doing well. Since the end of World War II it has lost its hegemony over Yugoslavia; suffered a disastrous breach with China; and its hegemony today over several East European states (Czechoslovakia and Poland) is maintained in some part by military threat. Its adventure in support of a failing client regime in Afghanistan is going on as badly as did several British adventures in that country in the last century.

In short, I see no evidence that the Soviet Union (which has an acute headache over Poland) has an appetite to gobble up more unruly nations in the West. Nor does it have, at this time, the economic or political influence to turn Western Europe into some kind of 'Finland'. On the contrary, the Soviet rulers are more anxious about the penetration of 'Western' influence into the East, and, if the Cold War were to come to an end, we might expect to see some 'Finlandisation' in reverse in Eastern Europe.

The panic scenarios which we are always being given, of hordes of Soviet tanks rolling towards the Channel ports, do not come out of reality but out of the Cold War textbooks of the past. What is needed now is the commencement of some healing-process between the two blocs—a diminution of the mutual sense of threat—which will, in due course, enable the Soviet and East European peoples to make whatever changes they wish in their own societies and in their own way. As for 'human rights', every time Mrs Thatcher or President Reagan rant about these (while at the same time hurrying forward new generations of threatening missiles) they are making the situation over on the other side *worse*. The cold warriors of the West are actually feeding and strengthening those very forces in the East which are holding back democratic change.

I have been watching this process very closely for a year, since we Western peace workers are in touch with independent-minded persons in the East, who are working in their own way and in the face of great difficulties for peace and for change. I have observed with sorrow the way, every time our Western cold warriors open their loud mouths, it makes the position of our friends on the other side worse. When Mr Heseltine does his show-biz at the Berlin Wall one can actually hear the prison-doors closing on the other side.

I said, some pages back, that I was unable to commence writing this pamphlet on Monday, May 23rd, because I had to make a quick day-trip for a private consultation with some Soviet friends in Vienna. These friends (whom I had never before met) were a young Soviet artist, called Sergei Batovrin, and his wife, Natasha. They are members of a small independent Soviet peace group which was set up, some eleven months ago, with the aim of promoting direct communication and exchanges between the citizens of the East and West, and, in particular, of Establishing Trust between the USA and the USSR.

This initiative was not liked by the Soviet authorities at all, partly because they dislike *any* private intiatives by their own citizens (unlicensed by State or Party) and particularly dislike direct communications between their citizens and the West (which they suspect as being channels for 'Western intelligence'), and especially, on this occasion, because working for peace in the Soviet Union is preserved as a State monopoly and is directed at opposing the aggressive and expansionist plans of the capitalist West.

In short, the Soviet authorities view the whole Cold War
scene *exactly* as does Mr Heseltine, only upside-down; but
since the Soviet Union is a tightly-controlled authoritarian
state, the Soviet authorities are in the happy position of
being able to hold down and control independent peace
initiatives more effectively than Mr Heseltine can do. And
instead of sending around libels on peace workers to Tory
parties and to the popular press (as Mr Heseltine was reduced
to doing), the Soviet authorities were able to send around to
Sergei and Natasha's apartment—again and again and again—
the officers of the KGB.

It has been an appalling scene, and if you get hold of
END's publications you can read about it there. The Moscow
Group, which has not given up and which does not intend to
give up, and whose support, not only in Moscow but in other
cities is actually growing, has been given a very rough passage.
All of Sergei's paintings have been confiscated, Natasha has
had to put up with KGB men pushing around her apartment
and upsetting the baby, Sergei was put for a month into
confinement in a psychiatric hospital, and, finally, he was
given, for the third time, the choice between imprisonment
and exile. After consultation with his friends he decided that
he must go. And he and Natasha, their baby and Sergei's
mother arrived, quite suddenly, in Vienna on May 19th.

There has not been a great hullabaloo about this in our
media, although one might have thought that the story was
good Cold War 'copy' and could have been used to beat up
the Western peace movement. This is perhaps because when
Sergei arrived at Vienna airport, and the microphones and
cameras were thrust before him, he simply said that he and
his friends were working for peace, and for 'trust' between
East and West, and he meant to continue with the work.

He did not call upon the West to build even bigger weapons, nor did he ask for boycotts, nor did he accuse Western
peace workers of being useful dupes of the Kremlin, and he
did not even ask us to help his people by ordering cruise
missiles. In short, the Western media found him to be a flop.

When Dorothy and I heard of the Batovrins' arrival we got

ourselves tickets to Vienna. It was a daft thing to do, and the most expensive day-trip of our lives, but it was a matter of impulse and not of thought at all. Our purpose was simply to take Natasha a bunch of English flowers. When your brothers and your sisters have been suffering in that way, and for the same cause, it seemed right that someone from our own peace movement should go and say thankyou and hello.

Sergei will be writing himself about his experiences and his Group's ideas. I will leave this to him. What he said to us, again and again, was that the work of peace was not only about halting missiles but also about dialogue between peoples, communication, and establishing 'trust'. Somehow or other, we must establish a new kind of relationship between the peoples of East and West. As for the Soviet people, they very certainly feared and hated any thought of war. If they supported their own rulers, it was because they supposed that they offered them 'Defence'. Just like us.

I put to Sergei the question raised by our objector. If Britain were to initiate disarmament, would there be a Soviet response? He did not know. He could give no certain assurance. But if Britain were to halt cruise missile deployment, the Soviet people would see that as 'an act of peace'. It might make more possible the real work, the work of establishing trust.

I regard this election, or *choice*, now before the British people as the most important in our time, not because I am an optimist but because I grow, with each month, more pessimistic as to civilisation's future.

The Soviet state is certainly a threat to liberty. But it is a threat, not to our liberties, but to the liberties of the Soviet and East European peoples—to people like Sergei and Natasha. We have, very urgently, to reverse this process and to create the conditions in which the cause of trust can grow.

The whole matter of cruise missiles seems to me now to be very simple. After all the numbers have been counted, and the balances have been struck, it is simply a case of leapfrog. If the arms race is to be frozen, or halted, it is inevitable that at the point of freeze either one side or the other will be ahead in this or that category of missiles.

It may be true that at the present moment the Soviet
Union is ahead in certain categories of Euromissiles (if they
are counted in certain ways), just as it is probably true that
the United States is ahead, in the number of warheads and in
refined technology, over the global scene. In any case, there
is so much surplus of killing power around on both sides
that all the arguments of balance have lost any sense at all.

The second simple point is that if NATO puts down cruise
missiles then the Soviet Union will put down its own
missiles in reply. Marshal Ogarkov has already promised as
much. So that everything will have got a great deal worse,
and we may even be into launch-on-warning systems, and on
our way, on both sides of the world, to becoming permanent
cave-dwellers or troglodytes.

But there is a third simple point, which even those candidates in this election who have admirable policies for peace
are not yet succeeding in getting across. And this is that we
may, truly, be coming to a point of final choice. If we miss
the bus this time around, there may not be another. And
that what we are making a choice between is also between
two kinds of Britain: a Britain which is independent and
which still has some influence and respect in the world, and
a Britain which is becoming little more than a servile NATO
security state.

When I was in the United States recently I noticed a
curious assumption which was coming, increasingly, from
the White House and its captive media. It was that the
question of cruise missiles was a matter which, in the last
analysis, would be decided by President Reagan. Either the
President would come to some bargain with Mr Andropov
or he will 'decide' to deploy cruise missiles to Europe.

But there is something a little strange in that assumption.
The cruise missiles may belong to the President, but we had
always supposed that the territory of Europe still belongs to
us. There may of course be some other secret agreement,
worked out many years ago and assented to by successive
administrations—but never published nor brought before our
parliament—under which we ceded our sovereignty to the

United States. If so, then well and good, and we can dispense with the comedy of elections.

But until some Ministry of Defence spokesman can show us this agreement, we must assume that we still own our own country. And since the matter of cruise missiles is being negotiated behind closed doors at Geneva, where no European nations are present, we have ourselves only one point at which we are able to enter the negotiations. And this is to refuse our territory for their use. That is the only way in which we can get into the negotiations at all.

The matter in Europe now stands like this. Holland will almost certainly refuse cruise missiles, because the Dutch people won't have them. That being so, the Belgians will probably refuse also. That is two down, with three still to go: Italy, West Germany and Britain. Meanwhile it is pretty clear that there will be no agreement at Geneva, and that, if we lose this election, the cruise missiles will start to come.

But if the British were to refuse cruise, then the entire situation in Europe would change. It would then become impossible to put the things down in Italy or Germany. There would *have* to be a whole new negotiation, and the European nations themselves would have to be parties to it. The Americans would have to be less pushy, and to regard the Europeans with a new respect. The Soviet Union would have, out of plain self-interest, to make some kind of response.

For the first time, in clear daylight, the whole logic which is carrying us to nuclear war would be checked and reversed by the conscious choice of a free people. No-one can say what this might lead on to. But if the peace movement of the world, which is now a powerful force, responded to the British choice and worked with effect, we might even move forward to Sergei's agenda: the making of a new relationship between East and West, the establishment of trust.

The British people have therefore had thrust into their hands a most awesome choice, which could, in a visible way, affect the future of the whole world: which might decide, indeed, whether that world, as a civilised place, goes on at all.

Behind this choice (it is becoming daily more clear) there is also another choice: a choice between two Britains. We have long been a declining power, and some good may come of that. In those old Victorian days, which Mrs Thatcher so loves, when we splashed red paint across the five continents, we were feared but we were not greatly loved. We still owe human debts to the peoples of Asia and Africa whom we pushed about and exploited which it will take a century or two to repay.

This is a time, however (when all our old imperial self-images have been shattered) to reconsider what kind of a nation we are. If we accept that we are now a second-class power, it does not have to follow that we have to be a client state of the USA (nor of a fiction called 'NATO'). Nor do we have to be second-rate. Nor do we have to maintain the inclination and the airs of a bully when we have long lost the power.

It is this which bothers me most about Mrs Thatcher and her chosen circle: Mr Heseltine, Mr Cecil Parkinson, Mr Norman Tebbitt and the rest. They have an appetite for our liberties. Since they have lost the power to rule over half the world, they would like to recapture the buzz by ruling over us.

The media these days has a great line in hunting 'extremists'. When they dislike anyone's ideas, then they set them up as extremists and pelt them day after day. They did this with Mr Benn, and with Mr Livingstone, and now they are doing it with Bruce Kent and the peace campers at Greenham Common.

Yet if I look around this country the most extreme people in our public life are Mrs Thatcher and her circle. I do not refer only to their policies on 'Defence', although there could not be any policy more extreme than perfecting and modern-ising the means to exterminate our human neighbours a few thousand miles away. They are extremists in their social and economic policies as well.

They are bent (under cover of the cry of 'freedom') to strengthen all the powers of the overmighty central State: to increase the powers of the police and the surveillance of citizens: to enlarge the Official Secrets Acts (which already make our press a laughing-stock on the other side of the Atlantic): to sell off the nation's assets: to interfere with our university autonomy: to interfere with our trade unions: to weaken the powers of our local authorities: to employ the resources of the civil service and of the public revenue in order to libel private citizens and to engage in party-political exercises (as Mr Heseltine has recently been doing).

In short, if the Soviet rulers are a threat to liberty—but to the liberty of the Soviet people—then we must also say that our rulers in Britain are a threat to liberty, but to our liberties at home.

There has taken place, quietly and little observed, a take-over of the old Conservative Party (I am thinking of the party of Harold Macmillan, of Butler, Heath and Lord Carrington) by a Tory Militant Faction. These rulers are now becoming deeply impatient with our democratic forms. They regard the rest of us, not as their fellow-citizens, but as their subjects.

The crisis of this came when the British people's attention was diverted to the South Atlantic last year. Differing views can be held about that whole sad episode, which is very far from finished and which Mrs Thatcher means to keep going as long as she can. But there can be little dispute that this was the time at which, from the courage and the bloodshed of other people at the other end of the earth, Mrs Thatcher took on a new 'resolute' image. And there was then annointed by the media, and appointed to service as her Lieutenant upon all public occasions, a new officer in our life, 'The Falklands Factor'.

This 'Falklands Factor' has nothing to do with the Falkland Islanders, who seem to be a taciturn and slow set of people, and many of whom now want to leave their islands. It has everything to do with Mrs Thatcher's 'image' and the Central Office of the Conservative Party's projection of it. In this image, every act of heroism and endurance, by 2 Para or by helicopter pilots, are to be ascribed to Mrs Thatcher and to Mrs Thatcher alone.

In short, the Falklands War, coming at a time when our

The Archmedia of Mass Anointing the Falklands Factor

economy and our social life were visibly falling apart, was the greatest and most undeserved bonus which the Militant Faction of the Tory Party could get. And it made them more Militant, more factional, and more extreme.

The question is: is this really the kind of nation which we wish to be, and is this how we wish to be seen in the world? For I have travelled a bit since then, and have found that the Falklands War was regarded by most other nations in a very different light. It was seen as a bizarre episode, a sudden flush of imperial nostalgia, as if Britain had suddenly fallen through a time-warp into the 18th or 19th century. It made other peoples recall that Britain was still a nation to be *feared*. But fear is not the same thing as respect.

The Falklands War was the last episode of our old imperial past. It summoned up the nostalgias and the resentments of a nation in decline. It was played through by Mrs Thatcher with calculated gestures of Churchillian reminiscence. And there were times when this reminiscence caught the whole nation's breath—centuries of sea-born empire and piracy, and now once again the fleet putting out from Portsmouth, with the waving of flags and the watching crowds, on a mission to rescue our kith and kin from oppression at the uttermost ends of the earth. . .

Yet there is no way forward for any nation down the paths of nostalgia and reminiscence. That will become the rhetoric of rogues, and we will be screwed as their subjects. To become lost in the rehearsal of past grandeur (as Spain once did) is the path towards true decline.

That then is one kind of Britain we can choose: a security state, with a subjected people—a client state which still struts and postures in the world as a bully, which lets its staple industries decline while it exhausts its revenue upon an absurd and obscene great-power-symbol (the 'independent deterrent'), and whose written culture oscillates between cynicism and self-deluding nostalgia.

There has, however, always been an alternative Britain in these islands, and I suppose that my pamphlet may get through to some of them. I know all the dangers of national feeling, and I know more than most (since I am an historian) about Britain's imperial sins. Yet I cannot agree that the history of this island has been, in every way, a disgraceful one; nor that there is nothing in it that it is worth defending.

This has not only been a nation of bullies. It has also been a nation of poets and of inventers, of thinkers and of scientists, held in some regard in the world. It has been, for a time, no less than ancient Greece before us, a place of innovation in human culture. Here were worked out certain laws and democratic forms which have influenced the forms of States in every continent; here there were conducted, over centuries, great arguments of religious faith which were then carried across the Atlantic; here some of the first trade unions and co-operatives were formed, without whose example multitudes over the whole earth might still suffer extremities of exploitation; here, and in our neighbour, France, were worked out some of the clearest claims to human rights.

Therefore I say that the alternative Britain must stand to those rights now, and exercise them with the very greatest vigour. And in doing this we may be fortified by the knowledge that in defending ourselves, we may also be defending the future of the world.

Which Britain do we wish to be seen as in the eyes of international opinion? The Britain of the 'Falklands Factor', the strutting bully which made the world aghast by sinking the *General Belgrano*, an old battleship with a complement of more than one thousand souls, without warning and outside the exclusion zone which we ourselves had imposed and while it was steaming *away* from our fleet? Or the alternative Britain of citizens and not subjects which, summoned up all the strengths of its long democratic past and cut through the world's nuclear knot.

If we could only do that, then we could happily resign ourselves to leaving behind for ever the pretentions of a great power, leaving the world to say of our imperial past, as Malcolm said of the old Thane of Cawdor, 'nothing in his life became him like the leaving of it'.

You will recall that I have a padlock through my lips in the matter of the general election. I am not allowed to advise you as to how you should actually *vote*. I would advise you, of course, to vote for those candidates, of whatever party, which have the best policies for defending the lives and liberties of the British people.

These will best be defended by refusing cruise missiles and also by refusing a second term to Mrs Thatcher. Indeed, I would advise you to make your own judgments in every constituency, guided by two considerations only: the best way to refuse nuclear weapons, and the best way to ensure that Mrs Thatcher's administration is not returned.

I have a little difficulty with this last matter. It appears that if Mrs Thatcher is defeated, as a result of this pamphlet, which is not an authorised party-political production, then a breach of electoral law may be caused thereby. In which case it will be necessary to cancel the results of the entire general election and to play it through once again. But we have taken the advice of an eminent barrister, and, while it is a nice point and has not yet been argued in the higher courts, he thinks that the election might stand provided that I became a fugitive from the kingdom. He was very attentive to us, and gave us a full seven minutes of his advice, and he charged for his counsel only £800.

I have advised you what to vote *against*. As to what to vote for (apart from our defence) I can claim no clarity at all. I do not expect any alternative administration to work great wonders. I do not expect Mr Foot to be a 'strong' Prime Minister, but I expect him to be an honest and humane one which is something we presently stand greatly in need of. He is also a reading man, who knows something of our history and our democratic traditions; and to have such qualities in a Prime Minister would be a great novelty.

As for the other issues, and the issue of our employment most of all, it is not that I regard any one of them as unimportant. But all of them become trivial when set beside the defence of our liberties and our lives. And if these are not defended, then nothing can be solved. For we will move, with all our human neighbours, towards civilisation's 'final solution'.

This pamphlet was commenced in its writing at Worcester at 4 p.m. on Tuesday, May 24th and concluded on Thursday the 26th of May whence it was transported by messenger post-haste to Chilmark in the County of Wilts, three horses dying under the messenger on the way, and there set into type by Mistress Hems, whence it was taken by stage-coach to the City of London at the Merlin Press in the Isle of Dogges to be done by Master Eve into a little book.

▲ CRIMINAL PROCEEDINGS, ▲
OLD BELIAL SESSIONS*

by Our Crime Reporter

At the Old Belial last week Miss Jane Candide, a junior employee in government service, was convicted of offences under all seventy-seven sections of the Official Mendacity Acts.

When charged the defendant did not enter any plea. After some moments of silence Mr Justice Canting informed her that if she continued to stand mute then, according to the ancient practice of the land she would be subjected to the *peine forte et dure:* that is, she would be taken to a dark place and laid naked on her back while weights of iron and stone were placed upon her chest until she was pressed unto death. (Anticipation in court.)

As Mr Justice Canting was about to pronounce sentence, a court usher remarked that the prisoner might be better able to plead if the gag were removed from her mouth. When this was done she said something in a low voice which the Court took to be 'guilty', whereupon the gag was instantly replaced for the remainder of the proceedings.

Opening the prosecution for the Crown, Mr Percy Cute, QC, said that there was no dispute between himself and his learned friend, the counsel for the defence, as to the facts of this case. For some time Her Majesty's Government, in consultation with its closest allies, had been planning to import a consignment of American Cabbage-Patch Scarecrows.

---

* *New Society*, 5 April 1984.

These Scarecrows, of a new and advanced design, were necessary for the defence of the kingdom. By their fearsome aspect they would keep in awe the scarecrows of the Enemy. And, even more they would cow and render subordinate the Enemy within—that is, the disaffected natives of this country.

There was no secret whatsoever about the matter of these Scarecrows. Her Majesty's ministers had proclaimed their imminent arrival in the loudest possible terms. Since their entire purpose was to terrify both the Enemy and the natives, publicity was of the essence of the matter.

However the Secretary of State for Offence, who was particularly responsible for this operation, was placed in difficulties last autumn by the growth of disaffection among the general populace.

'The whole operation was placed in jeopardy,' said Mr Cute. 'What was to be done? In these perilous circumstances Mr Hushpuppy, the Minister for Offence, took the bold decision (under instruction from our Great Ally) to "put the boot in". He agreed to sneak in the first consignment of Cabbage-Patch Scarecrows six weeks in advance of the publicly-announced date.'

Mr Hushpuppy had dictated a memorandum to his closest colleagues in the Cabinet, announcing this decision and describing the measures which he would take to mislead Parliament, con the British people, and manipulate the media. In short, this was a perfectly normal ministerial memorandum, of the most mendacious intent, and as such every comma lay under the protection of the Official Mendacity Acts.

It was this document which Miss Candide had leaked to an unauthorised newsheet. Mr Cute acknowledged that the leaking of secret information was a regular practice, in which senior officials of the security services and indeed ministers themselves frequently engaged. But this was proper. It conduced to the management of the natives. The material so leaked was nearly always false or defamatory of defenceless individuals. It was leaked only to authorised persons and to authorised media.

Indeed, when this was taken into account, it only threw

into a darker light the heinous nature of Miss Candide's crimes. For she had leaked information to the public which could give the game away by revealing to them the means by which their minds were controlled. Mr Cute feared that even now Miss Candide did not understand the depravity of her conduct. For, when interviewed by Det. Chief Supt. Gotcher of Scotland Yard, she had replied that 'she did not believe in telling people lies'. (Sensation in court.)

By this confession Miss Candide stood condemned out of her own mouth as a person disqualified in the most essential point for any form of government service. He would rest the case for the prosecution upon her own confession.

Mr Pleamarket-Creep, QC, defending, said that there was no dispute between himself and his learned friend, the counsel for the Crown, as to the facts of the case nor as to the depravity of the offence. He supposed that there was no disagreement as to anything anywhere in the Court.

His defence was that his client was a moron. She was an animal and she was not a political one. She had no ideas of her own. She had never joined anything. That is why she had done so well when she was positively vetted. Indeed, if it had not been for this momentary and inexplicable lapse into honesty, she was exactly the kind of moron qualified to rise to the highest ranks of government service.

At this point Mr Pleamarket-Creep concluded his defence, wrapped his silk around him, and lay down on the floor, where he was observed to screw up his face and wink at Mr Cute and then at Mr Justice Canting.

Mr Justice Canting began his judgment. He addressed himself first to counsel for the defence and assured him that grovelling would be of no avail in this case, the most flagrant of any that had ever come before him.

It was true, that plea-bargaining was an established practice of the courts, and one which was often of great service to the Crown. Why was this? Because it brought matters to a term and excluded from the process that archaic relict of past times, the jury. Trial by jury occasioned time, expense, and (far worse) uncertainty of conviction. The useful invention of plea-bargaining enabled the Court to move directly from the

charge to the sentence. This was a great convenience. Indeed,
he was happy to say that by such means the Old Belial itself
might now be regarded as a Public Convenience.

He did not know whether there had been any bargain in
this case. Very probably not. However, it was clearly in the
interests of the Crown that there should be no jury in this
case. How could a jury be selected with absolute certainty
of conviction? His learned friend, the Attorney-General, had
assured him that every possible precaution was being taken
in the vetting of potential jurors. Even so, no certain way
could be found to exclude subversive persons, such as readers
of the unauthorised newsheet which had published Mr Hushpuppy's memorandum—every one of whom was an accomplice
after the fact.

In these circumstances it was politic and proper for the
Crown to take exceptional measures to ensure that Miss
Candide entered a plea of guilty. It was possible that they
had gone further than they had a warrant to do, in conveying
the suggestion that in return she would receive a non-custodial
sentence. But what of that? The object had been achieved,
and he now had the prisoner defenceless before him.

Mr Justice Canting then addressed Miss Candide: 'Your
offence is the most monstrous in living memory. I will deal
with it under three heads.'

'First, by revealing the plan to sneak in Cabbage-Patch
Scarecrows into this country you set in motion a train of
consequences among the disaffected populace which could
have led on to riot, rapine, arson, violent confrontation and
blood flowing through the country lanes. It is true—and I will
frankly acknowledge this—that when in fact the Scarecrows
did arrive there was no riot, rapine, blood nor arson.'

'But it is an ancient practice of our courts that any old
buffer who occupies this bench may introduce the most
lurid and improbable worst-case hypotheses into his judgment
and then give these fantasies full weight in his sentencing.'

'Prisoner at the bar, we must judge you not on the basis
of what *did* happen, which was rather little. We must speculate
upon what *could* have happened, when viewed by a fevered
imagination, and then sentence you accordingly. So that I

must, in respect of my own ghastly fantasies, regard you as standing before me convicted of arson, rapine, riot, burglary, barratry, bigamy, buggery, bastardy, battery, bankruptcy, and whatever else I can imagine.

'Second, by your action you have weakened the confidence of this country's allies in the trustworthiness of the Government. I use the plural only out of form. You well know which Great Ally I refer to. It is a matter of high import that this Ally should know everything about the most secret affairs of this country but that the British people should not.

'Until lately only inferior degrees of treason have been known to our laws, such as high treason, petty treason and the like. But the courts now recognise an infinitely graver degree of treason. This is Super Treason, or lack of deference to our Great Ally. You stand now before me convicted of super-treachery. Indeed, I am aghast. . .' (At this point Mr Justice Canting was overcome by emotion and raised his eyes to the United States flag which now hangs in the courtroom of the Old Belial.)

Concluding his judgment Mr Justice Canting said that Miss Candide's offence, under the third head, was even more grave (if that was possible) than the first two. She had flouted the Official Mendacity Acts, without whose salutary operation no government could continue.

These Acts had a venerable history of precedents reaching back to the thirteenth century. They were a staple of English Common Law. It had long been a principle of government to regard literacy or the provision of public education as a threat to public order. His learned predecessors had done everything in their power to prevent the people from reading the Bible in English. For several centuries they had succeeded in conducting proceedings in the courts in archaic Latin forms so that the condemned did not even know for what they were being hanged. The government had conducted a stubborn resistance to the publication of the proceedings of Parliament. Had it not been for the interference of a certain Alderman Wilkes and of other ruffians in the City of London (in the case of *Rex versus Hansard*), the public would remain in blissful ignorance of debates in the House of

Commons to this present day.

'But, alas! The floodgates of democracy have now been thrown open! On every side authority is menaced by public education and public prints! How, in the face of these hazards, is order to be maintained unless by the skilful exercise of mendacity, and the constant provision to the public of pre-masticated public information?'

In an impassioned conclusion Mr Justice Canting described the Official Mendacity Acts as a last dyke thrown up against the inrush of anarchy. The grand purpose of these Acts was well-known. It was not to deny information to the Enemy, who had his own means of finding out. It was not even to deny information to the natives of this country, although the Acts took care of this matter. It was to enable the Government to feed the public with a wholesome and regular diet of *dis*information.

'Great God!', Mr Justice Canting continued: 'The crimes of the prisoner endanger the very fabric of civilised life. If the operations of government are to be thrown open to every Tom, Dick and Harry—nay, as the fashion now is, to every Jill and Jane' (consternation in court) 'and if the criminal infection of truth-telling were to become common, how could any rule continue? How could we ensure the security of any Scarecrows? How could we prevent the displeasure of our Great Ally? Nay, how could we ensure the secure tenure of our own salaries and fees. . .?' (At this point Mr Justice Canting broke off and wept copiously into his wig.)

When he had composed himself, Mr Justice Canting delivered sentence. 'Jane Candide, you have been found guilty of riot, arson, rapine, super treason, and of truth-telling in contempt of all seventy-seven sections of the Official Mendacity Acts. These are all capital offences, but by some oversight the legislature has not provided for the capital penalty. The sentence is seventy-seven years of imprisonment.'

▲ LAW REPORT : COURT OF APPEAL ▲

Regina versus Herself, Ex parte the British People

Before Lord Cain (Lord Chief Justice), Lord Justice Shuffel and Lord Justice Flay.

Actions taken by Government effectually withdrawing all human rights from the British people were clearly actions taken on the grounds of national security. Therefore the court was not entitled to inquire into the actions which were taken in the exercise of the Royal Prerogative.

The Court of Appeal so held when allowing an appeal by Herself against the decision of Mr Justice Playfair, who had granted in the High Court a declaration of invalidity of an instruction issued by Herself that the constitutional rights of British citizens should be suspended during Her Good Pleasure.

The Lord Chief Justice, giving judgment, said that it was intolerable that the time of their Lordships should be taken with such trivial and factitious matters. An action might well lie against the British people and their counsel for barratry. An action might lie against Mr Justice Playfair for insubordination—he would refer that matter to the Lord Chancellor.

What were the facts in this case? For many years a vast, complex and exceedingly expensive organisation known as HAPPYFARM had been employed by the Government to poke and pry into the communications of our neighbours, our allies, and whomsoever the Government nominate as our enemies (which of necessity included a great part of the British people). For reasons of national security successive Ministers had lied through their back teeth about this operation, and had repeatedly assured both parliament and the public that HAPPYFARM was a low-cost operation exclusively concerned with sending food parcels to the Third World.

The importance of HAPPYFARM's functions and its delicate and confidential nature was obvious and needed no emphasis. There could be no dispute but that the activities were of paramount importance and must be protected from any public inquiry.

Unfortunately the cover of HAPPYFARM had been blown when a postal worker blurted out to the press that no food parcels were ever sent from there through the post-office. This had been a most serious breach of the Official Secrets Acts.

In these circumstances it became inevitable that the true functions of HAPPYFARM (i.e. general piracy of the air, telephone and post) should be officially acknowledged. And ministers took the view that thenceforth security would be best obtained by chaining all civilian operatives to their desks and by forbidding any conversation between them except in the presence of an accredited security officer.

These condign regulations were issued by Herself upon the authority of the Royal Prerogative. Counsel for the respondents (the British people) had argued in the High Court that these regulations were contrary to the letter and spirit of a great number of statutes enacted by parliament in the past two hundred years, and by some accident they had lighted on a judge (Mr Justice Playfair) who had upheld their plea.

His Lordship said that although his patience was already exhausted he would, nevertheless, for form's sake, attend to certain submissions of counsel for the respondents.

Respondents had argued that this nation was governed through a 'parliamentary democracy', and that parliament alone was empowered to abridge the liberties of the British people.

His Lordship agreed that parliament was indeed one among a number of authorities so empowered. Parliament had in recent years been mindful of its duties in this respect, and had brought forward several admirable statutes which had enlarged police powers, curbed the trade unions, taken away rights from metropolitan authorities and juries, etc.

But parliament was a strictly subordinate organ of the State, and it shared the power to abridge liberties with many other subordinate organs such as the National Coal Board and the Metropolitan Police Commissioner. The notion that parliament was anything more than an historic ornament was an outmoded and archaic doctrine.

The function of government was to govern according to law and law must be certain. But parliament was constituted through an electoral process which, despite every precaution, remained arbitrary and uncertain. Parliament must therefore itself be governed and be subjected to law: that is, to their Lordships themselves.

Counsel had also argued that over several centuries the Royal Prerogative had been abridged, citing among other precedents the case of *English Commonwealth versus Charles I.* It was true that there was some abridgement to be found here; indeed, he might say that in that case the Royal Prerogative had been cut short. (Sniggering in court.) But it was well known that this breach in the body politic had been repaired by 13 Ch. II St. 1, c. 1.

It had further been argued that the Royal Prerogative had been subjected to the authority of parliament in 1 Will. & Mary, Sess. 2, Cap. 2, vulgarly known as 'The Bill of Rights'. His Lordship had little time for such musty precedents. That document had not been drawn by judges or by lawyers. It included many loose phrases as to 'Vindicating and Asserting the Auntient Rights and Liberties of our Auncestors', which purported liberties could not be found in any book of law.

In particular respondents had cited the first proposition of the Bill of Rights: 'That the pretended Power of Suspending of Laws or the Execution of Laws by Regall Authority without consent of Parlyament is illegal.' And they had supported this by citing 'The Case of the Seven Bishops' (1688) in which the jury had found against the exercise of the Royal Prerogative to suspend and dispense with existing laws.

But all these statutes and cases were no more than regrettable necessities. They were sops thrown to a turbulent and disaffected populace as a means of quietening their minds.

They did not represent the true intentions of the governors. Indeed, in 'The Case of the Seven Bishops' the jury had found against the clear direction of the court. These precedents had long been set aside.

Finally, counsel had submitted that the Royal Prerogative had been invoked as a fiction by Herself in the pursuit of Her own ambitions, and that Her Majesty the Queen had neither been informed nor consulted and might indeed have disapproved of this exercise of the Prerogative in her name.

It was true, Lord Cain said, that this matter was not wholly satisfactory. In recent years the Royal Prerogative had passed over from Her Majesty to Herself, along with much of the deference and allegiance previously owing to the monarch. He was aware that it had been proposed that the forms and the reality should be brought into a match, and that Herself should be duly crowned and enthroned.

However, it would be foolhardy to meddle with the ornamental forms of the monarchy so long as the arbitrary and uncertain process of parliamentary election (to which he had just referred) had not been curbed and brought under a rule. What if some shocking accident were to occur and Herself be unseated? What if some popular fellow should attain not only to the post of Prime Minister but also, thereby, to the Prerogative? It might then be a time when the Royal Prerogative should revert once again to the person of the monarch, as a hedge against anarchy.

Indeed, when Lord Cain considered the hazards of a merely-biological succession (the Royal Family), he wondered whether some more certain safeguard of law and property might be devised? Even in the best of families there could be disputes, or persons who did not come up to the mark, as he had once had to make clear with some force to his learned brother, Mr Justice Abel. Might it not be wiser if the Royal Prerogative were to be vested in the office and the person of the Lord Chief Justice?

In conclusion the Lord Chief Justice said that the matter before them was clear and allowed for no argument. The object of government was to govern the British people. No power could reside in the governed. The Government of this nation consisted of a separation of powers in three parts, *viz.:* (1) The Director of the Security Services, (2) Herself, and (3) Himself (in the Office of Lord Chief Justice).

The name of the Director was always withheld from public knowledge as an Awful Secret. He was generally—although this was not essential to his functions—the agent of a foreign power, such as the USSR or the USA. He might not be questioned by parliament and he was responsible only to Herself. The function of Himself was to confirm, in arcane and pompous language, whatever the Director or Herself decided upon, and to act as a screen between them and the public.

Since the interests of national security were paramount (and were the true seat of power in this nation), it was the duty of the courts to endorse any action taken under the Royal Prerogative 'which could truly be said to have been taken in the interests of national security to protect this country from its enemies or potential enemies' (*Times* Law Report, 7 August 1984). Such enemies might be without this country or (more probably) within. And how was the truth of what was said to be determined? His Lordship found no difficulty here. Whatever Herself chose to say might, by definition, 'truly be said', since Herself had truly said it. Any further inquiry into this by the courts would be dangerous.

It was true that he could find no certain definition of 'national security' in his books. But what matter? He would enter certain *dicta* for the guidance of the courts. National security was whatever the Government pretended it to be. This matter had already been made clear by his learned predecessor in this office, Lord Chief Justice Lane, who had found (*Times* Law Report, 7 August 1984) that 'the ministers were the sole judges of what the national security required'. All that was necessary, in any exercise of the Prerogative, was that Government should indicate that it 'thought' that national security required these measures, and that this 'thought' arose from 'a *bona fide* belief'. Since Herself was distinguished by the strength of her *bona fide* beliefs we could be assured of firm government during her lifetime.

As for the Royal Prerogative, Lord Cain noted that it was a convenient fiction to enlarge the powers of Herself. The Prerogative covered not only national security but also the conduct of foreign affairs, the armed forces and the police, the regulation of the civil service, the inland revenue, the interception of citizens on Herself's highways, and by extension whatever else She wished.

Counsel's submissions as to infractions of 'human' and 'constitutional' rights were an intolerable abuse of the courts. Their Lordships could not find any 'rights' in their books. The law was concerned with persons in their view as obedient subjects and not in any supposed view as 'humans'. Their Lordships could not find any 'humans' in their books.

Nor could they find any British 'Constitution' in their books. While certain suppositious 'rights' had from time to time been granted as a means of managing disaffected opinion, these could at any time be suspended, and usually they were. Indeed, their Lordships recollected that until recent times Governments had very often suspended not only the purported 'rights' but also the bodies of their subjects, and for all their Lordships cared they might soon start doing this again.

The appeal by Herself was allowed. The respondents were ordered to pay all costs as well as the costs of HAPPYFARM and of the Trident programme. Lord Justice Shuffel and Lord Justice Flay remained mute throughout the proceedings.

Law Reporter: E.P. Thompson

THE DIVISION
OF EUROPE

▲ A BASIC QUESTION ▲

Fifty-six years come tomorrow
Was Workers' October—kingdom of necessity
Turned arse-over-tit, kingdom of freedom come.

Let me look at my watch.
It seems a long time for the kingdom of freedom
To have shown the world nothing but its backside.

Comrade Central Committee, comrade high official
Of the Writers' Union, letter-signers, informers,
Stuck in half-a-century of backwards postures:
You bore us to distraction.

You're right: this *is* a bitter old capitalist world.
It needs changing. Some of us are trying.
But not in your way, arse-forwards,
Offering it to the world as a fully-human bottom.

Perhaps fully-human bases have superstructures?

May we talk to your other end?

September, 1973.

119

▲ THE SOVIET UNION: DÉTENTE ▲
AND DISSENT (1974)*

Roy Medvedev's measured appraisals provoke in my mind reflections upon two moments in my own political experience.

The first moment is that of the crisis of the Second World War: the years 1942-45. Soviet intellectuals are now examining the evidence of these years, and are uncovering a record of diplomatic miscalculation, destructive terror, and military and administrative mismanagement whose consequences were appalling. Medvedev himself, in his discussion of *Gulag Archipelago*, focuses attention on Stalin's personal responsibilities: his 'criminal miscalculations, his inability to prepare either the army or the country for war, his ludicrously foolish orders at the outbreak of hostilities, his desertion of his post in the first week of war, and his prior destruction of experienced commanders and commissars. . .' all of which resulted in the loss or capture of some 4,000,000 troops.

Some Western socialist intellectuals have tended to focus attention less on the military conduct of the war than upon the diplomatic bargaining in Yalta and at Potsdam which determined the balance of power at its conclusion: the trading of spheres of influence, which resulted in the division of Europe which endures to this day, and which entailed, on

* From *Détente and Socialist Democracy: a Discussion with Roy Medvedev*, edited by Ken Coates (Spokesman, 1975).

the one hand, the imposition by Soviet arms of a military and bureaucratic 'socialism' upon the peoples of Eastern European countries, and, on the other, the consignment of certain Western European countries to a United States sphere of influence (whose consequences, in Greece and in Spain, can be seen to this day).

Both these lines of enquiry seem to me to be important. But there is a sense in which, for a man of my generation, neither of them falls at the exact centre of the experience of those years. For the experience was—as one lived it—that 'the war' was 'won', and that it might very well have been lost. It is true that as Solzhenitsyn, Medvedev and others show, it was 'won' at a cost immensely and tragically higher than might have been necessary. And it is true also, as many younger Western socialists and Trotskyists insist, that in the moment of 'winning' the war many of the democratic and socialist objectives of the popular victors were betrayed by their own leaders.

But neither of these reservations cancel out the historical event: that the Allied armies and not the armed power of Fascism emerged in control of Europe. The generations who did not live through those years perhaps assume this outcome too easily. If the outcome had been the opposite, they would now be making very different kinds of assumption. For if Franco, in the more exposed and precarious circumstances of Spain, has been able to survive the war for thirty years, I can see no overwhelming reason why Nazism and Fascism should not have endured over the whole of Europe into the 1970s: at the best one might have hoped for inner nationalist fractures resulting in terrible internecine conflicts between rival élites; at the worst a Euro-Nazism, armed with nuclear weapons, might have submerged the entire world in imperialist wars. In any case, those of us who survived in the 1970s would not be discussing these matters, since we would have access neither to any printing-press nor to sources of objective scholarship.

So that a 'victory', even if at tragic cost and partially-betrayed, remains different from that kind of defeat. And since no Western writer with the genius of Solzhenitsyn has ever composed a *Gulag Archipelago* which takes into a single view the repression in this century of intellectuals, Jews, trade unionists, socialists, liberals, communists, and ordinary people of all persuasions in Western and Southern Europe, it follows that the matter is not as vividly present in the imagination of those under 40 years of age as it remains to those of us who are over 40.

It may follow also that there is a certain difference at a deep, almost sub-conscious level—a level of experiential assumption—in attitudes towards the Soviet Union. Put in the simplest way: I cannot in the end rid myself of some kind of very deep affirmative feeling towards 'the Soviet Union', as the country whose valour saved all of us from a future of Euro-Nazism. If the Western Allied forces and the resistance movements contributed something to this outcome—and perhaps contributed rather more than Russian school-children are now told in their lessons on 'The Great Patriotic War'—none of us can doubt that the Soviet people bore the greatest part. So that all of us now living, including those who were not yet born at the time of the battle of Stalingrad, live by virtue of a transfusion from that Soviet blood.

At any rate, between 1942 and 1944 it appeared very simple when one looked at a map. Nazism possessed absolute control over an area and resources larger than the present European Common Market: every unrestrained political and administrative means was employed to fashion a military machine of formidable efficiency and power. While the Allied forces engaged in peripheral campaigns or in lengthy prepara-tions for the opening of a 'Second Front' in Europe (content, in fact, to see 'Germany' and 'Russia' bleed each other white) the markers on the map moved to the edge of Leningrad and of Moscow and deeply towards the Urals. Then they began to move back, in a way in which, from the time of the assumption of power by Mussolini, Hitler and Franco, they had never moved back in Europe before. They moved back with astonishing rapidity, as this hitherto invincible political and military machine met, for the first time, its match; and whole armies were encircled and engulfed. Even the simplest Allied soldier, listening to the news in South Italy or on the

South Coast of England, knew the meaning of these gigantic German reverses. They offered expectation of ultimate victory: an enhanced chance of survival for himself or his family: a war which might not (as one had come to suppose) endure for decades but which might reach a more proximate termination.

For the Soviet people this achievement may have taken place *despite* Stalin and Stalinism, although this was not so easy to see from the West at that time. And the resilience of the people may have stemmed from patriotic rather than communist resources. But however this is seen, some residue of affirmative feeling towards something called loosely 'the Soviet Union' must always remain in my experience. Even when confronted by *Gulag Archipelago*—perhaps at such times most of all—one thinks of the Soviet people as a people with extraordinary, inexhaustible reserves; with an irrational resilience; a people who, when by every logic they are defeated, are capable of moving the markers back across the map once again.

For some of us, in those years, admiration was indiscriminate and self-betraying; and we can now see clearly Stalinism as the enemy of Soviet and Western revolutionaries alike. We can also see Soviet 'dissidents' in all their variety—Solzhenitsyn, Sakharov or Medvedev—as emblems of this astonishing resilience; driven back into the Urals of Soviet culture, they have decided, when defeat had seemed inevitable, to give not an inch more of ground. They are hemmed in in their own Stalingrad. Will we see, once again, those liberating markers moving back across the map? This is what Medvedev asks. I have tried to explain why this question calls up in some of us an ancient sense of solidarity.

The other moment in my own political experience which Medvedev provokes me to reflect upon lies in the years 1956-61. In the aftermath of the 20th Congress Western Communist Parties were thrown into turbulence, with major secessions of 'revisionists' and 'dissidents'. In Britain some of the seceders (the *New Reasoner* group) formed an alliance with younger socialist elements which gave rise to the 'New Left'. These events coincided with the influential presence of the Campaign for Nuclear Disarmament: in itself an induction of a new political generation into affirmative action.

The Campaign advocated the immediate, unilateral renunciation by Britain of the manufacture or possession of nuclear weapons. By some—indeed by all—this was seen, in part, as 'a moral gesture'; an initiative towards general disarmament and détente. But opinions were divided as to the political and diplomatic context of this policy. Some supporters of CND advocated the open or tacit continuation of Britain within the strategies of NATO. This would have entailed a continuing dependence, in the last resort, upon a United States 'nuclear shield' which, in the view of some of us, deprived unilateral nuclear disarmament of either moral or political credibility. We in the New Left advocated the policies of CND *plus* 'positive neutralism': that is, a policy which entailed also British renunciation of NATO and the adoption of mediating, neutralist policies aligned to those of Yugoslavia, India and the emergent Third World.

It was a critical part of our advocacy that we argued that with each effective movement of détente there would follow a relaxation in military and bureaucratic pressures within both the United States and the Soviet Union. Thus the relaxation of Cold War tensions was a precondition for further de-Stalinisation, and a precondition for resuming socialist and democratic advances, East or West. I was myself especially associated with this advocacy; and since recent events have thrown this whole perspective into doubt, I should perhaps convict myself out of my own mouth.

Thus I wrote in *Universities and Left Review* (No. 4, Summer 1958):

. . . with each month that the Cold War continues, a terrible distorting force is exercised upon every field of life. As it drags on the half-frozen antagonists become more sluggish in their reactions. Political and economic life is constricted, militarism and reaction are infused with new blood, reaction and the subordination of the individual to the state are intensified, and the crooked ceremonies of destructive power permeate our cultural and intellectual life.

The relaxation of the Cold War would create conditions 'in which healthy popular initiatives will multiply' and (in the words of the Programme of the Yugoslav Communists in the same year) 'shatter the basis upon which bureaucracy thrives and assist the more rapid and less painful development of the socialist countries'. If the British Labour Movement were to adopt the policies of unilateral disarmament plus active neutrality (outside of NATO) this would contribute simultaneously to the acceleration of processes of democratisation in the East and to the resumption of socialist progress in the West. The same perspective was still presented in the British *May Day Manifesto* (1968).

As Medvedev shows, we have been witnessing in 1973-4 an altogether different process. Summit agreements between United States and Soviet leaders, accompanied by some regularisation of relations and limitation of Cold War tensions, have intensified pressures upon Soviet 'dissent' and have been accompanied by the increasing discipline of intellectual and cultural life throughout the Communist world. Does this mean that our original argument was wrong, and was based upon a merely sentimental and wishful appraisal of realities?

Such a conclusion would be premature. It is mistaken to be too impatient in our expectations. There are inner contradictions to be expected within any wider political process. The logic which we proposed—that relaxation of Cold War tensions provides a precondition for socialist democratisation—has, although in a very general and uneven way, been seen at work between 1954 and 1974: and notably in the evolution of Eastern Europe. But insofar as democratisation threatens ruling bureaucracies and also the military-diplomatic controls of the Soviet Union, we have seen a zig-zag movement with very severe setbacks—notably in Czechoslovakia, 1968.

In the Soviet Union the contradictions are especially acute. On the one hand, the repressive institutions and the repressive ideology of pseudo-Marxism have found, for decades, their major source of justification in the function of the ruling bureaucracy (and of its organs of police and of intellectual control) in defending the Soviet people from the threat of attack, from without or from within. It therefore follows that if Nixon and Kissinger can be seen driving through the streets of Moscow—and if the threat from Western imperialism can no longer be seen as immediate— then the function of the bureaucracy is itself called in question, and its repressive ideology loses further credibility. Hence 'détente' is simultaneously a moment of enhanced danger to all those whose privileged and unrepresentative positions rests upon the invocation of this function. Hence the post-Stalinist bureaucracy finds that its legitimacy is called in question, not because our earlier argument was wrong, but because it was right. If the threat from the West appears to diminish, then the old functions can only be sustained by emphasising the threat from China. (But this also involves tormented readjustments of ideological ortho- doxy, and of expectations as to from which quarter to expect 'the main enemy' within.)

Thus what we are now witnessing is a limited and calcula- ted agreement, a détente based upon the regulation of great power interests from above. Both parties to the agreement wish to keep this détente firmly within control and to prevent the unleashing of popular initiatives. But insofar as *any* détente strips the reigning Soviet bureaucracy of its prime function and legitimation, this is sensed as a moment of acute danger. Controls over the life of the Soviet people are tightened at exactly this moment, to prevent that un- controlled and self-generating liberation of (in the first place) intellectual and cultural forces which would, in the end, call in question this bureaucracy itself.

If this analysis is correct, then it also suggests to us certain lines of action which European socialists should take. What we are observing in the Soviet Union at the moment need not indicate a genuine and profound reversal of the tendencies towards democratisation but a temporary arrest to a process which, at any time, may be resumed. Since so much depends upon contingencies—as well as upon the jockeying for power of different interest-groups within the Soviet leadership itself—it would be foolish to attempt any prediction as to

whether this arrest will prove to be long or short. What has
to be challenged is the complacency of those Western socialists and liberals who assume that they are only spectators in
this auditorium, and that the outcome will be determined
solely by events in the Soviet Union or in Eastern Europe.
So long as Western social-democracy remains confined
(whether by active ideological complicity or by effective
impotence) within the strategies of NATO and of a 'Europe'
which excludes not only Moscow but also Prague, Belgrade
and Warsaw, it is itself contributing to the outcome which it
deplores. It is very easy for the Western intellectual to
applaud those Soviet intellectuals who have the courage to
challenge their own statist orthodoxy. But since Western
intellectuals, for all their vaunted (and valued) freedoms,
have been unable to detach decisively one single Western
society from the military and diplomatic definitions of the
Cold War era, the applause has an empty sound to it.

There have of course been gestures towards such a detachment: in French truculence towards NATO, in Brandt's
ostpolitik, and (at the level of annual conference decisions)
in the professed policies of the British Labour Party. Gestures
and professions are better than nothing; and they indicate
that, with greater resolution, actions may ensue. If only one
Western nation were to effect a democratic transition to a
socialist society, were to detach itself decisively from NATO
and from dependence on the United States, and were to
initiate an active, probing, self-confident diplomacy, offering
manifold exchanges in trade and in ideas with 'the East',
this might serve as a significant catalyst. An initiative of this
kind—supported by popular initiatives, exchanges by trade
unionists and intellectuals, exchanges in education and in
tourism—could not be presented by orthodox Soviet ideologists as the old kind of threat to 'subvert' the Soviet system.
It might give great encouragement to the most affirmative
elements in Soviet and Eastern European 'dissent'; and, by
breaking down the old ideological deadlock, by which we are
offered the alternatives of a statist and repressive 'communism' or of substantial democratic rights and defensive
liberties within a capitalist society, it would point towards

further perspectives of socialist internationalism.

It is of course true that such an initiative—if taken by France, Britain, West Germany or Italy—would entail an element of risk. Militarist elements in the Soviet leadership might take it as evidence of 'weakness' in 'the West' and seek to exploit it accordingly. Thus we are supposing that, if such an initiative were to succeed, it would meet with corresponding initiatives from progressive forces in 'the East', at least strong enough to hold their more regressive and militaristic leaders in restraint. And the risks would be greatly enhanced by the diplomatic and economic sanctions brought to bear by the United States and NATO powers upon any defaulting member; by the consequent exposure of this defaulter to immediate economic and social crisis, accompanied by intensified internal class struggle. But the continued division of Europe and of the world entails much greater and continuing risks, which may be regulated temporarily but which can never be permanently ended by great power agreements. We can never move out of this international polarisation except through a process which, at the moment of depolarisation, entails great risk: and it is important that these risks be taken, not as a result of unforeseen accidents; but in a context of mounting popular internationalist initiatives.

This is to restate, in the context of the mid-1970s, perspectives which were argued in the late 1950s by Claude Bourdet and the French *Nouvelle Gauche*; by 'positive neutralists' within the Campaign for Nuclear Disarmament in Britain; by C. Wright Mills in the United States; and by Imre Nagy and the Yugoslav League of Communists. It is sobering to realise that, after fifteen years, the perspectives appear to many to be more, rather than less, utopian. Not many Western socialists today appear to have any confidence in the possibility of a peaceful and democratic transition to socialism; indeed, few appear to be examining what such a transition would entail and many would appear (from their actions) to consider that such a transition would be undesirable, preferring to develop the defensive institutions and the redistributive policies of the labour movement, so that they can get some milk from the capitalist cow for as long as she has milk to give. At the same time the younger Marxist Left, in all its varieties, falls back upon a rhetoric of 'revolution' which supposes a dramatic and violent transition to a socialism whose democratic features are problematic—a rhetoric which, whether one finds it distasteful or not, offers a perspective a good deal more utopian than the one I have sketched above. Finally, many dissidents in 'the East'—or many of those whose voices have been heard most clearly in recent years in the West—no longer hold to the perspectives of a regenerated socialist democracy which, to one degree or another, informed the Polish revisionists in 1956, Imre Nagy, the Yugoslav Communists of 1958, or Dubcek. One or two of them (if we are to judge by recent statements of Solzhenitsyn) might actually oppose any Western advance towards socialism, and would (like the Pentagon) see the detachment of any Western power from NATO strategies as a symptom of weakness.

Utopian or not, I think it is worth re-stating this old perspective for two reasons. First, it may serve to correct the rather self-satisfied stance of some Western liberals and socialists. For if one proposes this perspective, it can at once be seen that it might prove to be as difficult for a Western nation to resume initiatives independent of great-power polarities as it proved to be for Czechoslovakia in 1968. A comparable effort of self-emancipation by any Western nation has scarcely been attempted. While this does not in any way call in question the value of Western freedoms, it does suggest that Western intellectuals have efficiently preserved these freedoms for their own consumption by virtue of the fact that they have been ineffectual in using them to challenge the overall boundaries within which such self-expression remains 'safe'.

The limits of Western tolerance have not yet been exposed to a Dubcek-type test; or, if they have, that test was made in unusual circumstances in the southern hemisphere. And when Allende pressed against those limits, neither he nor any Western freedoms survived the test.

Second, the perspective only appears utopian because it is

presented in a way which proposes that an action be taken in advance of the necessary preconditions for that action. These preconditions are, exactly, an initial rebirth of socialist internationalism; a growing discourse between 'dissident' voices in both the East and the West; a discourse which, by proposing alternatives to the present polarisation of power, itself begins to create such an alternative, in a reawakened internationalist conscience, and in feasible national strategies. This is why one must attach the greatest significance to Roy Medvedev's initiatives. Honest political exchanges between Soviet or East European dissidents and Western socialists, unmediated by party officials and uninhibited by ideological imperatives, are a precondition for Eastern democratisation and for Western socialist advance alike.

This leads me to my final points as to how such exchanges might be conducted. If exchanges enlarge they will turn out to be deeply confusing, to overthrow many cherished expectations; to break down many ideological pre-suppositions. There is a sense in which the Soviet Union, after fifty years of severe intellectual repression and discipline, is a de-structured political community. Or it is, in one sense, altogether de-structured; and in another sense, it has only one, obligatory political structure, through the Soviet Communist Party. We are fortunate, in conversing with Roy Medvedev, to be conversing with a man who relates at many points to our own Western socialist traditions, and specifically to a Marxist tradition: we recognise common terms and signposts. But it cannot be expected that all conversation will be like this. On the one hand, from the de-structured political community we must expect that a people who have suffered from innumerable crimes which have been justified by a mandatory statist Marxist orthodoxy will show a profound distaste, not only for Stalinism, but also for all Marxist forms and terms. The Christian tradition will seem to some—as it seems to Solzhenitsyn—to have offered greater resources in defending the individual and the human conscience than any resources within Marxism. The children whose teeth have been set on edge by the sour grapes of paternal statist ortho-

doxy may suffer very large illusions as to the liberalism of the
West, and they may be (as Solzhenitsyn seems to have been)
seriously misinformed as to certain Western realities. In
contrast to statist ideology the Voice of America may be
mistaken for the voice of truth.

On the other hand, insofar as the only legitimate
structuring of political life is through the Soviet Communist
Party, we may expect to see unexpected and unpredictable
things here also. Any historian knows that social contradictions and tensions have a way of working themselves out,
not in neat predictable ways, but through whatever forms are
available. People make use of whatever forms history has
given to them to use. In a Durham pit-village in the 19th
century the very conservative Methodist chapel may turn
out to be the training school for a militant miners' leader; in
Catholic Fascist Spain we may find important radical and
liberation elements within the Catholic Church; and so on.
Since the inheritance of the Soviet Communist Party is in
fact enormously richer than its official ideological forms
would suggest, we can expect repeated evidence of social
tensions working their way through within—or despite—
these forms. The rhetoric of statist Marxism may be authoritarian and empty; but it remains, in form, a Marxist rhetoric,
and there are strong libertarian elements within the Marxist
tradition. To suppress those elements would involve (among
other things) suppressing the collected work of Marx.

This is why it is foolish to criticise Medvedev because he
has some expectations of renewed democratic changes initiated by elements within the Soviet Communist Party. But in
fact I find it foolish and beside the point for any Western
socialist or Marxist to spend time, at this particular stage, in
criticising Medvedev or any other dissident in any way at all.
What we ought to be doing is *listening*. In the first place,
and in the second place, we have to express solidarity, assist
our Soviet comrades in their efforts to consolidate a position
from which any dialogue becomes possible, listen carefully,
learn, attempt to understand the new ideas and the new
sensibility which has been growing up like tundra beneath
the orthodox snows.

The particular privilege enjoyed by the Western Marxist or Leftist intelligentsia is the privilege of irresponsibility. Since our actions are largely verbal and command few real social consequences, we can say what we like in the way that we like. An error of political judgment, an ill-advised telephone call, lack of security with an address-list, will not bring down the arrest of colleagues or their dismissal from employment. Still less will it plunge a whole movement into disarray. Some of us have got so used to this displaced, intellectualised context of Leftist discourse that we indulge in the luxuries of mutual denunciation at the drop of a hat. In the pursuit of a 'correct line' which might be followed, at the very most, by a few thousand people—and more often by a few score intellectuals—we denounce A. because he has a wrong formulation on Soviet State Capitalism and B. because he shows a tendency to humanism and moralising. Well, if we want to be like that, and if the discourse between East and West opens up further, we shall find a great deal to denounce. It will keep us happy for some years. There will be, for example, quite a lot of Soviet humanism and moralising, since a nation which has had a great many millions of people wrongfully and arbitrarily killed or imprisoned has got something to moralise about, and some knotty problems about morality, politics, the State and the individual conscience, to clear up. It will seem to some that the matter is not wholly closed by coming to the fine point of a correct formulation.

It seems to me that any helpful discourse between Soviet dissidents and Western socialists must be conducted in a receptive and provisional way. For the time being we should not be impatient for it to have an outcome in any agreed opinions or agreed internationalist strategy; the open and rational discourse—and the information and mutual understanding which this will bring—will remain as a sufficient objective. And if some of those from the East who join the discourse turn out to be deeply hostile to all Marxism, and in search of non-Marxist spiritual values, I hope the discourse will continue all the same. Indeed, when I read some self-styled Western Marxists—for example, the school of

M. Althusser, which appears to continue on its way oblivious of the fact that the history of the Soviet Union raises certain 'moral' questions—I think that it would not matter all that much if Marxism was Christianised a little. Or, again, perhaps the problem is that as a State or doctrinal orthodoxy it has already been Churchified too much.

As regards the supposed failure of dissident Soviet intellectuals to agitate among the masses. . . Perhaps I may end with an historical analogy which might afford a little encouragement. When in 1792 Tom Paine published in England *Rights of Man* every official and quasi-official means was taken to suppress the man and his ideas. Paine was indicted and driven into exile. The book was burned by the public hangman. House-to-house enquiries were made as to his readers or supporters. Resolutions were passed at county meetings. In nearly every town and most villages in Britain there were public bonfires, when Paine was burned in effigy, and the populace were given drink to toast the 'Church and King'. And all this worked very well. The chauvinist and regressive impulses of the crowd (who had never had an opportunity to read Paine) were flattered. Those intellectuals and artisans who supported him were isolated in a sea of public hostility. But a year or two later? What the authorities had overlooked was that they had engaged in a superb advertising campaign. Every old woman (as one reformer noted, in an isolated country town) had heard about Tom Paine and wondered what he had really written. The ideas and the pamphlets began to circulate in the wake of an aroused national curiosity. Soon a book had become a popular movement. I could not say whether this is a relevant analogy or not. I know little about the complexities of life in the Soviet Union. But I do know that in history exiles have a way of returning as heroes; and that at night bonfires light up the surrounding countryside.

▲ EXTERMINISM REVIEWED* ▲

My 'Notes on Exterminism'[1] were written in May 1980, in the aftermath of the NATO 'modernisation' decision and of the Soviet invasion of Afghanistan (both in December 1979), and against the background of the US failure to ratify SALT II and of a bellicose and seemingly 'consensual' all-party militarist hullabaloo in Britain (*Protect and Survive* and so on). There was then no effective peace movement in Europe—something in Holland and in Norway, a first stirring of the new movement in Britain, but as yet very little in West Germany or Italy. The peace movement in the Far East was also quiescent. And Solidarity did not yet know its name.

The times favoured intellectual pessimism. I can accept the reproof of Raymond Williams and of those other contributors who detect some sentences in my 'Notes' that could support a determinism according to which the rival weapons systems, by themselves, and by their reciprocal logic, must bring us to extermination. I ought to have known better than to have gestured at Marx's suggestive image of the hand-mill and the steam-mill. Yet the 'Notes' did not only suggest that: there was also, already, in the European Nuclear Disarmament Appeal, the outlines of a strategy of resistance, and my essay concluded with a conspectus of this alternative—a conspectus which has taken on flesh in the past two years, in the realities

---

* Abridged from my concluding essay responding to the discussions of the notion of 'exterminism' in the volume *Exterminism and Cold War* (Verso Editions/NLB, 1982).

of the peace movements.

If the times are not quite as dark today, they are still dark enough. And I am unwilling to abandon the category of 'exterminism' without at least a tentative defence. The term itself does not matter: it is ugly and over-rhetorical. What matters is the problem that it points towards. There remains something, in the inertial thrust and the reciprocal logic of the opposed weapons systems—and the configuration of material, political, ideological and security interests attendant upon them—which cannot be explained within the categories of 'imperialism' or 'international class struggle'. And there are some plain misunderstandings of my argument.

Thus Roy and Zhores Medvedev[2] challenge my view that 'a situation could ever reach the point in the Soviet Union when "hair-trigger military technology annihilated the very moment of 'politics' "'.' And they argue, in response, that 'the Soviet system is too conservative and densely bureaucratised for this to happen'. If the Party exercises comprehensive control of most sensitive aspects of intellectual and social life, 'how can one imagine that those military experts who manage the Soviet Union's ICBMs could possibly launch them in an emergency without collective decisions at the highest levels of the Party and state?' And the Medvedevs conclude that 'strict and comprehensive safeguards exist against any possibility of either a mistaken or deliberate initiative by any level of the military hierarchy alone'.

That may be so, if we stress *initiative*, although even here there is room for little accidents which perhaps do not receive Politbureau sanction, such as the episode of the Soviet submarine in sensitive Swedish waters. But if we accept the Medvedev's arguments in a literal sense, then we can only conclude that the Soviet Union is doomed by its bureaucratic and conservative procedures to be the loser in any nuclear exchange. For military-technological considerations have already shrunk the time in which any collective decisions of Party or state can be made. Nuclear weapons are so devastating that response to an attack—or pre-emption of an anticipated attack—must be almost instantaneous. And the whole absurd theory of 'deterrence' demands that such near-instantaneous capabilities can be displayed. In one example, the Pershing II is advertised as a highly accurate and swift weapon: if sited, as planned, in West Germany it will be seen as a potential weapon for first strike, capable of taking out Soviet ICBMs and command and communication centres in the western Soviet Union in a few minutes of flight. In the view of one well-informed American authority, Arthur Macy Cox, such a threat could be met by the Soviet military only by the introduction of LOW (Launch-On-Warning) automated systems, which would despatch a nuclear counter-strike on the trigger of an electronic alert signal. The collective decisions of Party and state would then be pre-empted within the circuits of a computer. And an influential lobby for LOW systems exists in the USA as well. Where would be the moment of 'politics' then?

This question ought to remain open for analysis a little longer. New contributions on this question, some of them coming from positions rather far from those of the traditional 'left'—notably Jonathan Schell's *The Fate of the Earth*—will ensure that it will not be tidied away. Schell is asking whether advanced civilisation may not be falling subject to a tendency towards its own self-extinction—a tendency which, if not reversed within a decade or so, might become irreversible? That is much the same question as is proposed in my 'Notes'. What name, then, are we to give to such a tendency? And what *is* a 'tendency'? Is this moment simply the product of an accidental coincidence—the coincidental invention of an appalling new military technology superimposed upon a particular episode of world-wide political confrontation? Or can we speak of entering—at some point after 1945—into a distinct historical epoch (perhaps a terminal one), with distinct characteristics governed by the reciprocal non-dialectical contradiction between two military blocs whose competition, at every stage, reinforces their mutual hostility and their exterminist resources—an epoch which requires a new category for its analysis?

I proposed the term 'exterminism' because, in my view, the second of these alternatives may be correct. I have rehearsed the argument recently, but without recourse to the term, in my lecture *Beyond the Cold War:*

'The Cold War has become a habit, an addiction. But it is a habit supported by very powerful material interests in each bloc: the military-industrial and research establishments of both sides, the security services and intelligence operations, and the political servants of these interests. These interests command a large (and growing) allocation of the skills and resources of each society; they influence the direction of each society's economic and social development; and it is in the interest *of* those interests to increase that allocation and to influence this direction even more.'

I don't mean to argue for an *identity* of process in the United States and the Soviet Union, nor for a perfect symmetry of forms. There are major divergencies, not only in political forms and controls, but also as between the steady expansionism of bureaucracy and the avarice of private capital. I mean to stress, rather, the *reciprocal* and inter-active character of the process. It is in the very nature of this Cold War show that there must be two adversaries: and each move by one must be matched by the other. This is the inner dynamic of the Cold War which determines that its military and security establishments are *self-reproducing.* Their missiles summon forward our missiles which summon forward their missiles in turn. NATO's hawks feed the hawks of the Warsaw bloc.

For the ideology of the Cold War is self-reproducing also. That is, the military and the security service and their political servants *need* the Cold War. They have a direct interest in its continuance.

If we do require a new category to define this distinct epoch of nuclear-confrontational history, yet it goes without saying that this does not, by some gesture of a wand, mean that all previous categories are dispensed with or all prior historical forces cease to be operative. That may also be a misunderstanding which my 'Notes' invited upon themselves. Imperialisms and class struggles, nationalisms and confrontations between publics and bureaucracies, will all operate with their customary vigour; they may continue to dominate this historical episode or that. It will mean, rather, that a new, featureless and threatening, figure has joined the *dramatis personae* of history, a figure which throws a more abrupt and darker shadow than any other. And that we are already within the shadow of that extreme danger. For as the shadow falls upon us, we are impelled to take on the role of that character ourselves.

Roy and Zhores Medvedev turn away from this mode of analysis. As Soviet patriots (albeit 'dissident' ones) they react rather strongly against any notion of co-responsibility by the superpowers for the current crisis or of 'symmetry' of any structural kind induced in the rival powers by three decades of confrontation. They offer a different analysis, of a historical character, in which Soviet militarisation is shown to be in reaction (sometimes *over*-reaction) to the military threat of NATO, and especially the USA.

I found their contribution to be in every respect illuminating, as well as positive and encouraging. I welcome especially the sense of solidarity with which they write, and the patience with which they explore disagreements. If I explore these disagreements further (and from the weak position of a greatly inferior knowledge of Soviet history and reality) it is because of the extreme importance of the issues, and the urgency with which the European and American peace movements await a discourse of genuine internationalism with wider sections of the Soviet public. And for this to take place we must first remove certain road-blocks and controls which the Medvedevs scarcely mention.

I learned much from the Medvedevs' essay and have few and insignificant disagreements with it. Yet it leaves much unsaid, and in doing so it could close off some lines of inquiry prematurely. The Medvedevs are viewing history as rational *causation*, whereas I am viewing the contemporary opposed militarist structures as historical *consequences*; so that some of our arguments are flying past each others' ears. Everything the Medvedevs say about the prior responsibility of 'the West' for militaristic pace-making may be true; yet the consequence of three decades of Soviet response to that may have been to enstructure militarism deeply in Soviet society also.

The Medvedevs argue that the Soviet Union has militarised itself reluctantly, defensively, that the Party remains in control of all organs of the state. Yet history is full of examples of the way in which deeper processes can override or co-opt such controls and intentions. It simply is not possible for a major economy to be inflected towards military priorities for some three decades (and more) without profound consequences in social, political and ideological life.

The Medvedevs argue that 'military-industrial-research interests in the Soviet Union. . . do not constitute a "state within the state" as they do in the United States, but remain a subordinate part of the state'. I am surprised they can argue with such confidence, in view of the opacity of Soviet state structures and the paucity of published information—which they are the first to acknowledge. 'Subordinate', in any case, to what? To a Party which itself must in some part represent these interests (to which some 15 per cent of the GNP is allocated) and some of whose leading executives are recruited from the military-industrial-security areas? There are some scraps of evidence known to me (many more weighty evidences must be known to the Medvedevs) which suggest that 'isomorphic' replication of militarist priorities is not unknown in Soviet life. Thus 'Boris Komarov', the Soviet ecologist, refers repeatedly to the ways in which 'defence' priorities can always over-rule the well-intended environmental regulations of Soviet authorities. The sad story of the pollution of Lake Baikal commenced when 'the Ministry of Defence needed new durable cord for heavy bomber tyres. Such things are referred to tersely as "strategic interests of the country" and are not subject for discussion even within the Council of Ministers. The immunity of the Baikal projects to any criticism is explained by these "strategic interests".' And recounting the story of the poisoning of wild life by PCB (polychlorinated biphenyls) he concludes that 'the secret of PCB, as might have been expected, was buried in one of the defence ministries. PCB was required for extra-strong insulation for military equipment: its composition and hazards were concealed for reasons of military secrecy: 'Here too "strategic interests" prevailed. In the most literal sense strategic interests pervade our whole being whether we want them or not'. And to all this 'Komarov' provides some lighter footnotes. He describes the wholesale slaughter of wild life by high- (and even low-) placed military, overriding every protective regulation: 'eagles, hobbies, kites, and other birds of prey are wiped out from military helicopters just for practice; Marshal Chuikov has even been known to sweep through whole areas with a column of all-terrain vehicles, field kitchens, etcetera, slaughtering every bird and beast in sight; polar bears have been hunted by helicopter; and so on.[3] It is all reminiscent of the safaris of British officers in Kenya or in the Indian princedoms, thirty or fifty years ago.

The Medvedevs will understand that I do not introduce this evidence with 'anti-Soviet' intent. I am simply insisting that one cannot divert huge resources to secretive and protected military areas without incurring huge social consequences; that the same consequences which are felt here in Britain at Stornoway or at West Wycombe are felt there at Baikal or at Kyzyl-Agach. When 'strategic interests of the country' are not even subject for discussion within the Council of Ministers, in what sense are these then 'a subordinate part of the state'? Is this not only too familiar to us in 'the free West'?

If polychlorinated biphenyls, protected by 'strategic interests', can poison the water and grass of the Soviet Union, I would think it probable also that similar toxic ideological compounds, also protected by 'strategic interests', will be poisoning or confusing the minds of the Soviet people, just as these poison minds in the West. The ideological PCBs commonly found on this side are those which offer partisan, alarmist, or directly nationalistic descriptions of reality—which justify each and every measure of militarisation in the name of 'deterrence' and the threat of the Other—which directly inhibit genuine international discourse, and which repress or inhibit critical reflection and discussion as threats to the 'security' of the state. One need not read very far in the literature on contemporary Soviet reality to learn that such toxic compounds are widely dispersed, on that side as on this.

This does not mean that we should look for structural symmetries in the opposed superpowers. I have argued, not for this, but for reciprocal and interactive modes of strategic and ideological confrontation. If symmetry now, in the 1980s, begins to appear, this is consequence and not causation. We are entering upon extremely uneasy times, and we ought not to refuse consideration of the possibility that one of the options still open for a resolution of the political problems of the Soviet Union is a military one. It is already apparent that some sections of the ruling establishment there are displaying anxiety lest the peace movement should infect Soviet youth, but in a form critical of Soviet reality. In the past few months there has been an assault upon 'pacifist' tendencies weakening the 'heroic-patriotic' faith of Soviet youth. Boris Pastukhov, a leader of the Comsomol, has called for 'Undertaking with yet greater clarity of purpose the military-patriotic upbringing, the moral, political, psychological and technical preparation of youth for service in the ranks of the armed forces, to instil in young people courage, the will and readiness to perform heroic deeds. . .'[4] This is the moralistic and nationalist claptrap of all armed states. But even if it is argued that these necessary ideological measures are imposed upon Soviet authorities by the aggressive postures of the West in association with China, the consequence must be nationalistic and militaristic indoctrination. And behind this claptrap, is it not possible to distinguish the features of a distinct militarist lobby? Marshal Ogarkov, the Soviet Chief of Staff, has recently published a book, *Always Ready to Defend the Fatherland*, which advocates the demands of the military in an unusually open way. He advocates, like his NATO analogues, not only a massive programme of weapons 'modernisation', but also advanced preparations for switching 'the entire economy to a war footing': 'In order to increase the military preparedness of the country, today as never before it is necessary to co-ordinate mobilisation and deployment of the armed forces and the entire economy. . .' To achieve these objectives 'is

not possible without a stable centralised system of leadership of the country and the armed forces. . . an even greater
concentration of management'.[5]

This centralised management, this stable and concentrated
system of leadership of the-country-and-the-armed-forces,
looks rather like some kind of military junta to me. Because
Marshal Ogarkov has given a thought to this possibility it
does not mean that it will come about. But we have seen
already, in Poland, a military junta displace the Party in
power: and while this was a Polish solution arising from
Polish conditions, it establishes a new precedent nonetheless.
For the radical political weakness of the Soviet Union and of
every Warsaw Pact state is to be found in the weakness of
civil society; it is sixty-five years on from the Revolution,
and yet civil society in the Soviet Union has a sparse and
insecure presence, existing within the controls and by the
permission of the Party and the security police; and it is
precisely where civil society is weak that the military (in
alliance with other interests) can most swiftly enter in. It is
not just a question of force: it is a question of legitimacy.
Where no form of power is legitimated by civil accountability
and due and open process, then one form of power might
just as well give way to another. Each is as legitimate or as
illegitimate as the other.

I hope, profoundly, that the Medvedevs are right and that
my own fantasy is wrong. Yet for it to be proved wrong may
at least require that the possibility be steadily faced, so that
action may be taken to prevent it. And what disturbed me
most about the Medvedevs' brilliant essay was a sense that
the accumulation of absences and silences amounted even to
complacency. This is so far out of character in these two
indomitable and uncomplacent authors that I must be
wrong. Yet the sense lingered with me, especially at the
article's conclusion—in the section sub-headed 'The Responsibility of the Peace Movement'. And it turned out here that
this responsibility fell wholly, and without qualification,
upon the peace movements of NATO and of Western
European nations. The solution to the immediate crisis will
(it seems) be met by the pressure 'for unilateral nuclear

disarmament in Europe' but for 'Europe' it seems that we
should read 'Western Europe' and nothing whatsoever is said
about the need for any peace movement, or even reciprocal
strategy of agitation, in the East. So that while the Medvedevs' analysis is very much more rich and flexible than any
from apologists of the Soviet state, yet their conclusions are
pat and even orthodox.

Now this is a matter which, for our very survival, must be
honestly faced and openly argued out. For the Medvedevs,
in the first pages of their essay, suggest an immense Soviet
audience—an ordinary Soviet public, and also partisans of
socialist democracy like themselves, Soviet citizens who
attend to the work of the Western peace movement and who
share its concerns. Let us trust that this is so. It may even be
so. Yet something, somehow, has become skewed. For one
of the most remarkable facts of the past two-and-a-half years
has been the Soviet *absence* from the European peace movement. What Soviet citizens have taken in its discourse, or
been willing to engage, upon equal terms, in its councils?
A handful of doctors: Roy and Zhores Medvedev; that is all.
   No doubt a host of other Soviet citizens might wish to do
so but are inhibited by bureaucratic constraints. These constraints are not—or are not only—those imposed by the West.
They belong to the long-standing ideological self-blockade,
by Communist states, of their own citizenry: the Communist
international default. To examine, as rational causation, the
history of this default might give us a very different historical
answer to the question of co-responsibility for the Cold War
than does a history confined to the arms race. A history of
the arms race can be offered, as the Medvedevs offer it, in
terms of NATO action and Warsaw Pact reaction: this tends
then to the complacent conclusion that if NATO should halt
its provocative actions the Warsaw Pact will instantly cease
to react, and the peace-loving intentions of the Soviet Union
will then become plain to all mankind (except, perhaps, to
some Afghan tribesmen). But a history of the ideological
confrontation of the two blocs, which has contributed as
much as military measures to the adversary posture under-

pinning the Cold War, must result in more ambiguous conclusions. It has to be said, again and again, and in terms which demand a Soviet response, that the repression of the Prague Spring (1968) was as much the action of irresponsible warmongers as was the NATO 'modernisation' decision of 12 December 1979. And if it is the responsibility of the Western peace movement to contest with every resource the latter decision, it is the responsibility of the Soviet people also to contest the ideological and security structures which poison the political discourse of Europe, enforce its division into 'two camps', and legitimate the Communist international default.

I will not attempt to sketch this alternative ideological history here, although I have gestured towards it in *Beyond the Cold War*. But the presence of this history, as consequence, is manifest in Europe today. By 'Communist international default' I mean the refusal of the Communist apparatuses of the Soviet Union and of the Warsaw bloc to permit direct international discourse between citizens or groups, unregulated by their own security and ideological controls; their insistence that all exchange, even between peace movements, takes place upon their own favoured ideological terrain; the radical insecurity which inhibits any manifestation within the Warsaw bloc which might express a critical view of any aspect of Soviet reality; and the very damaging attempts to manipulate, or to divide, Western democratic movements, including Western Communist parties, trade unions and peace movements themselves, in order to subordinate them to the diplomacies of the Soviet state.

All this has a complex and bitter history. After 1945 there was the severance of ten thousand strands of international discourse, each severance causing confusion and pain. I can recall that moment, when the frame-up of the Hungarian Communist leader Laszlo Rajk was announced, and when we opened our papers in surprise to discover that Konni Zilliacus (the Labour Party's leading internationalist MP, expelled from the PLP for his stubborn work for peace), Basil Davidson and Claud Cockburn (two of the most able, internationally

expert journalists of the British left) had all been 'unmasked'
as imperialist agents. And so it has gone on. Frame-ups and
the unmasking of imperialist agents are less in fashion now.
But the same arrogant authoritarianism, the same bureaucratic manipulation, and the same fear of any East–West
discourse taking place outside the authorised forums and the
permitted ideological terrain—all these remain in force.

The World Peace Council congeals some of that history
and protracts it into the present. I am aware that many
younger members of the European peace movement cannot
understand the distaste with which some of us grey-headed
ones regard that mendacious bureaucratic organisation and
its national subsidiaries: these quasi-official state 'Peace
Committees' appear to them as plausible places for international communication; and their efficiency as travel agents
for visiting delegations eliminates many of the difficulties
and costs of less structured exchanges. I will only say that
some of us still active in the peace movement have had
twenty-five or thirty years of experience of the WPC's
manipulations and bad faith—a Council which, in all that
time, has never found fault with a single Soviet action—and
that the subject has become merely boring. It is an organisation whose function is to structure authorised East–West
exchanges and to blockade all others. It is a satire upon any
authentic internationalist discourse. The son of the traduced
and executed Laszlo Rajk now runs a *samizdat* bookshop
in Budapest. Any honest East–West discourse must hold
a place open for him.

Let us propose this in a more positive way. The conditions
which threaten us today—which throw the shadow of extermination upon us all—are military, political and ideological.
For more than two years an influential peace movement has
been developing, in Western Europe, Japan, Australia, the
United States, from the spontaneous and democratic initiatives of the public. This has been contesting, in the first
place, the menacing military and political dispositions of the
NATO powers. What might give to this movement truly
impressive strength—what might even bring some victory
within reach—would be a junction between the Western peace

movement and some congruent movement of opinion in the Soviet Union and in Eastern Europe.

This cannot come from travel and conference-promoting agencies subordinate to the *realpolitik* of the Warsaw Pact states. The present position is absurd. The orthodox Communist media, in the East, welcome and publicise the manifestations of the Western peace movements while at the same time censoring their demands and inhibiting an equivalent discourse in their own nations. If the articles or pamphlets of Bahro or Magri or Chomsky or my own *Beyond the Cold War* appear in Eastern Europe they will appear in *samizdat* and at the publishers' risk.

The Soviet state may not have co-equal responsibility for the thirty years of arms race, but it does have—and at this moment it has—co-responsibility for the continued ideological division of Europe, the Cold War. Europeans await, with increasing anxiety, the return of Soviet citizens to an international discourse: youth must be able to travel, writers to publish, peace movements to confer and to canvas alternative strategies, without attending upon some Office of Orthodoxy. It is not good enough that the gifted citizens of one of the greatest nations of the earth should cower secretively behind security barricades, and excuse themselves from all responsibility for this predicament with apologetic histories which always place the blame upon the shoulders of others.

We accept this blame: we in the West are contesting the policies of our own states. We ask the Soviet people to accept their responsibilities also: only their initiatives can begin to dismantle their own security and ideological barricades and repair the Communist international default. And the matter is urgent: the peace movement in the West, which anxiously awaits their response, cannot guarantee the continued vitality of its presence if that response fails to come. One cannot maintain the morale of a movement so inchoate and so moody without some signs of success, and one can imagine more than one scenario (a deterioration of the situation in Poland, a NATO adventure in Libya or the Middle East, a show trial of Czech 'dissidents' or a submarine disaster off Stornoway or in the Black Sea) which would check it or throw it into reverse.

Peace depends now and in the immediate future upon the élan and the continual enlargement of the democratic internationalism of the non-aligned peace movement. It depends upon the forging of a new internationalism, unmediated by state structures, between the citizenry West and East. The opportunity is open, now, and the response from Soviet citizens must begin to show itself before the end of 1982.[6] We must find ways to signal this urgently to the Soviet public in the coming months. There is no need, of course, to signal this to Roy and Zhores Medvedev: they are themselves evidence of the internationalism of Soviet citizens, and pledges that the junction between autonomous movements for peace and for socialist democracy, East and West, can still take place.

In conclusion, let us briefly consider relations between the Cold War, Europe, and the Third World. I have been criticised by several contributors for awarding such pre-eminence in my analysis to the fracture of power and of ideology through the heart of Europe as 'the central locus of the opposed exterminist thrusts': the place of origin of the Cold War and the place where its adversary postures are continually regenerated and refreshed. I am persuaded that I must take the criticism into account. It is not so much that I find my proposal to be wrong as that I am now unclear as to the proposal's status: I do not know what evidence would be required either to support it or to refute it.

It would be better if I stood the proposal on its head: *Europe, in the 1980s, is the weak link in the Cold War.* The question now is not whether Europe is the locus which generates the Cold War but whether Europe may not be the continent on which, as Erhard Eppler has said, the 'chain of armaments' might be struck through. Europe is now the locus of opportunity; and for this reason Europeans now carry a responsibility to the rest of the world—to the Third World in particular—to realise whatever opportunity allows.

Certainly Europe is menaced by particular military dispositions, by a density of weaponry, and by strategies which threaten a limited theatre war. But that is not all that has brought the new peace movements into being, as some North American observers may have supposed. There are also particular political and ideological conditions peculiar to Europe which make the fracture of its political culture seem increasingly arbitrary and insupportable. As direct conflicts of interest between the confronting blocs recede into insignificance in the heart of the continent, so congruent economic and cultural interests assert themselves. No 'global class struggle' divides the workers of Gdansk from those in Newcastle, or the peasantries of Hungary and Greece. The old ideological compulsions of the Cold War are losing their hold upon the rising generation. As impulses for socialist democracy or for civil rights find expression in the East so these can meet with a response in the peace and labour movements of the West. Increasingly it appears, in common-sense political perception, that the adversary structures of the armed blocs are all that are holding this confluence back. All this is a theme of my *Beyond the Cold War*.

To say that the Cold War is now perpetuated by its own self-reproducing inertia—that it is about itself—is perhaps a European perception. It is small comfort to those in El Salvador, Afghanistan, or Namibia. Yet it may be, within Europe's own context and conditions, true—as a perception which is challenging rather than complacent or Eurocentric. It is here that the chain might be struck through: but it is here also that new transformations, of the most radical and affirmative import for the rest of the world, might commence.

I am unwilling to predict what form these transformations might take, if the best case came about. I would predict only that we would have to devise new categories to explain them. In a general and loose sense I would agree with Halliday: socialist democracy, in some sense, might be the vocabulary of change in both worlds. But it would have to be more sharply anti-statist and libertarian than anything in the dominant Communist or Social Democratic traditions, or in Marxist theoretical orthodoxy: nothing less will be tough enough to meet the opposition, and maybe repression, of the opposed militarised states. It is likely also that (following

Bahro) it will be informed by an alert ecological consciousness since the congruent struggles, West and East, will be
founded upon the human ecological imperative. That being
so, it will shatter or transform or transcend the ritualised and
long-inert categories of 'Communism' and of 'Social Democracy', whatever historical legacy or detritus is left in the
institutions and forms of particular nations. It is not that the
Second International will make it up and enter a marriage
with the Third. New forces and new forms will replace
them both.

That is the best case, and the worst case remains at least
as probable. This best case is argued eloquently by Lucio
Magri,[7] with whom I express my solidarity and accord. I
welcome most especially his definition of the possible
relationship between the advanced and the underdeveloped
worlds. His definition of the matter is superb and I urge
readers to return to it again and again: 'Any new relationship with the Third World presupposes a qualitative change
in our own type of development. Such a change would have
to involve a reorientation of the European economies away
from the quantitative multiplication of goods for consumption
and export, and the wastage of natural resources that goes
with it, towards another style of development: one that was
sober in its consumption, exported technology and knowledge rather than commodities, sought a reduction in labour-
time performed, gave priority to improvements in the quality
of living.'

The arms race is a theft of resources from the Third World.
The export of arms, military infrastructures, and of militarist
ideologies (some of them disguised as Marxisms) from the
advanced world to the Third World is a way of distorting
social process, of aborting revolutions or of stifling their
potential at birth. This is not only an era of permanent
revolution but an era in which every revolution is screwed up
as every nation is dragged into the polarities of the Cold
War. If Europeans could strike through the chain of
armaments—and the diplomacies and ideologies that go
with it—and find a third way then in that moment the
possibility would open up of a new non-exploitative relation-

ship with the Third World, bringing material and cultural reinforcements to the strategy of non-alignment and affording more space to Third World nations to pilot their own course of development independently of either bloc.

I end with a confession of uncertainty. I will not fight for the category of 'exterminism' provided that the problem it indicates is not tidied away. We are at the end of an epoch, when every old category begins to have a hollow sound, and when we are groping in the dusk to discover the new. Some of us must be content to offer unfinished 'Notes', or may risk (as Bahro sometimes does) provocations and prophecies. I distrust only those who (after Cambodia, after Solidarity and Polish martial law) are satisfied with the old categories and who offer to explain overmuch.

We are engaged in an international discourse of extraordinary complexity. We are trying to construct, out of the collapse of earlier traditions, a new internationalist constituency and one capable of acting urgently and with effect. We cannot write our recipes at leisure in the drawing-room and pass them on to the servants' hall (although some try to do that still). We must improvise our recipes as we sweat before the kitchen fires. Even in Europe, to assemble that internationalist constituency into a common peace movement—from so many nations, traditions, and from two adversary blocs hung around with misrecognitions—requires extraordinary skills. Intellectuals and communicators have particular responsibilities and roles in putting that internationalism together in these early stages. They are the couriers who must take the first messages across the frontiers of ideologies. And they must be self-mobilised; they must find their own routes; they cannot wait upon any High Command of party or of peace movement to tell them what to do. It is in this spirit that the editors and contributors to this volume have acted, and I salute their work.

NOTES

1. My 'Notes on Exterminism, the Last Stage of Civilisation' first appeared in *New Left Review*, no. 121, May–June 1980, and were republished in *Zero Option* (Merlin Press, 1982), and *Beyond the Cold War* (Pantheon, New York, 1982).

2. Roy and Zhores Medvedev, 'The USSR and the Arms Race' in *Exterminism and Cold War* (Verso Editions/NLB, 1982), pp. 153-174; also published in *The Nation*, January 16, 1982.

3. 'Boris Komarov', *The Destruction of Nature in the Soviet Union* (London, 1980), pp. 7, 33-4, 77, 87-9. Zhores Medvedev, in a private communication, has persuaded me that there are serious reasons to doubt the authenticity of 'Komarov's' account. But the general trend of his evidence can be confirmed from other sources.

4. *Christian Science Monitor*, 11 March 1982.

5. *Guardian*, 12 April 1982.

6. Such a response did show itself, in the Moscow Group for the Establishment of Trust between the USSR and USA (and similar groups in provincial cities) in the summer of 1982. As I argue in other essays in this book, the tormented history of these groups and their repression by Soviet security organs, and the failure of any respondant 'thaw' in the East, were contributory factors in the (temporary?) defeat of the Western peace movement in its campaign against NATO modernisation.

7. In *Exterminism and Cold War*, pp. 117-134.

▲ THE POLISH DEBATE* ▲

The argument of your letter turns upon Poland; and, while your facts are often wrong and your quotations wrested out of context, some of your questions are fair. You are wholly wrong when you say that not a single 'unofficial person' from END travelled to Warsaw while Solidarity was overground. I trust that you will not expect me to name names or occasions. As it happens, one of the first British visitors to the Hotel Morski in Gdansk, early in September 1980, carried in his pocket a message of solidarity with Solidarity, which I had moved at a packed END public meeting in Newcastle-on-Tyne a few days before. This visitor, John Taylor—a temporarily unemployed WEA tutor travelling on his own savings and not, as *Trybuna Ludu* was subsequently to fulminate, a 'wealthy businessman'—moved in to Solidarity's Gdansk headquarters to help in any way he could (he assisted Solidarity to obtain some of their first printing equipment) until he was told by the Polish authorities to leave five months later. His account will be found in *Five Months with Solidarity* (Wildwood, 1981).

What John Taylor found was that Solidarity was preoccupied, twenty-four hours a day, with its work as a union. 'Foreign affairs' or disarmament were not on its agenda, and (as you say) the matter of the Warsaw Pact was a question

---

* From the *Spectator*, 30 October 1982, responding to an 'Open Letter' to me by Timothy Garton Ash, *Spectator*, 21 August 1982.

153

too sensitive to add to that agenda. This was what other
visitors, supporters of CND or END or Western peace movements, found in that first year: for example, Dennis McShane,
Solidarity (Spokesman, 1981). (You will notice that I am
only citing published and readily available sources.)

This 'self-limiting' (your own phrase) character of
Solidarity's agenda was understood and respected by END.
We never attempted to intervene, nor (unlike some Western
cold warriors) to thrust our recipes upon them, and, despite
the tenor of your argument, we never claimed Solidarity as a
part of the 'peace movement'. Those of us who gave our
public support to the movement did so as trade unionists and
as supporters of civil rights, and without conditions. We have
never said, '*if* you support the peace movement, we will
support you'. It is true that we saw also in the Polish renewal,
with its opening to more fluent communication with Western
movements, a pre-figurement of a process that will blur the
edges of the blocs, although the term 'objectively' (which
provokes your scorn) is not mine but M. Balibar's. Despite all
that has happened in the past ten months, I refuse to accept
that this opening has been finally closed.

We did, however, with insufficient vigour, offer a public
argument. This was that the right response by Western
democracy to the Polish crisis was to relax military tension
in Central Europe (in several statements we tried to disinter
the bones of the Rapacki Plan), to stop leaning on the
Eastern bloc with plans for Cruise and Pershing II, and to
afford the Polish nation more space for autonomy. Our proposals met with little response within Poland, and we did not
pretend that they did. In Solidarity's last open months more
interest in this dialogue was shown. You state, with your
habitual over-confidence, that Solidarity 'to the end
scrupulously refrained from attacking any aspect of Poland's
defence policy'. In fact the matter was debated, briefly, at
Solidarity's last open Congress, when Bogdan Lis (who is
now the underground leader of the Gdansk district) argued
for a cut in the arms budget, disclaimed any particular
criticism of either bloc, and concluded: 'We will always be
against armaments, whether in the West or East.' (*Guardian*,

2 October 1981). An official Solidarity delegation took part in the huge Amsterdam peace demonstration, a few weeks before martial law shut the gates.

I don't think that the Western peace movements did enough to keep those gates open. But failure does not necessarily disprove an argument: it may only underline that forces are unequal. NATO also signally failed to keep them open. It is my view that Reagan, Weinberger and Thatcher, with their bluster and political capitalisation of the Polish crisis, did a great deal to thrust the gates shut. You disagree. You argue that 'the dramatic warnings addressed to the Kremlin by NATO and Western leaders' did a great deal to hold back (in December 1980) the half-million Warsaw Pact troops on Poland's frontiers. How do you know? These were not the only warnings addressed to the Kremlin: there were warnings also from the Yugoslav government, from the Italian Communist Party, from the Western peace movement. There was even a warning from E.P. Thompson (*Guardian*, letters, 11 December, 1980) that 'Soviet or Warsaw power action in Poland would have the most disastrous repercussions on the European peace movement'.

How do you or I know which warnings may have been attended to? The *Daily Telegraph*, in a remarkable editorial just over a year ago, attributed Soviet military restraint to the Soviet leaders' fear of alienating the peace movement. It is not a claim which we would ever make ourselves. But you wish to bully readers—and whatever Polish opinion you can reach—into believing that your answer must be the only right one. You say, with satisfaction, that you have met 'more supporters of Reagan in Warsaw than in West Berlin'. This may, in recent months, be true. If I must add 'alas!', and if I repeat that some Polish trade unionists and democrats have been looking to the 'wrong friends' in the West, this is part of a public and open argument which we, in the Western peace movement, are entitled to put. We do not present it as a Polish argument, but as our own. It is possible to admire the courage of Polish democrats, and to express unconditional solidarity with them in their democratic objectives, but at the same time to argue with them about

their analysis and their international alliances. Solidarity is
not a one-way road.

It is at this point that you pass over to misrepresentation.
You cite a half-sentence of mine in which I say that martial
law was 'a Polish solution', and go on indignantly to document the Soviet pressure brought upon the Jaruzelski regime.
I cannot conceive why you should suppose that I need
persuading of this. To say that Soviet pressure was mediated
through (and also partly shielded by) Jaruzelski is not an
'apologists' phrase': it is a plain statement of political fact.
I regard martial law as a condition of enthroned anarchy, and
a confession of total political bankruptcy: but if you want
to know the difference between Soviet intervention and this
present Polish interval, you need only ask a Czech. Nor is the
situation in Poland today to be regarded, even in the short
run, as a settled episode.

You also cite an article which I wrote in the *Times* five days
after martial law was proclaimed in which I said: 'General
Jaruzelski is a patriot: he has pledged himself to avoid bloodshed.' I have a problem here, in my technique as a writer. I
had always supposed that irony was an available resource of
English letters, from at least the time of Chaucer, and that
one might presume a reading public sensitive to its reception.
This assumption has betrayed me into many difficulties in
translation, and now I am finding that the privilege of irony
is refused by English readers also, who perhaps have been
bludgeoned into insensibility by the prose of *Private Eye*,
Auberon Waugh and the Militant Tendency (of Right or
Left).

If you read that article again with candour, and with
Professor I.A. Richards' four kinds of meaning in mind, you
will see that it commences with a long passage (including
your chosen citation) of bitter irony, mocking the conventional wisdom (even relief) with which some part of our
press (including the *Financial Times*) had received the news
of martial law. The conclusion which I reach, in the immediately following paragraph, is that none of this wish-
fulfilling wisdom 'can survive even one week of martial law'.

You may defend that misrepresentation by a plea of generational insensibility to tone, but your next misrepresentation is indefensible. You cite me as writing, in *Exterminism and the Cold War*, that Solidarity had features (Catholicism, nationalism, etc.) 'which might wrinkle the nose of a purist', and you then proceed to offer this as a straight statement of my own wrinkled-nosed opinions. For pity's sake, permit me to place the citation in its context:

> Solidarity's life-cycle is one of the most remarkable and authentic examples of self-activity in history, and without doubt the most massive and purposive working-class movement in any advanced society since the Second World War. To be sure, it had certain features which might wrinkle the nose of a purist: it was nationalist, Catholic, predominantly male, and in its last months over-confident. Its internationalist perspectives were confined and confused. But my point, at this moment, is that an analysis of the contemporary crisis in terms of the global class struggle which cannot find any place for this astonishing episode of class struggle has somehow lost its way. Can the struggle have been between the wrong classes and in the wrong part of the globe?

I ask again—did you consciously misrepresent me, or has your generation lost the capacity to read? Surely it is not possible to read this paragraph as a whole without realising, first, that I am taking the mickey out of one or two Marxist grand theorists, and second, that it is an expression of profound humility before the historical experience of Solidarnosc? I am, after all, a historian of working-class movements, with one or two yardsticks in my memory, and my commitment to working-class movements and to trade unionism has been somewhat more long-lasting (and perhaps less suspect) than some of Solidarity's most vocal and self-advertising Western admirers.

I will allow that you do care, in earnest, about civil and trade union rights, and that you are as anxious about Poland's and Solidarity's future as I am now. I hope you are also concerned about these rights on this side of the Cold War divide: for example, in Turkey. But what would you have us do? We have conducted an open argument, both with official and with some 'dissident' voices in the East. We have given our advice that Europe has no future, except nuclear war, unless forces making for democracy and forces making for peace can recognise each other and learn to act together. We signalled that a military take-over in Poland would be 'a devastating defeat for peace'. And we, with Solidarity, suffered that political defeat. Defeat need not be final: it proves that our strategy is difficult (which we knew) but not that it is impossible.

It is not I but you, and a host of interpreters like you, who presume to speak for voiceless thousands in the East. What you do is select from various voices those 'dissident' voices which are locked into a hostility to their own Communist regimes so implacable that they view the entire globe in an inverted image, mistake Reagan for Tom Paine, and suppose that Western nuclear arms are, in some never-explained way, instruments of liberation. These often are honourable and selfless persons, who are entitled to their place in the European discourse. But you have no right to select these voices only, and to suppress the diversity of Eastern political conversation, silencing that intermediate discourse which is looking, between the two armed blocs, for a transcontinental third way.

In doing this, you help to confirm these persons in an ideological blindsight like your own. You help to bend against each other those very forces which, if acting in mutual solidarity, might liberate Europe from her bonds. And the rulers of both sides still stand in need of these rival bonding forces, of fear and ideological rancour, both for internal political control and to keep in their stations their client states. It was a little infelicitous in you to write, in the year of the 'Falklands Factor' and of the Victory Parade, that 'Brezhnev needs the bonding effect of militarism and nationalism a great deal more than Mrs Thatcher does'. Perhaps. But if the Soviet Union had elections and Gallup polls, I doubt whether the 'Afghanistan Factor' would show up so strongly.

What puzzles me most is why writers of your ideological persuasion so ardently *wish* independent peace movements in the East to fail. It is not only that they wish to show that the perspective of a third way is difficult, or to puncture my rhetoric. It is more than that. They have got themselves into an ideological lock in which it is necessary for the lesson of the ineluctable adversary posture of the two blocs to be repeatedly confirmed. It is as if, should nations or peoples begin to move out of this Manichaean framework and search for alternatives, then the entire globe would suffer an identity crisis. As it is doing now.

In this they resemble their opposite numbers, the guardians of ideological orthodoxy in *Izvestia* or *Rude Pravo*. It amuses me that the arguments of END are viewed with equal distaste in the Ministries of Defence on both sides. But now that independent and non-aligned peace movements are showing vitality in the East—and very certainly in East Germany and Hungary—is it not time for you to put your scorn on the ground (at least for a little while) and try to *help?*

▲ WHAT KIND OF PARTNERSHIP?* ▲

I hold the view that the Cold War is about itself: that is, the crisis in Europe is at the same time its own cause.

This is not an exercise in metaphysics. Let me explain it more clearly. It is easy to suppose that great military forces are assembled on both sides of Europe, and that missiles are deployed against each other, because there is some 'crisis' which these are intended to meet. But what if the militarisation of our continent is *itself* the crisis? We need look then for no ulterior cause.

Of course there are other causes, which historians examine, for the origin and development of this crisis. But these have contributed to a general *state of crisis* which has an existence and logic of its own. The Cold War has become a habit, an addiction, within European political culture. The reason why it continues, and is daily reinforced, is that it is easier for ruling groups, East and West, to surrender to its inertia and to adjust its 'balance' than to risk the possible 'instability' which might follow upon any radical challenge to its logic.

---

* A contribution to a panel discussion on 'The Actual Crisis in Europe: its Causes and Ways to Overcome It' in Athens on February 7th, 1984. This conference, hosted by the government-supported Greek peace organisation, KEADEA, brought together for the first time representatives of the official Peace Councils of the Warsaw Pact nations and of the non-aligned Western peace movements. Mr Zhukov, chairman of the Soviet Peace Committee, was a fellow-panellist and took offence at my remarks. But in the view of many delegates it was constructive to have a face-to-face exchange of this kind, and to bring into the open these controversial issues.

Let me illustrate this in another way. One major cause of the actual crisis in Europe (which we are too polite to mention) is the overwhelming military presence on both sides of our continent of forces which have long over-stayed the historical occasion for their arrival. This points to a simple remedy. Let us invite the Soviet Union and the United States, by mutual agreement, to dismantle their bases and withdraw their forces within their own borders once more. We might recommend this to the Stockholm Conference as a helpful 'confidence-building measure'.

Such a measure would bring World War II at last to an end. And, as a combatant in that war, I am now weary of it. If one had told any combatant in 1944 that, forty years later, American and Soviet forces would still be deployed on foreign territory, one would have met with utter disbelief.

This remedy may not be taken for a year or two, although Greece promises to teach Europe by example. But it is a proper and normal objective to set before us, and one which is in the best interests of the superpowers themselves. It might be called the 'Austrian solution' to Europe's crisis, which has served Austria well for a quarter of a century.

To present Europe's crisis in this way is to emphasise that it is two-sided. The repair of the torn tissues of our continent cannot take place on one side alone.

This does not mean that always and in each episode both sides are equally 'to blame'. That would be absurd. It is to point out that the rulers of both blocs stand in a reciprocal crisis-relationship to each other; that they both worship the same Goddess of 'balance'; that each Cold War impulse calls forth a response in the same kind from the other; and, above all, that the crisis is not only a crisis of weaponry but is also a crisis of adversary ideologies, and of trust, which, no less than nuclear missiles, threaten our common existence.

I see no point in allocating blame. That can be left to future historians if we are so fortunate as to have a future. If you wish for my view, it is that the United States and the NATO powers must be awarded the greatest blame for the escalation and technological refinement of nuclear weaponry. In the episode of NATO weapons 'modernisation' they are greatly to blame; and the present United States administration is adventurous, threatening, and bidding for military superiority. But in terms of ideological confrontation, and in the repression of transcontinental dialogue and citizens' communication, the Warsaw powers must be awarded the greater blame.

I need say little of the first question, since the unequivocal and continuing contestation by the Western peace movement of NATO missile deployment is common knowledge. But I wish to address the second, and more sensitive, question—and I hope that this conference will not avoid sensitive questions —in the attempt to disclose certain problems to the representatives of the Warsaw bloc who are welcome participants here.

There are very real difficulties in the relations between Western peace movements and Eastern Peace Councils which must be laid open. These are not both 'peace movements' of the same kind. The Western movements are loosely-structured alliances of voluntary popular associations, directly contesting the policies of their own governments and confronting the hostility of much of their own media. The Eastern Councils are quasi-official institutions, endorsed by their own governments and applauded in the official media.

Put in another way, the Western peace movements are popular movements primarily engaged in opposing Western militarism. The Eastern Councils are government-endorsed institutions—which are also primarily (sometimes exclusively) engaged in opposing Western militarism. That does not offer a relationship between equals. We, in the West, cannot regard it as a 'fair swap'.

Of course we recognise that Eastern Councils perform useful functions of communication and diplomacy (just as certain quasi-official institutions do in the West). We do not doubt that their members and supporters abhor the idea of nuclear war. We welcome occasions to meet with them. But we cannot acknowledge them as equal partners* in a trans-

---

* My phrase, 'equal partners', gave great offence to the official Peace Council representatives from the East. My argument about unequal political relations was mistaken for an attempt to put them down as

continental peace movement.

To accept them as equal partners could only be upon the premise that the threat of war arises wholly and entirely from the aggressive designs of Western imperialism; that no responsibility of any kind for Europe's crisis lies with the Soviet Union or the Warsaw bloc; that no public voices are needed in the East to advise or restrain their own governments or military; and that the Western peace movements are or ought to be auxiliaries to Soviet peace-loving diplomacy.

If we were to accept such premises, then our business in meeting together need only be to chant in unison anathemas against President Reagan and NATO's aggressive designs. But let it be quite clear that one consequence would follow. This would reduce the Western peace movement to an insignificant pro-Soviet rump, and would alienate that majority opinion which stands on the different premises of non-alignment.

This unequal relationship has already contributed to our present crisis and to the closure of the blocs against each other. For throughout the past four years the credibility of the Western peace movement, in the eyes of the Western public, has depended upon our assertion that, if we in the West refused Pershing and cruise, this would initiate a reciprocal process of disarmament.

We needed two things to vindicate this assertion and to swing the balance of opinion to our side. The first would have been an affirmative response by the Soviet Union to our request that it should, in advance of NATO deployment, dismantle a number of its superfluous SS-20s (for these SS-20s were the only good arguments which NATO had). The response to our request was silence. Warsaw Pact leaders are at one with the leaders of NATO in their abhorrence of any 'unilateral' measures. Yet I remain convinced that we could, together, have brought to a halt this whole insane auction of missiles, for a down-payment in advance of some 80 dismantled SS-20s.

---

national or even human inferiors. This was not, of course, my meaning. And I accept the suggestion of some fellow-delegates from the West that 'symmetrical' might be preferable to 'equal'.

No credible transcontinental peace movement can be founded on the premise that identical weapons are barbaric and aggressive, if in one bloc, but innocent and purely-defensive if in the other. That is to smuggle partisan ideology into our midst. It is time to turn our backs on this rubbish.

The second way in which our credibility would have been vindicated would have been if we could have pointed to a visible partner on the other side, entering into open dialogue with us, and willing to voice—not 'equal blame'—but public criticisms of the military measures of the Warsaw powers. Not only have we been unable to point to such a fellow partner, but, worse than this, we have noted with dismay the harrassment of independent voices and peace movements (not only, in outrageous ways, in NATO's favoured ally, Turkey) but also in the East. The symbolic significance of these episodes has still not been understood. Thousands in the Western peace movements stand appalled at the sight of a great and powerful nation which cannot tolerate the inde-pendent voices of a handful of people—let us cite the case of Dr Olga Medvedkova—who, whether right or wrong, are recognised by us as courageous partisans of peace and of dialogue.

It is because the Cold War crisis is composed equally of military and of ideological hostilities that these matters acquire such significance. Let me add this. It is untrue that any responsible persons in the Western peace movement wish to 'interfere' in the internal affairs of the Warsaw powers or wish to promote 'destabilisation' of these societies. We wish, not to 'revise' the frontiers of 'Yalta', but to throw these frontiers more open. We wish to enlarge in every way communication and informal exchanges between citizens—exchanges which the medical profession has to its honour pioneered.

We are calling for a 'thaw' in human relations between the blocs. We are calling for it now. The Western peace move-ment represents exactly such a thaw in the frozen ideological postures of the Cold War. We are waiting for a thaw in response.

Such a thaw need not wait upon the outcome of delibera-

tions at Geneva or at Stockholm. It does not require the
signature of statesmen upon treaties. It is in the power of the
citizens of Europe to commence a healing-process for themselves. May it not now be the turn of the East to commence
some ideological disarmament? We invite our friends from
the Warsaw bloc to consider with us how we may remove
certain restraints upon the traffic of persons and of ideas, so
as to advance 'detente from below', which will in turn lay
the foundations of trust upon which statesmen in future
will build.

I will give one example. I find that it was exactly four
years ago, to this very week, that I first wrote the preliminary
draft of an Appeal to rid the entire continent of Europe of
nuclear weapons and bases. This Appeal, when it had been
improved by many hands, became the European Nuclear
Disarmament Appeal (or 'Russell Appeal') which was signed
by tens of thousands across Europe, contributed to the rebirth of the European peace movement, and remains an
influential document in its discussions.

Yet—and it is difficult to credit this—so far as I am aware,
after the passage of four years, this little four-page document
has never been published in any freely-available form in the
press of any Warsaw power except in *samizdat!* I must
suppose that this is because certain ideological advisors found
that there were 'formulations' in the document which were
considered to be 'incorrect'. Tens of thousands of column
inches and of photographs in the Eastern press have been
devoted to the actions of the Western peace movement
against NATO missiles: the demonstrations, the Greenham
Common women's peace camp. But the proposals and the
strategies of influential sections of this movement are passed
over in silence.

Friends, how is it possible for there to be honest dialogue
between peace activists, East and West, if every word must
first pass through the fine-meshed sieve of an ideological
censor? How is it possible to talk of partnership unless, as a
matter of course, we undertake to publish in our nations
each others' strategies for peace? This is not a marginal
matter. I hope that this question of the exchange of un-

censored publications will be considered in our discussions.

Let me turn from difficulties to a great point of common agreement. Our discussions on this panel are subordinate to the great question before this conference: the furtherance of a Balkan nuclear-weapons-free zone. At a time when the two halves of Europe are closing their doors against each other, it is a privilege to be here, at the invitation of KEADEA, and to find one part of Europe where the door to peace is being held open.

Since this is a nation where one of the first and most bitter episodes of the Cold War was played out—an episode in which my own nation played a discreditable part—it is right that this nation should also be one of the first to heal old wounds. And, as my Bulgarian fellow-panellist will know, I have a personal reason for regarding this strategy of healing with pleasure. For it throws my mind back, once more, to the year 1944, when there was a spirit abroad in Europe which, for a brief moment, transcended ideological divisions and looked forward to a continent united in a democratic peace.

Nowhere was this spirit more heroically evinced than in the mountains of the Balkan peninsula. It is therefore right that it should be here that the vision should be reborn and that Europe's healing-process should begin. We, in the peace movement of West Europe, salute your initiative. In bringing together into one zone-of-peace nations from the Warsaw Pact, from NATO, and non-aligned Yugoslavia, you are offering to all Europe a paradigm of the possible future. Let this bring about a zone, not only rid of the nuisance of nuclear weapons, but also a zone in which the more fluent communication of persons and of ideas takes place—a zone of human repair.

▲ THE TWO SIDES OF YALTA* ▲

Dear Dr Săbata

You were kind enough to address an open letter to me as long ago as last April. If I have delayed a reply for so long it has been for two reasons.

The first is that your important and encouraging letter allowed for no response except the single word, *Yes*. But you would scarcely have thanked me if that had been all that I had sent back to you at Brno.

You argue (as many of us in the West have also argued) that 'what we really need is a joint strategy for transforming Europe into a single entity', But this can only come about from 'a democratic transformation', which will entail a process more radical than that which is usually implied by 'detente' or 'convergence'.

The change which you wish us to work for together would involve 'a convergence of a quite different type':

---

* *New Statesman*, April 4, 1984. The text of Dr Jaroslav Săbata's 'Open Letter' to me is in *Voices from Prague* (Palach Press END, 1983). Dr Săbata, a philosopher and psychologist, was a member of the Czech Communist Party Presidium during the Prague Spring of 1968. Expelled from the CP in 1971, he served five years imprisonment for 'subversion of the Republic' (his offence was to distribute leaflets in the 1971 elections advising citizens of their right not to vote). Released in 1976 he was one of the first signatories of the civil rights organisation, Charter 77, and one of its official spokespersons in 1978. Arrested at the end of 1978 for communicating with Polish KOR activists, he served a further twenty-seven months of imprisonment. He now lives in retirement at Brno.

a coming together in a convergent strategy of social and political movements, traditional and less traditional, from both halves of our divided continent. Its long-term political strategy 'is the demand to *abolish* the undemocratic legacy of the post-war social and political settlement, *end* the division of Europe into two opposing systems and *unify* this artificially divided continent'—in short, 'a democratic peace'.

As I have said, I can only reply 'yes' to this. Yet there was a second reason why I have delayed my reply. Ever since I received your letter a slow and predictable nightmare has been unrolling before our eyes. I read your letter first last June, just as an election returned to power in my country a government truculently committed to deploying cruise missiles here—and to libelling the British peace movement as a witting or unwitting agency of Soviet interests.

From June until December the nightmare unrolled. Everything that we had warned against for more than three years came to pass according to our worst predictions. The superpowers and their client states performed to perfection their ascribed Cold War roles. The demonstrations of millions in West Europe and North America were powerless to affect the outcome. And, as we had also predicted, the Soviet military responded to this in the same vocabulary of confrontation and 'balance', and instantly set in motion the deployment of new missiles not only on Soviet territory but also—as if mimicking NATO—on the territory of certain of its client states in the Warsaw bloc.

Since the time that I received your letter the situation has degenerated. The blocs have closed against each other. And this has closed also the narrow political aperture through which your perspective of 'a democratic peace' could be glimpsed.

The beneficiaries of this closure are the security services and the obsessional ideologists of both sides. It is a reciprocal process with which we have long become familiar. Of course the strengthening of the security state does not take place on each side in exactly the same way. In the 'Free West' the erosion of our liberties does not occur with one single all-embracing decree from an all-wise Party Presidium, but in little lapping waves like a rising tide: trials and threats under the Official Secrets Acts, the deprivation of trade union rights of employees in sensitive areas, increasing pressures upon our civil servants and our media of communication.

You will perhaps find such examples to be trivial. It would not be discreet to invite you to exchange examples of similar precautions taken in your own country. Yet I draw attention to these matters to illustrate another aspect of 'convergence'. If, as you have written, the post-war history of our continent is the history of its militarisation, then the rival antagonists, like wrestlers locked in each others' nuclear arms, have been growing more alike.

Even the vocabulary of the antagonists has a weary similitude. For four years our NATO apologists have assured us that cruise and Pershing missiles are enforced and necessary measures of 'defence' against the expansionist aspirations of the Soviet Union. And now I notice that your own *Prace* (December 14th, 1983) has called on its readers to support 'the enforced and necessary measures of the CPCZ Central Committee Presidium and CSSR Government against the hegemonist aspirations and intimidation which the Reagan government and its armour-bearers in the offensive military NATO pact have called into being'.

The responsibility for this latest upthrust in the arms race lies heavily (although not exclusively) with the NATO powers. And NATO's apologists have, as always, sought to justify their measures in the language of 'human rights'. And, as usually happens, the consequence of the closure of the blocs against each other is that further restrictions are imposed upon the civil rights of citizens on both sides. We have learned with dismay of measures taken against independent peace activists on your side of the world. And we regard our own Cold Warriors as accomplices in this interactive process.

My response to you must therefore be somewhat tinged with pessimism. You write that we now have the task of formulating 'a common, universal, and all-embracing strategy for the democratic transformation of Europe'. I agree. But, with the new missiles now in place (and many many more coming on after these) where does our strategy start?

Perhaps we might now suspend the argument about the missiles and seek to go *behind* the missiles and find out what is moving them there? What is the Cold War now about? From what structures and from what ideologies do these growing armouries arise?

The Western peace movement has for several years been so preoccupied with nuclear weaponry itself, and with its annihilating potential, that it has been mesmerised by this. We set outselves the task of halting certain new NATO systems; and although we have succeeded in arousing a peace consciousness of massive dimensions, we have failed in that task.

I do not think that it was wrong for us to be so preoccupied. The weaponry itself, and the military options disclosed by the weapons, remain insanely dangerous. This understanding is a base-line for our thinking. But the preoccupation with cruise and Pershing missiles allowed us to neglect ulterior political questions.

For even missiles have to be considered also in the light of political symbols. They are, of course, symbols of 'face' and of 'posture' in the superpower confrontation. But they have increasingly become symbols of internal political confrontations also, within both blocs and within nations.

At a certain stage it became necessary for cruise and Pershing to be imposed upon a reluctant West European public, not because of any evident 'Soviet threat', but in order to symbolise the 'unity of NATO' and the hegemony of United States military power over its European allies. And it became essential for ruling groups in these countries (above all in Britain and West Germany) to impose these missiles in order to inflict a public defeat upon their own domestic opposition: that is, the peace movement. In this symbolic sense these missiles have been aimed, not at you, but at us.

The Soviet counter-deployments now going ahead employ the same vocabulary of symbolism. Their missiles also are symbols of 'posture' towards NATO. And they are also symbols of the 'unity of the Warsaw powers', and loyal demonstrations and petitions in their support are intended to drown any questioning voices. So that in this symbolic sense the SS-21s, 22s or 23s are aimed in the first place not against NATO but against any strivings towards greater national autonomy by any East European nation. In this sense the missiles of both sides are like props which lean against each other, enforcing the increasingly-irrational division of our continent, lest (if the props were removed) we might fall into each others' arms.

The Cold War today is a habit passed down from the past; and it is a habit to which the governing elites, on both sides, have become addicted, since they sense that its continuance is necessary to justify and sustain their own purchase upon power. Lip-service is paid, and on both sides, to the desirable objective of the dismantling by mutual consent of both NATO and the Warsaw Pact. But if any actual step in this direction is detected, on either side, it is instantly denounced as 'destabilising', and as a blasphemy against that Great Sacred Cow which both East and West must bow down before and worship: the 'Balance'. It is before the Sacred Balance that we sacrifice our little liberties and burn, for the delight of her nostrils, an ever-growing tribute of our taxes.

This Sacred Cow was the first-born calf of another great Cow who was sometimes worshipped by the name of 'Yalta'. The name was never accurate, but we know very well what 'Yalta' is taken to mean today: it describes the post-war settlement which passed down the division of Europe as we find it at this day—a division not only geographic but also political and ideological. In short, 'Yalta' is reverenced or execrated as the Mama of 'Balance'.

The assent of the Soviet Union to the Helsinki agreement was purchased by the assent of the NATO powers to the finality of the settlement of the 'Yalta' frontiers. This concession was earnestly desired by ruling groups in the Warsaw bloc, who had been tormented for years by the rhetoric of John Foster Dulles and others, as to the 'roll-back' of Soviet power. And it was equally desired by certain of these rulers because they were aware that their own tenure upon power was uncertain.

From this a stereotype has grown up—that 'Yalta' is a settlement greatly desired by the rulers of the Warsaw bloc but only grudgingly acceded to by the rulers of NATO, for reasons of opportunism or in the interests of detente. And ideologists on your side of the world have done a great deal to give this stereotype credibility. The mere mention of the word is taken as a 'provocation'. And they insist, as a precondition of any discussion, that the inviolability of a particular historical adjustment of spheres of influence must also be extended to a pledge of the inviolability in perpetuity of the particular political systems now in being—but only in their half of Europe.

Anything less than this is, as you say, suspected as a 'call to arms'. In Western Europe far-reaching political changes are to be expected, and we have witnessed such changes, accomplished with maturity and with the minimum of bloodshed, in Portugal, Spain and Greece. But any change of a political order in your half of Europe—for example a change which offered to enlarge the potential of a democratic socialist society, as the Prague Spring promised to do—is ruled out of order as an outrage against Her Sacred Presence, the Balance.

However, I think that this stereotype is misleading. The true historical meaning of 'Yalta' is far more double-sided than it suggests. And if one digs a little beneath the rhetoric of the ideologists of NATO one discovers that they are no less fiercely committed to both 'Yalta' and the 'Balance' than are their Warsaw Pact analogues.

For the 'Yalta' settlement, in its fullest historical meaning, did not only license the Soviet military presence in East and Central Europe. It also licensed a very powerful hegemonic United States presence in Western Europe—a presence which has always dominated the councils of NATO and which has grown with each decade more dominant along with the growth in nuclear weapons systems.

The Soviet and American presences in Europe have of course been of a different order. If we leave aside the case of Greece (1945-50) the United States presence has not imposed regimes of its choice by military force. But while operating in a different mode and under different constraints, it has been an immensely powerful and distorting presence nonetheless.

It has by no means been a presence conducive to the advancement of human rights. It coexisted happily with totalitarian regimes in Portugal and Spain and with military regimes in Greece and Turkey. It is true that there were no American tanks in Madrid or Athens to prevent their peoples from liberating themselves from tyranny. We acknowledge this with relief, while at the same time noting that the same restraint has by no means been evident upon United States support for tyrannies in Latin America and Asia.

The United States military presence on our continent remains immensely strong, nearly forty years after the end of World War II. What is it doing here? How long does it have licence to remain? There are United States military, air and naval bases in Spain, Italy, Greece, Turkey, Norway, Holland, Belgium, Iceland and scores of bases and installations in West Germany and Britain. American warships (some armed with nuclear weapons) patrol the North Atlantic and Mediterranean waters. As I write, an American fleet is sailing up and down the coast of the Lebanon, and has been firing heavy salvos into the interior of that unhappy country. Cruise and Pershing missiles on our territory are owned and operated by United States personnel.

This is the other side of the 'Yalta' settlement. And it is jealously defended by the ideologues of NATO. One strategy which West European peace movements have been seeking to advance is that of staged disengagement on our continent, by means of nuclear-weapons-free zones: in the Baltic, the Balkans, or a zone or corridor in Central Europe.

Of course it can be said that such zones might only be 'symbolic'. But we prefer the symbolism of disengagement to the barbaric symbolism of missiles. And the symbolism might then be extended, to the progressive mutual withdrawal of conventional forces also—and thence to the more fluent movement of persons and ideas: the repair of the torn tissues of Europe.

What is remarkable is the hostility which has been evinced, from start to finish, to all such proposals by the leaders of the NATO powers. I suggest that this is because they are seen as a threat to the other side of 'Yalta': that is, to the iron premise that every part of Europe that is not to the East of the Yalta division must be drawn by all possible means within the military and diplomatic structures of United States hegemony.

This premise is also inviolable. Thus when the Swedish proposals for a nuclear-free corridor in Central Europe were introduced to the Stockholm Conference, Mr Alois Mertes, the West German Minister of State for Foreign Affairs, commented that such a corridor 'is not compatible with the indivisibility of the territory of the European–American alliance'. And a fellow West German official chided Sweden for failing to 'honour the vital security interests of the member states of the Atlantic alliance' (*New York Times*, 21 January 1984).

The proposals for nuclear-free zones (which should entail reciprocal concessions from each bloc) can take their place in a European healing-process, and I commend them to you as a part of our common strategy. Yet, as you well know, something must be added to them, and this could be added now, in advance of any agreement between states. The healing of Europe does not have to wait for signatures inscribed in the Kremlin and the White House. As you have written, 'detente will not lead to the dissolution of the military-political blocs unless a political discourse is established, one that will "grow" into a new political bloc'. In short, the traffic of ideas and of persons can precede any treaty whatsoever, and the establishment of trust may be the necessary precondition for any treaty.

This is not to call for the 'revision' of the 'frontiers of Yalta'. It is a call to throw these frontiers open, and (wherever this is possible) to commence to act as if these arbitrary frontiers did not exist. What is preventing this? It is, first, that the rulers on both sides are the last people who are able to advance this healing-process, since their very function is ascribed to them by the rituals of the Cold War. And it is, second, the fear of unregulated social or intellectual change, and of possible 'destabilisation', which inhibits these rulers' breasts.

If NATO carries the major blame for the upwards armament auction, then we must award the prize to the rulers of the Warsaw Pact for their activity in the repression of transcontinental dialogue. I think that they do desire to achieve some nuclear disarmament, but at the same time they wish every instrument of ideological armament to remain in place. They might endorse a nuclear-free corridor in Central Europe, but they would hope that the corridor would be wide enough to prevent the two-way flow of ideas from running across it. They do not wish the causes of peace and of liberty to recognise each other and to search for a common convergence.

Yet even now, as this recognition is beginning to take place, our 'common strategy' remains indistinct. For 'Yalta' has two sides, and one side will not be unravelled unless we also unravel the other. If that Sacred Cow, the Balance, is preposterous in its military form, yet I fear that we must pay some deference to her in our political strategy. For whenever initiatives arise on either side, the rulers of the opposing bloc will try to turn these to their own advantage. So that, if we are to find a reciprocal common strategy, we must learn not only how to support the initiatives of each other but also how to refuse advantage to either bloc, even if this entails exercises of patience and self-restraint.

It was the failure to find this common strategy which contributed to the defeat (however temporary) of the two most powerful popular impulses on our continent in the past three years: those of Polish Solidarnosc and of the Western peace movement's resistance to NATO modernisation. These are both complex questions. I will only say that those NATO ideologues who celebrated the feats of Solidarnosc at the same time did their best to destroy it by seeking to harvest their own advantage and by hastening forward cruise and Pershing missiles. Even the French public, which generously contributed food and medicine to the Polish people, might have helped them more if they had—as a symbolic gesture towards the relief of East–West tension—dismantled some part of their own *force de frappe*. But there was no Western statesman, at any time, who suggested that Polish liberties were worthy of the price of one dismantled Western nuclear weapon.

This is a stern logic. But I think it a realistic one. Was it probable that the Soviet Union would permit its influence in Poland quietly to lapse at the same time as the American offensive military posture in West Germany was steadily *rising*? What we ought to have done, East and West, was to seize that moment to turn our political worlds upside-down in the effort to bring back onto the stage some new variant of Adam Rapacki's old plan, in which a demilitarised zone would take in, not only Poland, Czechoslovakia and the GDR, but West Germany as well. And only on some such precondition do I think it likely that your other desideratum —a peace treaty resolving the status of both Germanys—could come about. Is it not evident that the price of greater Polish autonomy must be some military concession from the West? Yet in 1981 scarcely a head in Poland, and few enough heads in the Western peace movement, were turned that way.

In 1983 the Western peace movements bruised their heels against the same inexorable logic. Throughout the year public opinion swayed in the balance. And what tipped the margin against us was not only the effective propaganda of our own governments but the superfluity of SS-20s. I am not disowning those sections of the Western peace movement which called for a 'unilateral' halt in Western deployment; on the contrary, I am convinced that only such unilateral initiatives will ever get a reciprocal process of disarmament going. Yet there must be a credible expectation that such a reciprocal process will ensue, and that measures of disarmament on one side will not simply be swallowed gratefully to enlarge the advantage of the other.

I remain convinced that if at any time before the autumn of 1983 the Soviet Union had responded to requests from the Western peace movement to commence to dismantle a number of its superfluous SS-20s, then the balance of opinion in the West would have halted NATO's deployments.

But, as we know, the Soviet rulers, looking across the heads of Europeans to their superpower antagonist, and pre-occupied with 'face' and 'posture', would have 'nothing to do with unilateralism'. In this article of faith the worshippers of the Divine Balance have always been at one.

An influential part of Western opinion found our advocacy of disarmament to be 'one-sided' because they could not observe comparable movements in the East, capable of restraining Eastern militarism from turning the event to its own advantage. And this mistrust was fed by the evidence of the harassment of those independent movements and voices on your side which offered an open dialogue with us: harassment which has acquired a great symbolic significance. I believe that such forces exist, although the structures of power deny them visibility, and that they will grow in strength in the immediate future. And at the moment that a truly transcontinental peace movement becomes visible, then our objective of a 'democratic peace' will move from utopia into the world of practical possibility.

Both of these examples illustrate that a common strategy which seeks to heal the tissues of Europe cannot succeed unless it presses against the structures and ideologies of both blocs. It is necessary that I should make this explicit. For Mr George Shultz, the American Secretary of State, in his opening speech at the Stockholm Conference, has made his own intervention in our discussion. 'Let me be very clear,' he said. 'The United States does not recognize the legitimacy of the artificially-imposed division of Europe. This division is the essence of Europe's security and human rights problem and we all know it.' And he went on, in language which seemed to echo our own, to talk of 'an artificial barrier' which has 'cruelly divided this great continent—and indeed heartlessly divided one of its great nations.'

This was a mischievous speech. Coming only one month after the deployment of cruise and Pershing missiles, which have divided Europe even more cruelly and Germany more heartlessly, it was a speech of consummate hypocrisy, whose aim was to perpetuate the division of Europe. For, of course, the United States has little intention of doing anything more than meddling, or 'stirring the pot', in Eastern Europe. And even this is subordinate to the more important aim, foremost in the minds of President Reagan and Mr Shultz, which is stirring the pot of the United States elections.

The immediate effect of Mr Shultz's speech has been to make more difficult the pursuit of our common strategy. The speech might have been calculated to meddle in the affairs of advocates of 'human rights' in the East, by pointing them out to the attention of the security services as possible friends of Western forces which may still cherish an appetite to 'roll back Yalta'. At the same time the speech was received by many in the Western peace movement with dismay. They have been searching for a strategy to break down the blocs. Now they fear that this could play into the hands of NATO's propagandists.

Mr Shultz is trying to prise apart the forces making for 'a democratic peace'. These forces have no part to play in the prescribed rituals of the Cold War. But this reminds me that while the United States is a great and—for some aspects of its history—an honoured neighbour of Europe, it is not a European nation. And the people of Europe might find their way better towards a healing-process without Mr Shultz's intervention. For the United States' presence in West Europe is one half of the European problem.

It is now time that World War II was brought to an end. Thirty-nine years of abnormal conditions and of the presence of foreign troops upon our territories is long enough. Let the goal of our common strategy be the withdrawal of all United States and Soviet forces and bases back within their own national frontiers.

This is the only realistic way in which 'Yalta' can be superceded: not by its one-sided 'revision' (which will not happen) but by removing military pressures on both sides at the same time as the dividing frontiers are thrown more open. This will not come about at once, all in a lump. There will be phases, as new spaces, corridors or zones open up between the blocs; as individual nations, East or West, loosen their bloc-bondage and attain more autonomy; as the direct political discourse for which you call begins to establish confidence. There will be, at some point along the way, a place for Summit meetings and for conferences of European nations with a more serious agenda than the present Stockholm farce.

It will be an excessively difficult process. It is quite possible that Europe will blow up before we can succeed. At every stage one or the other bloc will try to turn events to its own advantage. If the United States should commence to withdraw its forces (as Mr Kissinger is now recommending) this might trigger off a compensating resurgence in West European militarism. If any East European nation sought to move into too close an association with the West, it might bring down upon itself a re-enactment of the events of 1968 which you will only too well remember. To achieve our common objective will require an unprecedented maturity in those popular movements, West and East, which seek to pace and to monitor the transition, and to limit the episodes of 'destabilisation'.

Yet this is not just one possible way forward. It is, I am convinced, the *only* way. The alternative is the convergence on collision-course of two vast over-armoured security states towards the probable terminus of nuclear war. We do not have an alternative. Either our civilisation will perish, or we must make the entire political world over anew. And our rulers will never do that for us.

If we can work together, if we can support each other, we have an outside chance of success. I do not know what we would then discover, on the other side of 'Yalta'. I do not think it would be some new Eurobloc. Distinct differences in socio-economic and political systems will remain. I would look forward to European diversity (and Russia is a part of Europe) not to bureaucratic 'unity': and to the deconstruction, on both sides, of certain forms of state power.

I agree with you on two essential matters. First, this new Europe of our imaginations could not possibly exist without a radical transformation in its relations with the Third World, which would in turn (as you have argued) assist in the transformation of that world itself. And, second, such a resolution would be profoundly in the interests of the people of the United States and the Soviet Union as well. It would relieve both nations from vast expenditures and occasions for confrontation. It would strengthen those forces contesting the militarisation of their own societies. And, rather than expelling their citizens from our continent, it would welcome them back as respected neighbours to our common discourse.

Jaroslav Săbata, I thank you again for writing. I fear that the events of the past two years have left me pessimistic. It is possible that Europe is already within the valley of the shadow of death. But this very crisis of the twin militarisms is arousing on every side forces of resistance, which might lead on towards the 'convergence of a quite different type' for which you call. And if the Western peace movement is dismayed, I can assure you that it is very far from being defeated. Such voices as your own give us new heart to continue in our common pursuit for a democratic peace.

Yours sincerely,
Edward Thompson

March 1984

▲ THE LIBERATION OF PERUGIA ▲

This appears to be the season for reminiscences of World War II, when every veteran is licensed to 'strip his sleeve and show his scars'. And since I have just returned from the Third Convention for European Nuclear Disarmament, which met in the beautiful city of Perugia, this is evidently the right moment for me to disclose my own part in the liberation of that city.

It is true that the Italian campaign, which preceded D-Day by more than a year, has fallen into some memory hole. But it is at least remembered in our media more often than those vast engagements on the Soviet front which had, for three years before D-Day, cost the lives of millions of soldiers and civilians. I may therefore assume that, while the Italian campaign is boring, it is not for some political reason unmentionable.

In one of his less happy flourishes Sir Winston Churchill described Italy as 'the soft underbelly of the Axis beast'. Soft it was not. Italy has a singularly rugged spine and the successive mountains and rivers provided barriers behind which the German armies could execute an orderly withdrawal while their well-disciplined rearguard inflicted, day after day, sharp casualties on the advancing Allied armies. It was a preposterous error to plant large motorised armies in the toe of Italy and then to fight, mile by mile, up the boot. It may be because the whole campaign was so misconceived that it is rarely mentioned.

In between very heavy set battles (Salerno, Anzio, the battles of Cassino, etc.) there was a ritual of cautious forward advance, of temporary check, and then of forward probing once again. Our tanks would go northwards up the roads until the leading tank hit a mine or was stopped by a blown-up bridge or came under fire. Then infantry and engineers were hurried forward to push back the German rearguard so that, in a day or two, the tanks could move on. The predictable casualties on each day's advance of this kind, along each road, would be the leading tank and some infantry and engineers. As well as whoever happened to get in the way of the incessant shelling which fell behind the lines—perhaps an ambulanceman or signalman, a padre, an old peasant and his donkey, a brigadier.

For reasons which will soon be clear I had to write a formal account of one episode in the liberation of Perugia, and this is how it starts:

> At approximately 18.30 hours on 19 June 1944 my troop was lead-ing the advance into the village of Fontioeggi. When the leading tank, commanded by Sjt. S. started to enter the village, it was penetrated by armour-piercing shot from a gun sited up the road, and also engaged by enemy infantry weapons from houses on the left. After attempting to reverse, Sjt. S. ordered his crew to evacuate the tank, but was unable to get any member other than the gunner, Trooper W., out of the tank...

One remembers very much less, after forty years, than the writers of reminiscences pretend. What I can recall is this. My squadron of tanks had been sitting on top of a low hill several miles south-west of Perugia all day. A squadron is normally 15 tanks, but we were already depleted by losses and mechanical breakdowns.

We were a very visible target and we were being shelled (mainly by howitzers and mortars) the whole day. Ordinary shellfire didn't do much harm to a tank unless the shells scored a direct hit. But it was advisable for tank commanders to keep their heads inside the turrets. Every five minutes or so we moved around a few score yards on our little plateau, perhaps to unsettle the enemy gunners, perhaps to settle our own nerves.

It was a really hot day. The sun baked the armour of our tanks and, as we brewed up tea with a primus on the floor of the turret, we all got dozy. I distinctly recall that sense of drowsy diminished reality which comes with heat, exhaustion, and nervous tension protracted for so long that the nerves become unresponsive. I remember popping my head out of the turret from time to time to look at the towers of Perugia or at the state of the other tanks, even though (with a sniper in a nearby leafy tree) each time I did so invited entry into eternity. On one occasion a shell splinter made a dent in my tin helmet. But we were all so dozy that we seemed to have drifted to the edge of an unreal eternity already.

At approximately 18.30 hours, minus a few minutes, two of the remaining nine tanks were so hot that they refused to start and another two had had their tracks blown off by shellfire. So that when the order came to advance into Perugia there were only five working tanks left in the squadron, two of which were of my own troop.

The Squadron Leader ordered my troop to lead the advance. There followed a hesitant incident inside my own head. The standard rule-book procedure was this: in any advance, out of the three tanks in each troop, either the serjeant's or the corporal's tank would take the lead, and the lieutenant's tank (that is, my own) would take second place, from which middle position command was presumably best exercised.

But my corporal's tank was disabled, my troop was down to two, and the rule-book was vague about such eventualities. I therefore came up on the wireless and asked my Squadron Leader: 'Shall I lead?' There was no reply: either the Squadron Leader did not wish to reply or he had switched his set onto another frequency. I can recall a momentary chill of indecision. Then I leaned from the turret and signalled my serjeant to lead the advance.

I don't know whether I did this out of deference to the rule-book or because I was afraid. We all knew that the first tank down the road would probably be knocked out. It was because of this that I felt that I 'ought' to go first, although according to military rules the 'ought' probably went the other way. I had been placed at a point in the sequence of military decision at which I was momentarily endowed with the powers of life and death: to enhance the chances of life for some (including myself) and to diminish them for others.

We trundled down a long road into a suburb of Perugia at about ten or fifteen miles an hour. At the point where we started there were vineyards and gardens on each side of the road, but we were entering a built-up street with a bend at the bottom. As we approached the bend my serjeant's tank, some eighty yards ahead, jolted, rocked and stopped, a wisp of grey smoke hanging in the air. There was a roar of engines as it sought to reverse, and then it jolted and rocked once more. I saw the tank commander, Serjeant S., duck down into the turret. Then he leaped out, followed by the gunner, Trooper W. The two ran back to me, and the serjeant called out: 'I can't get the others out. I think they've had it.' 'Are you sure?' 'Quite sure. I called out to them. We got hit twice.'

I told my gunner to take command of my tank and I ran forward to the inert machine ahead. I remember my binoculars bumping against my chest as I ran. Jumping on the tank's back I peered into the darkness of the turret, my eyes half-blinded by the full Italian sun on the dusty white road. I called out and received no answer. I was being fired upon from a house nearby and it seemed impolitic to stay around.

I am still not clear why I made that little gesture. It was unwise to leave my own tank when it might itself come under fire. And I could scarcely have lugged a wounded man out of the tank while under small-arms fire. I suppose that the gesture was made, not only on an impulse of trying to bring some aid to my fellows, but also to assuage my own guilt at having been the instrument of sending them there.

That is all that I can recall about June 19th. The German rearguard evacuated the city in the small hours, and we entered Perugia on the 20th, passing the blackened carcass of my serjeant's tank as we went in. There were some cheering crowds in the city streets but my spirits were too heavy to be lifted. Compared with the spontaneous delight of the peasantry in many of the villages we had passed through, the welcome of the Perugia crowds seemed somewhat reserved. The city had been an administrative centre for Fascism—for police and lawyers, tax-collectors and rentiers, officers and ecclesiastics—and Perugia had been one of Mussolini's pets. There was a long anti-fascist tradition in the city—but perhaps the people were waiting to see how far 'liberation' would go?

The complement of a Sherman tank was five, so that three men had been left in that inert machine. I went back later on the 20th and inspected the tank, finding a pile of ashes, still moulding the shape of the lower half of a man, in the driver's seat. I talked with civilians in nearby houses, including a plucky nun in a convent just beside the tank. She had witnessed the whole episode from a window and had even, later that evening, run out into the street and called out to see if anyone was alive. Later she had seen a German soldier throw a hand-grenade into the turret, look inside, pour in petrol and set the tank on fire. I was satisfied beyond any doubt that the driver, co-driver and wireless-operator were all dead.

Army Records were not satisfied and the next-of-kin of the three men were informed that they were 'Missing, Believed Killed'. As their immediate commanding officer it became my duty to correspond with the next-of-kin over several months. Perhaps this is why, although I witnessed far more violent episodes, this small event at Perugia haunts me to this day as a symbol of the chances of war.

For the dead to be posted as 'Missing' is a protraction of the pain of bereavement. The imagination strains after impossible hopes of survival so that, as each hope is disallowed, the grief of bereavement is renewed time after time. 'He was our only child so you can see how we feel about it, if it is really true,' one father wrote to me. And the mother of another wrote:

> I know how busy you must be but we have received a very disquieting note, saying 'missing believed killed' and it has upset me again most terribly—surely if you know my darling is buried he cannot be 'missing'? Please forgive me—I am in the depths of despair

and my mind is in torture. My darling boy saved his mother's
thoughts until the last, his lovely cheering letters always assured his
mother he was alright. . .

I was as callous as any young soldier had to be in order to
survive (my substitute for emotional responses took the form
of outbreaks of skin disease) but I could scarcely bear to read
these rather formal, self-effacing, ever-courteous letters:

My brother was all I had in the world we had lived together the last
ten years since losing our mother and I would like to know a few
more details, if the spot where he is buried is marked or did an
explosion make this impossible?

'Please did one of his friends pick some wild flowers and
place on his grave?' And always, whenever I sent the least
scrap of news, this was received with pitiful expressions of
gratitude from the kin of these troopers. They seemed to be
astonished to receive any attention from anyone in authority:
'Hope I am not asking too much of your time. . .', 'I am so
sorry to trouble you. . .',

Will you try and do me a kindness and see that his personal belong-
ings are sent back to me and if you really could get me a photo of
his grave it would set my wife's mind at rest as she is greatly grieved. . .

With all the weight of my twenty years I did what I could
to offer comfort and to abbreviate the grief of my enquirers
by giving to these deaths a definite term. I remember these
letter-writers (whom I never met) better than I can how recall
the three dead troopers. Or, rather, these letters gave to the
soldiers a quite new and disquieting dimension. They could
no longer be defined only by rank and number and rôle and
by the humours and quiddities which they disclosed within
our small functional social group. I recall that I liked them
all, and (so far as I could know across the gap of army
rank) they none of them had any reason to dislike me. They
had shared in the resigned complicity of military life and had
joined in the repartee of ironies as we camped in the evenings

beside our tanks in the beautiful countryside of May and June. But I did not tell their next-of-kin that, in the causal sequence of command, I had directed them towards their deaths—at that moment when I had beckoned forward the serjeant's tank to take the lead, and had sentenced them, instead of my own crew, to the consequence.

Why do I set this down now, forty years later, when the Third Convention for European Nuclear Disarmament has assembled in Perugia? I am aware that my petty episode of warfare is so inconsequential that I could tack onto it whatever moral I might like.

What I will tack onto it is, first, that much of the experience of modern warfare is as personal and inconsequential as that. All the wide-angle plural renderings which we see on film or telly scarcely connect with any war veteran's authentic experience. The individual moments of experience are recycled as a collective subject, 'war', which is something none of us knew much about.

'War' is a collective abstraction, a matter for romance or for disgust. Post-war generations in Europe are preoccupied with war in this abstract sense, and most thoughtful and sensitive people are quite properly on the side of disgust.

What is sometimes overlooked is that the soldiers were disgusted also, for good reasons. Did that large collective noun, the army, have a collective purpose? Yes it did. It was to finish the war and then go home. Did the individuals comprising that collective share any personal aims? Yes they did. These were to survive the war if possible, but the 'possible' included reservations as to fulfilling certain necessary duties and loyalties as well as avoiding shame and self-accusation.

These reservations were often large enough to cancel out the possibility of personal survival. Some of my younger friends, including feminist friends whose actions for peace I greatly admire, suppose that there is a simple cause of war in male structures and male aggro. This message is sometimes associated with 'Greenham' and it met with fervent applause from the youthful audience at the Labour Party's rally for a Nuclear-Free Europe at Wembley on June 3rd, 1984.

It may be right that the younger generations should feel this to be so. If we have reached a point where the human species must refuse war, then we must draw upon our cultural resources. The antithetical poles of warfare and of nurture have often been expressed in art and poetic imagery in compelling sexual imagery: the opposition of Mars and the Madonna. A fragment in William Blake's notebook expresses it all:

> The sword sung on the barren heath
> The sickle in the fruitful field:
> The sword he sung a song of death,
> But could not make the sickle yield.

'Greenham' has drawn with effect upon this powerful symbolic inheritance.

In modern societies warfare has occasioned the sharpest dissociation, and often antiphony, of gender roles and alternative cultural forms, with consequences which have endured in time of peace and entered peace-time structures. These consequences may be contributory, yet they should not be confused with causes. For history (in my view) does not disclose segregated and antithetical gender cultures, but, rather, a plurality of emphases (class, racial, gender or occupational) within a unitary sum. And in any complex society the causes of war can never be explained by biological reductionism. The 'barren heath' and the 'fruitful field' lie intermingled with each other.

These are fascinating questions whose strict examination must lie within the disciplines of social history and social anthropology. The examination has scarcely yet been made, and feminists are right to propose the questions, although the good-hearted assertion of feminist feelings cannot substitute for the examination. The moods and the imperatives of the present may be admirable and necessary to our survival. But they cannot be smuggled back as universals into the interpretation of the past.

If we say, as some simplistic voices are saying now so

loudly that few dare to answer back, that there is something essentially male about war (all war, universal war), and that a feminist culture would never have sanctioned warfare, then we are smuggling in also the premise that 'war' (being male) has, always, in every historical eventuality, been wrong or disgusting or unnecessary, and that some non-violent feminist alternative was always available. I do not know that this is so, nor how it could ever be shown to be so.

Of course, more considered feminist analysis does not follow this simplistic biological explanation of the causes of war. But the view is very much around today. And it has arrived, through a feminist door, at the position of absolutist and universal pacifism. That is a respectable position, which is endorsed by some part of today's peace movement. But it is one which the majority of my generation in occupied Europe forty years ago considered and rejected. That generation comprised, as is usually the case, both sexes, and the women who served in the Resistance or in the Allied forces, whether in combatant roles in the Serbian mountains, the Warsaw ghetto, or with the French Maquis, or whether in sustained political and economic engagement in non-combatant rôles, would not thank their younger sisters today for accusing them of having been surrogate males.

I labour the point, although it is perhaps now of interest only to my own generation. The present time discloses quite different alternatives, and the imperative of resistance to nuclear weapons has become absolute. But because we endorse wholeheartedly the spirit of 'Greenham' are we therefore obliged to undertake a wholesale retrospective rehash of the past, including our own past, and disown our loyalties to those who, in a different age, decided differently and sealed the decision with their deaths?

In any case I cannot recall much evidence of male aggro in my own experience of war. On the contrary, the soldier (more often officer) who displayed martial *macho* was not only generally disliked but was also feared since he was likely to lead others into futile acts of theatre and un-functional deaths. I would still prefer the old-fashioned diagnosis of the causes of war within the political economies

of states, the ambitions of ruling groups, and the irrationalisms of nationalisms and of ideologies: and, on that occasion,
of the Nazi and Fascist ideologies most of all. And (to give
back my argument to the care of more complex feminist
analysis) let it be noted that those Nazi ideologies and those
Fascist structures were as aggressively racist, martial and
masculine (albeit with substantial feminine cultural
complicity) as any in modern history.

Of course when the media recycle 'war experience' they do
not always give us wide-angle plural stuff. Sometimes
narrator or camera zoom in on a few rugged individuals.
The deception here is to show us 'war' in terms of individual
agency: these photogenic individuals displaying cunning or
heroism and thereby becoming the actors who 'won' the war.
For example, by breaking enemy codes at Bletchley.
    There may have been, in olden tymes, wars of that kind,
when the course of a battle was turned by the example
and exploits of—

> Harry the king, Bletchley and Exeter,
> Warwick and Talbot, Heseltine and Gloster. . .

Those times have long gone by, except perhaps in the low-
technology fighting of 'partisans'.
    Modern warfare is the ultimate negation of human agency.
Much of the killing in World War II was done at long-distance
between enemies who rarely ever saw each other. In World
War III they will never see each other at all, but only a blip
on a radar screen.
    What is decisive in modern warfare is military technology,
logistics, economic resources and so on. Beside these,
individual agency scarcely matters. And the chances of
survival or death are altogether casual and arbitrary. If
human purposive agency survives—but we are descending into
a technological determinism in which the matter is thrown
in doubt—then it is not in the 'war' but behind and before
the war, in the political culture of the warring states. If we
wish to be agents in the next war then we must be agents

now. At the moment when it starts all space for agency will have closed.

Another moral which I will draw from my episode is self-evident. The 'war' which contemporary resurrectionists on our media delight in showing is two-dimensional. It is quite flat. It leaves out the dimension of bereavement. This is always somewhere behind the camera crew, outside the margin of the book. The script has no place for the pain of the parents and lovers and kin.

Two generations of Europeans—those of my parents and my grandparents—had to endure this monstrous thing: the knowledge that their children, scarcely out of school, faced death at any time. They lived in fear of the postman, in fear of the newspaper, in fear of the radio news. I hold myself and my generation in Europe (although not in Asia, Latin America or Africa) to be greatly fortunate that we have never had to endure that kind of aching fear on behalf of our own.

To be sure, this is now a somewhat archaic reflection. For the Third World War, if it should come, will at least spare us this differential generational or gender suffering. Already in World War II the amazing technological refinements of gas-ovens and aerial bombing of cities were equalising all pain. Next time the babe in arms, the mother, the son and the grandparents will at least all go together.

Current suggestions that 'conventional' weapons are somehow more tolerable than nuclear weapons are also misleading. The conventional weapons of the first two world wars were hideous and their 'modernised' successors will be hideous in the extreme. Taboos against the massacre of noncombatants have already been broken beyond repair. And since as we are often told—nuclear weapons 'cannot be disinvented' we can be quite sure that, in any battle between the blocs which starts with 'conventional' arms, the losing side will, at the point of defeat, summon the nukes back.

It follows that it is no longer sufficient to clamour for nuclear disarmament. If European nations should go to war then the distinction between the nuclear and the conventional will soon be lost. We must therefore enlarge our objectives.

We must work to disallow any kind of recourse to war.

We Europeans are packed into this small continent, our armouries overflowing with every modernised instrument of murder, while the two hostile blocs lie against each other as closely as lovers in a bed. The bland news presenters and the public images of politicians no longer deceive us. There is already a rising hysteria in Europe, like fog rising on a frosty evening from the culverts and drains. Let there be one lurch towards war, and the gods of the opposed ideologies will display a ferocity even more crazed than the ferocity of the gods of Iraq and Iran.

Certainly nuclear weapons are the most odious symbols of our predicament. They will remain prominent in our concerns. But the peace movement must now move beyond its obsession with these and become a movement for the making of European peace.

Perhaps only historians will appreciate how unlikely of achievement this objective is. European history has been marked at every stage by warfare, whether on this continent or whether exported to others, and the wars of this century have been as merciless and as indiscriminate as any and on the largest scale. Warfare has been a normal element in the polity of the clan, the city-state, the Roman empire, the cause of Christendom, the trading metropolis, the nation-state, the expansionist empire. At predictable intervals the young have been sent out to fight, and predictably they have been ready to go. War has been a normal function of all types of European society, the menace of war has been a normal instrument of diplomacy, and the expectation of war has been habitual within European culture.

It follows that a peace movement, if it is to *make* peace and not only make protest, must set itself an agenda which extends into every nook and cranny of our culture and our polity. It has to be an affirmative movement of an unprecedented kind.

If our movement is to make peace, and not only offer a rearguard resistance to the increment in the weapons of war, then it must address itself to the political and ideological conditions within which the next world war is maturing. It must learn the skills of communication across the blocs, where the lines of hostility are sharpest. It must concern itself not only with material disarmament but also with political and ideological disarmament.

That is why the questions of the division of Europe—and of the presence of foreign military forces and bases outside their own territory in both halves of Europe—must move forward in the peace movement's agenda. To say that there can be no prospect of peace until we overcome the division of Europe, to say that there must be some 'historic compromise' between the hostile polities and ideologies of the adversary blocs (and between the USA and USSR), is to reveal the actual size of our problem. Yet it is also to propose an objective more attainable than that of eliminating all 'male structures' from the world scene within two or three decades (which is all the extent of the reprieve which I judge to be left to us), or than that of removing all nuclear, chemical and biological weapons-systems on both sides while at the same time all the hostilities and structures of the Cold War itself are left intact.

It is entirely right that the millions who have been rousing themselves throughout the world in recent years should see themselves as a peace movement, as a movement of affirmation challenging the structures of the Cold War. Some Soviet ideologists, with their allies, have recently been attempting to re-baptise us as an 'anti-war movement'. But that will never be enough.

By an 'anti-war movement' they intend a movement which is limited in its agenda to matters of military posture and procurements only and from which all questions of ideology, polity and culture are excluded. That is, we are to meet together (the self-activating independent movements of the West and the official peace council diplomats of the East as equal partners) with an agenda which replicates the agendas of the arms-controllers and diplomats of the armed states.

We are permitted to run through this agenda: no first use, a test ban treaty, which missiles are to be controlled first and in which order, how an equitable 'balance' may be

maintained. The agenda is so constructed that it generally
turns out that what must be demanded are Western concessions only, and since the Western military posture is
currently atrocious the Western peace movement is willing
to go along with that.

But when we attempt to extend the agenda from the
symptoms of militarism to its causes, when we propose
measures to overcome now (and not in some utopian
future) the arbitrary division of our continent, when we ask
to discuss together cooperation in a healing-process by means
of the opening of frontiers, increasing cultural and human
exchanges, and the disarmament of security services and
malevolent ideologists, we are instantly ruled out-of-order.

It is not only that we are told that all such questions are
'ideological intrusions' which have 'nothing in common'
with the purpose of the anti-war movement. We are told this
in menacing and bitterly-divisive tones. Mr Zhukov, the
Chairman of the Soviet Peace Committee, has been kind
enough to inform the readers of CND's monthly, *Sanity*,
that my object is to 'bury the peace movement'. He has also
recently in *Pravda* (March 11th) lampooned the arguments
of thousands in the Western peace movements as the products of 'US and NATO psychological war agencies'. It has
been insinuated that END and the Dutch Interchurch Peace
Council may be instruments of the CIA. Activists from
Western peace movements have been denied visas or have
been summarily expelled from East European countries.
All the foul and paranoid suggestions of conspiracy which
marked the Stalinist zenith have been deployed to create
divisions and to sow suspicions of treason within the Western
movement. In one secret briefing document of the Czechoslovak Communist Party (prepared before the Prague Peace
Assembly in 1983), my own name featured with that of
Enrico Berlinguer towards the top of a list of malign influences within the anti-war movement—which I take to be
a signal honour.

Another internal document of the Czechoslovak Party
commences: 'Imperialism recently attempts to weaken the
peace movement by infiltrating it with ideas, persons and

whole organisations whose clear aim is to break the peace movement, to prevent its unification, etc.' Since my own organisation, END, is (with the Russell Peace Foundation) especially singled out as an example, we must suppose that END, whose first Appeal in April 1980 for a nuclear-free Europe helped to initiate today's movements—an Appeal which was the direct precursor of the recent Convention in Perugia—was a prescient pre-emptive ploy by 'NATO psychological war agencies' to 'infiltrate' a movement which did not then exist.

I do not know how long it is possible to continue to sit down in the same room with people who are guilty of bad faith, libel and the pollution of political relations, and to pretend that nothing is going on. I try to be patient still. I try to remember that these people are only bureaucrats in the service of armed states, and if they are not better then at least they are no worse than the bureaucrats of NATO. They are doing the job they are paid to do. This job is to try to co-opt the Western peace movement as an auxiliary to Soviet diplomacy just as the job of their NATO analogues is to try to co-opt Solidarnosc and human rights movements in the East as auxiliaries of the 'Free West'.

But they have not been, in the past year or two, the kind of functionaries who can help us to make peace. They have often been, precisely, the emissaries of ideology. It is easier to talk with any Soviet or Czech citizen—with scientists, musicians, teachers or even with diplomats—about the real problems of overcoming bloc division than it has been to talk with some members of these 'peace councils'.

For this has not been their office. Their office has been to write agendas which disallow the discussion of these problems as 'ideological intrusions'. Their office has been to present Warsaw bloc policies as, on every occasion, the most perfect and peace-loving known to history, and to demand their endorsement by all. Their office has demanded that they and they alone must be the channel for relations between Western peace movements and their own peoples, and if unstructured dialogue takes place with 'unofficial' voices then their legitimacy is called in question. Their function has been not to open dialogue but to police it and place it under Party controls.

Perhaps the recent Perugia Convention has shown the first signs of cracks in this old Stalinist mould, and of an entry at last into genuine dialogue with the West. It must be as difficult for Warsaw bloc bureaucrats to break with the forty-or-more-year-old habits of political manipulation as it would be for their NATO analogues. And yet, if the Cold War and the division of Europe are ever to be brought to an end, then at some point the bureaucracies of both sides must be persuaded to be consenting parties.

It is not possible that some of these men and women, on both sides, do not know the gravity of the predicament into which the blocs have become locked. They must suspect that the question of *making* peace, of an 'historic compromise'* between the blocs, is the only alternative to terminal nuclear war. One or two of them may even suspect, when they consider our divided continent, that they are themselves a part of the problem.

If this understanding is now stirring in some minds, and if we are seeing the first evidence of a genuine response within orthodox Communist ideology to the pressures of the Western peace movement, then the East–West exchanges at the Perugia Convention may be counted a small success. As for the Western peace movement's own resistance to NATO's formidable militarisation, this is already in hand and it will grow in strength. We require no instructions on these matters from the officers of the East.

I have strayed far from my theme, and Europe herself has come a long way since that day, in June 1944, when I drowsed inside my tank on the outskirts of Perugia. It is not easy to join into a single theme those episodes from the last war and the strategies for preventing another. If these things sometimes run together in my mind, yet I cannot expect the post-war generations to understand.

---

* The phrase is that of George Konrad, the independent-minded Hungarian novelist, in his *Antipolitics* (Quartet Books).

Revulsion against war among the young is a necessary moment in our culture if our species is to pass from its pre-history of barbarism to the first ledges of civilisation. Yet the revulsion extends also to the past, where it engulfs my twenty-year-old self and my fellow soldiers as we trundled in our tanks down the road to Fontioeggi. Because we were fighting-men we must be objects of pity or disgust. It is un-necessary to ask what were our views of war nor what we supposed we were fighting about. We must either have been victims or else doing our *macho* thing.

But I do not think that we were either. We had a certain hardness towards ourselves and we had little self-pity. We were disgusted by war but we assented to its political necessity, a necessity which might—although we hoped most ardently that it would not—entail our own deaths. That is why I see— although the post-war generations cannot and perhaps should not see—the anti-Fascist alliance of World War II as having some political affinity with the peace movement of today.

It may seem absurd to see those Allied armies, the Resist-ance movement in the mountains and the cities, or the 'home front' where the women and the old laboured in munitions works and were bombed and bereaved, as precursors of today's peace activists. It is easier to see the victims of Belsen and of Auschwitz as precursors of the German peace move-ment, as indeed in some sense they were.

Yet the sense of some affinity persists. Then as now there was an active democratic temper throughout Europe. There was a submission of self to a collective good. Then as now there was a purposive alliance of resistance to power, a 'popular front' which had not yet been disfigured by bad faith. And there was also an authentic mood of international-ism which touched the peasants in the Umbrian villages and the troopers in our tanks.

The division of Europe (for which I hold the rulers on both sides responsible) was a betrayal of all this: of demo-cracy, of internationalism, of personal sacrifice. It turned those famous victories into a pile of shit. In 1944 all of Europe, from the Urals to the Atlantic, was moved by a consensual expectation of a democratic and peaceful post-war continent. We supposed that the old gangs of money, privilege and militarism would go. Most of us supposed that the nations of West and Southern Europe would conduct their anti-Fascist alliances towards some form of socialism. Most of us (including many of the Communists of those countries) supposed that the nations of Eastern Europe would be governed by some form of authentic socialist popular front. We all supposed that the people of the Soviet Union (before whose measureless sacrifices we felt humility) and the people of the rest of Europe would cohabit on the same continent agreeably as good neighbours. It was brave rhetoric, and we bought it, and some bought it with their lives.

That is why I return to 1944, before Europe was struck into two halves. I feel a distinction must be made between the long casualty-lists of World War I and of World War II. I can only see the dead of the First World War as victims, futile losses in the ledgers of rival imperialisms. But I hold the now-unfashionable view that the last war was, for the Allied armies and the Resistance, an anti-Fascist war, not only in rhetoric but also in the intentions of the dead.

So long as Europe remains divided, so long as hostile militarisms occupy both halves, those intentions are being violated. It is not their past credulity but our present inaction which reduces those intentions to futility. My fellow soldiers who were burned in that tank were not ardent politicians. But they were democrats and anti-Fascists. They knew what they fought for, and it was not for the division of Europe, nor was it for the domination of our continent by two arrogant superpowers.

Nor was this the spirit which animated the freshly-risen democracy in Perugia in 1944 and 1945, and which still can be felt in that well-governed Communist municipality today. The spirit which breathed through the *Corriere di Perugia*, the organ of the Umbrian Committee of National Liberation which was founded within a month of the city's liberation, was that of the popular front and of democratic self-government ('l'autogoverno democratico'). It was edited by Aldo Capitini, a leader of the local Resistance who was committed to the methods of non-violence. His editorial celebrating the end of World War II (7 May 1945) is headed 'Mondo Aperto': Open World. The greatest war known in history must now give rise to the greatest and most complex peace, with nations subordinating their sovereignty within federal institutions and with a developing internationalist culture informed by 'l'anima aperta', an open spirit.

We have to return to that time, before the division of our continent, and search for that 'Mondo Aperto' once again. If the Convention at Perugia did something to help this healing-process on, then it will have done more than place wild flowers on those distant anti-Fascist graves. It will have liberated the intentions of the dead.

DOUBLE
EXPOSURE

To

Zdena Tomin

▲ INTRODUCTION ▲

In the last months of 1984, when I was preparing a collection called *The Heavy Dancers* for the press, it occurred to me that some of the matters discussed in those pages concealed a 'hidden narrative' of the non-aligned peace movement of the past five years.

This narrative has been hidden simply because the actors have been too busy to write it. It concerns the origins of a part of that movement; the increasingly sharp attacks (and calumnies) visited upon it by orthodox Western critics; the co-operation between Western peace movements and independent peace groups in the East; and the sharp and confrontational response to this from official sources in the Communist apparatus.

While some part of this record is known to many active members of Western peace movements, only a few hundred people have been centrally involved in these events. It seemed to be time to make the record more public. But when I sat down to write an introduction to *The Heavy Dancers*, it turned out that matters were too complex to despatch in a few pages. My fingers became trapped in my typewriter for weeks.

This essay is the result. It is a companion to *The Heavy Dancers*, but it is also a distinct study in itself and one which is addressed in particular to persons active in the peace movement. It is not offered as an objective narrative of the past five years. No-one is competent to write that yet, and it would require research into numerous national histories and movements. Yet, since something needed to be written, I decided to write this in a more personal way. Because I have exposed my views often in publication, I have drawn upon myself numerous attacks, some of a quite personal nature. Most of them have been too trivial or too bigoted to answer; yet replying to some of them has given me a gate-of-entry into general questions of history and of ideology of more public interest.

There is also the difficulty that a writer cannot always (without some auto-suppression) argue out difficult points as a representative of some collectivity: a Campaign or a Committee. Political, moral, and philosphical matters raised here are not ones as to which organisations have 'positions'. The positions are my own. And, where narrative enters in, I have also drawn directly on my own personal experience. No doubt in that part of this essay which considers East/ West relations, a much fuller (and richer) account could be given by those who have had direct experience of Soviet, Polish, GDR or Czechoslovak exchanges. But in keeping with the manner of this essay I have confined my examples to matters which came most directly within my own observation.

This essay therefore should not be taken as expressing the views of 'the peace movement' or of CND or END. But it could not have been written without their collective work and experience. This is so much the case that it is impossible to single out individuals for acknowledgement—and a few of them, on 'the other side', might not thank me for doing so. I will only say that I owe most of all to my colleagues in the British Committee of END (European Nuclear Disarmament), and, in the second half of this essay, to those specialist groups of END which have made it their work to monitor developments and to communicate with citizens on 'the other side'. Some passages of Chapter Five have appeared in *END Journal* (October 1984) and in a fuller essay on 'Star Wars' in the *Guardian*, 18 February 1985.

Worcester   E.P.T.
January 1985

▲ 'A HANDFUL OF SCOUNDRELS' ▲

On April 25th, 1983, General Bernard Rogers, the Supreme Allied Commander, NATO, was giving evidence before the House of Representatives Committee on Armed Services, Procurement and Military Nuclear Systems in Washington. A major argument against the freeze movement in the United States (he said),

> . . . is the support that the freeze gives to those movements in Western Europe that are counterproductive to our efforts, because they look back and they say, 'look at what's going on in the United States, we have got support there'. It plays right into the hands of a man named Thompson, who heads the campaign for nuclear disarmament in the U.K., who has come out and said as much. Just the fact that you are considering such a freeze, you see, plays into his hands.

It is flattering to know that I have come to the notice of someone so eminent as General Rogers, although it suggests an alarming state of incompetence in NATO's intelligence services that they have not yet been able to identify who 'heads' CND. And I was equally flattered to learn a few months later that I had also come to the notice of Mr Georgi Arbatov, the director of Moscow's Institute of US and Canadian Studies. In private discussions with both Dutch and Belgian peace workers, in the summer of 1983, he referred to me and to END (European Nuclear Disarmament) somewhat curtly as 'affairs of the CIA'.

It is not only General Rogers and Mr Arbatov to whom I
have given offence. I have had, in 1983 and 1984, a
sensationally bad press from ideologists on both sides of the
Cold War: from *Encounter* and *Commentary* (which both
come from stables which, in the first Cold War, received
laundered subventions from the CIA—although, in the case
of *Encounter*, the torch of subvention was later handed
on to the British Arts Council); and from such journals as
Rude Pravo, *Pravda* and *International Life* in the East. For
an advocate of peace, and of a healing-process between the
blocs, this is discouraging. Indeed, I have been the target of
so much abuse that I have often thought that it would most
contribute to the peace of the world, as well as to my own
peace-of-mind, if I just shut up.

Yet at a time when the superpowers can agree on almost
nothing, I and some of my friends have at least provided
them with a common bond. If the Geneva negotiations had
been, not about cruise, Pershing and SS-20s but about how
to rub out the non-aligned peace movements (including 'a
man named Thompson') then the negotiators would have
come out smiling and arm-in-arm.

I suppose that I do really know what makes both lots of
them so cross. First, it is essential to their world-view (and to
their arms procurements) that they should uphold a binary,
Us-versus-Them, definition of world politics. The very notion
that there might be alternative ways is threatening to them
both. Second, neither lot likes being called the 'ideological
look-alikes' of the other. This is deeply wounding to their
self-esteem. It might also give the game away—a game in
which they are partners as well as antagonists.

The Heavy Dancers chronicles these complex arguments
between peace movements and the war movement—and it
may be helpful to explain something of their context. One
way of doing this may be to comment on my critics.

From the West one kind of criticism falls into the category which I will define as 'political soft porn': that is, it
makes no pretence of confronting my arguments but ransacks
my writings over thirty and more years, pulling the odd
sentence or phrase out of context, and uses these to flash

lubricious signals suggestive of devious motives and of disguised complicity with Soviet strategies.

Since I am known as a vocal critic of official Soviet ideology and power, they hint that this is only a rhetorical device to make me the more persuasive as the proponent of a peace movement whose objective effect (if successful) would be to disarm 'the West' unilaterally and expose it to Soviet occupation or blackmail. It is left to readers to decide whether I am 'disingenuous' and a 'dangerous' undercover Soviet agent or merely 'self-deluded'.

In this category of political soft porn fall 'Portrait of a Peace-Fighter' by Gerald Frost in *Encounter*, May 1984, and 'The "Neutralism" of E.P. Thompson' by Scott McConnell in *Commentary* in the summer of 1983. Mr Frost is attributed with the high-sounding title of Executive Director of the Institute for European Defence and Strategic Studies, an 'Institute' with which Mr Roger Scruton is also associated but which turns out to be, not an academic foundation, but a private office in London. I have already replied to Mr Frost's scatter-shot (*Encounter*, 'Letters', July/August 1984). An example of Mr McConnell's technique (which verges on the political hard porn) may be taken to exemplify his method.

I counted some twenty-seven direct mis-statements or direct mis-representations in McConnell's seven pages; here is a characteristic example. McConnell is commenting on the fact that my central preoccupations changed in late 1979, 'in the aftermath of the NATO decision to deploy cruise and Pershing missiles':

One need not speculate on the particular events which prompted the change. It is true that Thompson focused his concern on the campaign for unilateral disarmament right after returning from a visit to Bulgaria, in the fall of 1979, where preparations were just beginning for the Soviet-sponsored World Peace Council festival, planned for Sofia the following year (preparations which, it has been noted, followed directly upon the Soviet decision to invade Afghanistan). But Thompson did, after all, have personal reasons for his visit (his brother died in Bulgaria during the war). Moreover, he had not been a party man for some time, and he was certainly

able to conceive of the significance of the peace issue without
higher guidance.

The intention of this passage is to discount the actual
reasons for my active involvement in the peace movement
in those months—the failure of the USA to ratify SALT II,
the NATO modernisation decisions, and the Soviet invasion
of Afghanistan were leading on to a dangerous bloc confrontation—reasons which were clearly stated by me in
articles in *New Society*, the *Guardian* and the *New Statesman* at the time. The passage insinuates that there must
have been ulterior reasons, which might be deduced—if all
were known—from his muddy passage about Bulgaria. The
suggestion is made that I might (or, again, I might not) have
received Soviet 'guidance' during this visit, and this suggestion is allowed to linger in the mind although it is, as proof
of McConnell's fair-mindedness, then partially withdrawn.
Since I had not been 'a party man for some time' (in fact
I had left the Communist Party in 1956, twenty-three years
before) I might have fallen within these Soviet guide-lines
of my own accord. (McConnell had already prepared for this
expectation by describing me as 'a sort of fellow-traveller
with his own car'). What is left behind with the reader is
the sense that something malodorous was going on.
The stench, however, comes from McConnell's own
insinuations, which entail a direct inversion of historical
sequence. I visited Bulgaria with my wife, Dorothy, not 'in
the fall' but in April 1979; we went as private tourists,
although on the invitation of the association of former
partisans of World War II. We were collecting information
both in South Serbia and Bulgaria, about my brother's part
as a British Liaison Officer (SOE) with the partisans, in
which he met his death; and in due course I hope to publish
a study of this odd corner of that war.
Our relations with the Bulgarian authorities were courteous
but formal and were exclusively related to this question. I
had never heard of cruise missiles or of NATO modernisation at that time. I do not remember hearing of the World
Peace Council event in Sofia (which took place eighteen

months later) until after it had happened. Moreover,
McConnell engages in extraordinary acrobatics in suggesting
that 'preparations' for the Sofia event were taking place 'in
the fall' of 1979 as a result of the Soviet invasion of
Afghanistan, which took place in December 1979, two weeks
after the NATO modernisation decision of December 12th.
The actual historical sequence (our visit to Bulgaria, April
1979; NATO modernisation decision, December 12, 1979,
Soviet invasion of Afghanistan, December 26, 1979; Sofia
World Peace Council conference, September 1980) is inverted
to insinuate that I received 'higher guidance' from the
organisers of a conference (at which I was not present and to
which I was not invited) which took place 18 months after
our visit.

To plant a libel by both offering it and disclaiming it is a
well-known technique of this kind of porn. But McConnell
is also suggesting an extraordinary conspiracy-theory of
politics. 'Preparations' for the Sofia conference 'it has been
noted, followed directly upon the Soviet decision to invade
Afghanistan'. The far-sighted engineers of Soviet subversion
(it seems) had already decided to invade Afghanistan (when?
in September 1979? or in April, when I was in Sofia?) and
were already winding-up the master-spring of the European
and American peace movements of the future. And this
conspiracy has 'already been noted'. Where? By whom?

I think that in this case I can provide the answer. Vladimir
Bukovsky had already published in *Commentary* in 1982 his
long article, *The Peace Movement and the Soviet Union*,
which was then republished in England, first in *The Times*,
and then, with an introduction by Winston S. Churchill,
MP, as a pamphlet promoted by the Coalition for Peace
through Security. It was also published in Holland, Germany,
and no doubt in other countries. The French edition, *Les
pacifistes contre la paix*, was a sensational success, and
week after week Bukovsky could be read pontificating on
Soviet strategy and on the peace movement in such intellectual organs as *Paris Match*. I think it possible that Bukovsky's
accusations that the peace movement was the creature of
Soviet agencies had an influence upon delaying the develop-

ment of an independent French movement.

Vladimir Bukovsky is a Soviet 'dissident' who was treated ferociously by the KGB and who, after long terms of imprisonment and of forcible commitment to psychiatric institutes was finally deported to the West (in a celebrated 'exchange' with the Chilean Communist leader, Luis Corvalan) in 1976. His experiences have been savage, and were endured with stoicism, and they entitle him to deploy some verbal savagery in arguments with opponents. Indeed, if he were testifying on matters within his direct experience, I could only attend to his testimony with humility.

He has however offered testimony on a great many other matters which lie far outside his experience. In the West he has bounced back like a rubber ball and he is full of ebullience. He enjoys the theatre of things, especially when he is centre-stage, and he has a charming way of gesturing, exaggerating for effect, and saying whatever comes into his head. He published in Paris in 1981 *Cette lancinante douleur de la liberté* (This Agonising Pain of Liberty), subtitled 'Letters of a Russian resister to Westerners', in which he chronicled the agonies, comedies and errors of finding his way in the Free West—mainly in England. It is clear that the Free West has not lived up to his expectations; we have disappointed him; the British did not let him bring in his dog from Switzerland since they were firmly persuaded that madness in animals comes from abroad and 'any island madness is quite unthinkable'.

In short, he takes the mickey out of us, it is good fun, and he has some perceptive comments as well. His style strives for effect, not for veracity. Contrasting the serious reading-habits of the average Soviet citizen with the English, he writes that 'when in 1978 I was looking for lodgings in Cambridge, I visited a hundred houses and I practically never saw any books except for telephone directories'. I can well believe the contrast, but I cannot believe that he really went to 100 houses looking for digs nor that almost none of them had any books.

I can suppose that if he had not crossed me in other ways I would have enjoyed an evening with Bukovsky, over a

in September 1979, 'the sky was cloudless'. 'There was no new escalation in the arms race. . . The Vienna summit meeting had just been successfully concluded with the signing of SALT II.' *Ergo:* the Soviet leaders must have already decided to invade Afghanistan, and with remarkable forethought set in motion at the same time a future Western peace movement to soften the future consequences.

I have met with this kind of ideological history, in which the actual events are contorted or inverted in order to encode the correct ideological message, fairly often from Soviet bloc apologists, but it is sad to see Bukovsky at the same trade. Bukovsky pretends to have tracked down 'the earliest traces' of the peace movement's revival to this Sofia event, and McConnell follows on in *Commentary* by taking Bukovsky's fiction for established fact. We have at least tracked down that source.

I have one qualification for discussing the 'earliest traces' of the revival of the movement which is denied to Bukovsky and McConnell: I was myself an 'earliest trace' and I was deeply involved in its formation. I do not intend to write this history, although its evidences still lie about me in my files or on my floor. But it should be noted, first, that the Sofia 'Parliament' had almost no influence on the generation of the Western movement (I do not recall it even being discussed), and, second, that many of that movement's key elements were active long before that event.

These elements owed little or nothing to 'Moscow', and most of them were strictly non-aligned. In Holland the crucially-influential IKV, or Interchurch Peace Council, funded by the major churches, was long-established, had a small expert staff, and also (which is more important than some peace activists suppose) had got ahead with its *thinking:* it had developed theories (which it continues to develop) of the principles of non-alignment, of East–West relations and of relations between North and South. It had campaigned with effect, alongside the Dutch 'No to Neutron Weapons' (at that time under some Communist influence) against the neutron bomb, as had also the non-aligned Norwegian movement. In Europe as a whole there were several networks of small non-aligned peace organisations: the International Confederation for Disarmament and Peace, with which Peggy Duff (the first General Secretary of CND) was associated, and which had had its own traumatic history maintaining independence from the World Peace Council; the International Peace Bureau; the War Resisters International; the Fellowship of Reconciliation; and others. (These organisations also had affiliates in the United States, Japan and Australia.) There were also substantial political forces searching for some alternative to the blocs, not least among them influential sections of Labour and Social-Democratic parties and those Eurocommunists in Italy and Spain whose first principle was *not* to be 'instructed directly from Moscow'.

In Britain, where most of these elements could be found, CND had declined over the previous decade to pitifully small numbers. But it still existed, in January 1980, was experiencing a revival, and had the great good fortune to find as General Secretary Bruce Kent. At that same moment a group of us (which included Bruce Kent and Peggy Duff) began meeting and corresponding with a view to launching a movement to clear all nuclear weapons out of Europe. The proposal was first made by Ken Coates. I drafted the original Appeal, which was then redrafted and revised by several hands, including Ken Coates, Mary Kaldor, Dan Smith, Dorothy Thompson, and with some advice from Claude Bourdet in Paris, Ulrich Albrecht in Berlin, Dr Zhores Medvedev and others. The END Appeal was as clear a statement of non-aligned perspectives as we could make it, and as such it still stands as the charter-document of three major Conventions of the European peace movements (Brussels, 1982; Berlin, 1983; Perugia, 1984):

> We must resist any attempt by the statesmen of East or West to manipulate this movement to their own advantage. We offer no advantage to either NATO or the Warsaw alliance. Our objectives must be to free Europe from confrontation, to enforce detente between the United States and the Soviet Union, and, ultimately, to dissolve both great power alliances.

From February 1980 onwards the work of collecting signatures to the Appeal went forward, under the energetic direction, not of Moscow, but of the Bertrand Russell Peace Foundation, an office in Nottingham with wide experience and international connections and with a record on 'human rights' which had often got up Moscow's nose. Both before and after April (when the Appeal was formally published) thousands of European signatures were collected, including those of prominent intellectuals, politicians and trade-unionists over a wide spectrum of opinion. And with the collection, European and then transatlantic networking increased.

This was an important contribution to the revival of the European peace movement and to its new form. It was, of course, only one contribution. The Dutch IKV, which was scarcely known to us then, was building its own network. Other groups were reaching outwards: the Greens in West Germany: the *Il Manifesto* group in Italy; women's networks; the older bodies and alliances which I have mentioned; and, on both sides of the Atlantic, the Quakers.*

In this thumbnail impression I mean only to emphasise that a complex social movement is made up of many elements, just as a great river is fed by many streams, and that the conspiracy theory favoured by Messrs Bukovsky, Churchill, McConnell and Frost is not only false but is absurd. All this had long been on the road, in 1980, before that Sofia conference (which none of us attended). Among the influential writings being discussed in Britain in 1980 (long before the World Peace Council resolutions which Bukovsky cites) were Lord Mountbatten's famous speech, articles by Lord Zuckerman and George Kennan and the Penguin collection, *Protest and Survive*, none of which were

* Diana Johnstone's *The Politics of Euromissiles* (Verso, 1984) gives valuable background to the development of the peace movement, less from the viewpoint of the kitchen (where we peace activists were sweating at the stove) than from that of the parlours where higher politics went on. Her treatment of Germany, Italy and Belgium is especially helpful, but her view of Holland, Britain and Scandinavia suffers from Parisian myopia. See also Ken Coates, *The Most Dangerous Decade* (Spokesman, 1984).

drafted in Moscow.

The West German movement developed more slowly, and Bukovsky will have it that the Bonn demonstration of October 1981 was set up in Sofia the year before. There was a little external influence upon Germany, of which I have poignant recollections. For in March 1981 the END Committee in Britain, on the initiative of Peggy Duff and Bruce Kent, called a small conference of European peace activists in Frankfurt.

This was Peggy's last conference, and it was, very much, her conference. She had used all her experience, and the network of the non-aligned ICDP, to bring the delegates together. It was at this conference that I first met many peace workers who have since become firm friends or allies, including Ilkka Taipale of the Finnish Peace Union, Gynt Krag of the Norwegian 'No to Nuclear Weapons', and Eva Quistorp of West German Women for Peace.

I travelled both ways with Peggy. She was riddled with cancer, and used a stick or a wheel-chair. We arrived very early at Frankfurt because of a cheap air ticket (none of the 'astronomical' Soviet subsidies which Bukovsky reports ever reached us) and went to the Spartan youth hostel which was not ready to receive us. I managed to get a room where Peggy could lie on a bunk: she had nothing to eat all day but a carton of milk. Then the first delegates started to arrive. I did not know whether to disturb Peggy, but she had ordered me to do so and (since we were all a little scared of her) I did. She hobbled down the passage, and as she saw her old (and new) friends assembling, an amazing power of the spirit seemed to lighten her eyes and to assume command over her for the next three days. It was a successful conference, and it was Peggy who chaired the final session, making sure that the talk ended in clear decisions. We travelled back together the next day, and we had time to talk over many things, including her many conflicts with the World Peace Council and 'the Russians'.

Peggy died within two months and we have missed her advice grievously ever since. I have put this down because, when I recall the kind of commitment which her life embodied, then the Bukovsky–McConnell-type fictions rise in my gorge. I will not claim that the Frankfurt END conference was the starter-motor of the West German movement. It was just one kick on that motor. And there were plenty of kicks in Germany itself. We had seven or eight different groups of West German activists present (women, war resisters, Easter marchers, Peace Society, supporters of the Krefeld Appeal, Rudolph Bahro from the Greens), who, at the end of the conference, met together for the first time and made plans. At about the same time the Dutch IKV was exerting its influence also, especially among the Protestant churches. The first real signal that the German movement had arrived was at the Protestant Church Day in Hamburg that June. Then came the amazing October demonstration in Bonn, whose youthfulness, good-humour and restraint seemed to signal a mutation in German culture, and whose formidable platform—General Bastian, Petra Kelly, Erhard Eppler, Heinrich Böll and also (please remember) Coretta King—could scarcely be described as 'a handful of scoundrels instructed directly from Moscow'.

For all that I know Bukovsky may really believe what he writes. As he says himself in his tract, 'sometimes it is very comfortable—even for professional intellectuals—not to know things. . .' But that does not excuse him of irresponsibility, in not trying to find out. I do not mean that there has been no pro-Moscow Communist influence in the Western peace movement. On the contrary, there has been, and there continues to be, and some of it does come directly from Moscow; it has been damaging and time-wasting and we will deal with it anon. In West Germany, for example, the influential Krefeld Appeal against NATO missiles was silent about Soviet weapons; it was backed by an alliance which included both the non-aligned Greens (Bastian and Kelly) and the DKP (German Communist Party)—an alliance which came under increasing strain until it fell apart. In other countries there have been splits between pro-Moscow and non-aligned movements: France, Denmark, Finland, Greece.

What I mean is that Bukovsky and his followers present the movements as a coarse lampoon and in crucial ways they invert the true history. The new peace movement was never a replay of the World Peace Council campaign of the Fifties. It discovered itself, from a multitude of sources, and from small non-aligned bases established in the previous decades (ICDP, IPB, Russell Foundation, IKV, CND, War Resisters). It was moving powerfully in Britain, Scandinavia, Holland and Belgium before whatever went on in Sofia, and from that time on the World Peace Council has been panting after it, trying to catch hold of its coat-tails and to claim it as its own.

Bukovsky's lampoon has been damaging to us, perhaps in France and perhaps also in those places in Eastern Europe where *Commentary* and *Encounter* are assiduously read, precisely because it serves to confirm and to enforce exactly the same ideological fiction which the Communist ideologues wish to impose: that the *true* peace movement is, or ought to be, the compliant ally of peace-loving Soviet diplomacy in the face of imperialist aggression, and that the non-aligned forces (who in fact started it off and who represent its major movements) are late-comers and 'infiltrators' of 'NATO agencies'.

The Cold War world is a merciless world and it sets these cruel traps for us all. But there are some of us who scarcely deserved this treatment at Bukovsky's hands. For, looking through old files, I notice a press release of the Bertrand Russell Peace Foundation in 1974. In this, there is an announcement of a series of Days of Protest on behalf of civil rights prisoners in Eastern Europe, and especially in the USSR and Czechoslovakia, called jointly by the Russell Foundation, Pavel Litvinov, Jiri Pelikan and Andrei Sakharov. General Grigorenko was to be the theme of protest on the first day (7 May 1974), Jaroslav Šabata and Jiri Muller of Czechoslovakia on the second day (27 November 1974), and on the third Day of Protest (29 March 1975)—Vladimir Bukovsky! And I also notice, in a letter from Ken Coates to the *Times Literary Supplement* (November 22, 1974) that I was one of the platform speakers at the meeting at Conway Hall for Šabata and Muller; and that a number of persons subsequently prominent in the revival of the peace movement (including Noam Chomsky, Daniel Ellsberg,

Christopher Hill and myself) were signatories to the general appeal. So far as I can remember I spoke on Bukovsky Day also, on a university campus, and very certainly the Russell Peace Foundation continued its work for our impatient author.

So that it turns out that Vladimir Bukovsky has lampooned as 'useful idiots' directly 'controlled from Moscow' a Foundation and individuals which both campaigned for his own release and which played a major role in launching the Appeal for a nuclear-free Europe. I am not making any complaint about 'ingratitude'. Those of us on the 'Left' in the past three decades who have busied ourselves with issues of human rights in Communist countries have got used to finding out that the first thing that certain 'dissidents' do when they get to the West is slap us across the face with a wet fish. Yet the question of civil rights is not a question of political trading; it is an absolute; we do not defend these prisoners because they will say what we want them to say but because they have the right to say what they want themselves. We do not lay upon anyone a debt of gratitude because we do what is our plain duty.

Direct East-West communication now is like a faint exchange on the radio against a mass of static and with the jamming of the ideologists of both sides. Yet now and then a message *does* get through, and these are moments without price. It is heartening to know that, in 1974, some of us held a Day of Protest for Jaroslav Šabata—a protest he may not have known about in his prison and may not know about today. Yet today his voice has come back to us, loud and clear through the static, in his remarkable letter to the peace movement in *Voices from Prague*.

We have drifted a long way from Messrs Frost and McConnell and it would be a drag to go back to them. What they are chiefly interested in doing, with respect to myself, is to flash upon the anxious reader's mind the fact that I was a member of the Communist Party as a young man (between 1942 and 1956) and to suggest that I have never been sufficiently penitent about this and therefore should be suspect as a possible accomplice of 'Moscow'.* The difficulty in meeting this kind of attack, which is mounted not against my arguments but against my own credibility, is that it can be answered only by going off into autobiography or apologia. I would have to dive into page after page of personal matters, and chew over once more the issues of thirty years ago—questions which have nothing to do with today's peace movement and the positions which we hold in common. I am damned if I can see why any of my colleagues in today's movement should feel bound to endorse my whole life's history, any more than I feel bound to endorse theirs.

I have written out, over the years, at inordinate length my own reflections on the whole Communist and ex-Communist experience, in the *Reasoner*, the *New Reasoner*, *The Poverty of Theory*, and elsewhere. It is true that I have not, and still do not, repent of everything that I did as a Communist between 1942 and 1956. After I had finished being a soldier (which I do not repent) my main political preoccupation was in work for peace. We opposed a series of almost forgotten wars (in Greece, Algeria, Malaya, Cyprus, and Kenya), and I served as Secretary of the Federation of West Yorkshire Peace Organisations and as editor of our occasional journal, the *Yorkshire Voice of Peace*, at the height of the Korean War and during the run-up to German re-armament. All these actions still seem to me to have been right and necessary. At the same time, as I have often written, the Communist apologetics for Stalin's Russia were grossly dishonest and self-deluding, entailed direct betrayals of principle and of persons, and the whole international (World Peace Council) and sometimes national framework into which our authentic grass-roots peace movement was slotted was manipulated—in the last resort from 'Moscow'.

When all this has been said, on both sides, there is still one question remaining: which is, 'What, in those years, was

---

* Heseltine flashed in the same way in the run-up to the General Election in 1983, employing the resources of a special section of the MOD to research the political biographies of members of CND Council and passing on the findings to the *Express*. Some civil servants thought his employment of public resources upon party-political porn to be an unconstitutional abuse.

the right and effective course of political action?' It may not be difficult to suggest theoretically 'correct' positions, such as those of the Fourth or Seventh International, or, perhaps, suicide. It is a good deal more difficult to suggest how anyone might have acted with *effect*. As NATO and the Warsaw Pact were set up against each other, the world (and certainly Europe) was divided not only in theory but in fact into Two Camps. And as more state papers are opened it is clear that on occasions the 'nuclear option' was certainly considered by the United States: very certainly during the Korean War. In Britain it may be forgotten how un-reservedly Labour's leaders were committed to NATO and the American alliance; there was no tolerance in the Labour Party towards third ways. I think that we had no alternative to work for peace in the ways that we did, simply because there was no political space in which an alternative could then be pressed with effect.

That is a pragmatic point, not a theoretical excuse. I was not then looking for that alternative space, although I can now see, in retrospect, that a few were trying to hold it open: perhaps A.J. Muste and I.F. Stone in America, Claude Bourdet in France, in Britain G.D.H. Cole. The space did not open until after Stalin's death and the Khrushchev 'thaw'. In 1956 there was a world-wide effort of internal Communist 'revision' or reform, both in the East (Poland, the Soviet Union itself, Hungary) and in Western parties. When this was checked within the old ideological and disciplinary norms, many thousands of Communists (of whom I was one) left their parties, and many of these sought to break open that alternative space. Many gave support to CND and to the new non-aligned peace movements of that generation. Some survivors from that moment are among the elements who put together the peace movement of today.

But this recantation and redirection falls far short of what is required by the sages of *Encounter* and *Commentary*. They would be satisfied with nothing less than abject apostasy. Rehabilitation requires that we should proclaim the whole of 'Communism' a contaminated area and call

down an anathema upon all its works. It is my offence, in
the eyes of Mr Frost and Mr McConnell, that I have stead-
fastly refused to do this. I have polemicised against Marxism
as ideology, but I have not disowned my debt to an open,
innovative Marxist tradition. I have pronounced my
anathemas upon Communist statism—and the mental controls
and all-intrusive and brutal security measures of the present
Soviet regime are beyond reach of any apology—but I have
also noted contradictory (and potentially democratic)
elements in the Communist inheritance, the capacity of some
Communist-ruled societies for some measure of self-reform
(Prague, 1968), and even for more dramatic popular renewal
(Poland and Solidarnosc).

Indeed, it is exactly within the contradiction between
repressive form and human potential in Communist societies
that one of the hopes for human survival may be found. If
one does not see a potential for internal transformation,
what future can a dedicated anti-Communist offer? What
future (let us say) can M. André Glucksmann offer? He can
offer only to pile up more and more 'deterrents', in a
delicious state of vertigo, in the hope that in some future all
Communists and all their rabbits will die. That is the
mentality of war, the mentality of abstract and ideologically-
obsessed anti-Communism.

But I see around us all the time the evidences of Communist contradiction. There has never been a time when
official Soviet ideology and the commonsense of lived Soviet
experience were more at odds than they are today. The
ideology of 'actually existing Socialism' is nothing but
patches and holes. Outside the Warsaw powers bloc we
observe all the variants of Eurocommunism. Visiting the
peace movement in Barcelona in 1984 I was struck by the
vigorous contribution to it made by members and ex-
members of the Catalan CP (mainly ex); Spanish Communists,
who suffered under Franco and whose party was brutally
treated by Stalin, know a thing or two about human rights.
They expressed the hope that one of the effects of a non-
aligned peace movement would be to offer alliances with
Solidarnosc and with Charter 77, and to assist forward the

Communist world's democratic self-transformation. And who will they be assisting? Some of those courageous spokespersons of human rights who are now making their voices heard by the Western peace movement through the ideological static (for example, Ladislav Lis and Jaroslav Šabata) are themselves—former Communists.

The world is not so tidy as M. Glucksmann or as *Commentary* suppose. Nor is it as abstract. I do not argue any special privilege for ex-Communists in the peace movement. It is significant that Mr George Kennan, who was of the opposite party during the first Cold War, is now an ex-*anti*-Communist and has come to the same conclusions from the other side. But if we are to heal this broken world, and introduce the forces making for peace and for democracy on both sides to each other, then ex-Communists and Eurocommunists (as well as ex-anti-Communists) have their role within that healing-process. And it may not be unhelpful to the peace movement to have among its members some persons who have learned, from sad experience, about both the 'tricks, pranks and stunts' of the Communist Party bureaucrats and about the contradictions between Communist forms and potentials.

▲ 'MORAL ENDS' AND AMERICA'S 'MISSION' ▲

It is a relief to turn aside from Messrs Frost, Bukovsky and McConnell and to turn to a writer who attends in earnest to arguments. Mr Leon Wieseltier wrote a long essay in the *New Republic* (January 10 & 17, 1983) which was then put out as a book, *Nuclear War, Nuclear Peace*. This was very warmly received by the United States establishment, including Dr Henry Kissinger and ('a masterwork') Senator Daniel Moynihan. Wieseltier's strategy is to set up a 'Party of Peace' on one side (Jonathan Schell, George Kennan and myself) and a 'Party of War' on the other side (Colin Gray, Edward Luttwack and others), to expose both parties as extremist, and then to hew a 'moderate' path between them in which he vindicates the theories of 'deterrence', moderated by superpower arms control. Wieseltier occupies that part of the 'moderate' spectrum in the United States that Professor Lawrence Freedman occupies in Britain: in short, he is very much in favour of NATO modernisation, Trident II, and other such measures to 'maintain deterrence', but he criticises certain excesses of NATO strategists in order to sustain an image of 'moderation'.

The rehabilitation of 'deterrence' is a booming industry on both sides of the Atlantic. It is agreed that nuclear war would be an unthinkable disaster; therefore we must strengthen 'deterrence', which is the only way to avoid it; to prevent nuclear war we must procure more nuclear weapons. What is surprising is that some of this rehabilitation has gone on in the *New York Review of Books*, where, alongside excellent writings by Kennan, Zuckerman and Emma Rothschild, there has been a good deal of patient rehearsal of deterrence theory, but always in a liberal, restrained, sensitive sort of way.

What there has never been (unless I have overlooked it) is any direct presentation or analysis of the political alternatives proposed by the European peace movement. These have simply been closed out, by brusque gestures of rejection. For example, Theodore Draper ('Nuclear Temptations', January 19, 1984) refers to me as 'the swami of the British antinuclear movement', and goes on:

> Thompson has a wildly inaccurate version of the origin of 'deterrence theory'; he seems to think that the theory came about *after* 'Poseidon and Polaris, the SS-20, the cruise missiles, the neutron bomb' in order 'to excuse all these things'.

The reference is to my essay on 'Deterrence and Addiction' which appears on page 5 of my last collection, and perhaps Mr Draper found the passage so offensive that he could not read further?

I was arguing in this essay two propositions. First, that deterrence theory 'is not an *operative* theory: that is, it does not direct any nation's behaviour. It appears always as a gloss, as an *ex post facto* apologia, as a theoretical legitimation of actions which are taken for quite different reasons'. First came the Bomb, the theory came after it. First came 'technology creep', and the refinement of deterrent theory followed. Of course, the origins of deterrence theory go back to those earliest days, notably in the work of Bernard Brodie. But Brodie's essay (in *The Absolute Weapon*, 1946) was not the occasion for strategy meetings in the Pentagon and the Kremlin. As I stated in the same place, and at page 4 (which Draper surely read?), 'it was only *after* the Soviet Union also developed thermo-nuclear weapons that the theory of deterrence came into vogue'.

I was arguing, secondly, that deterrence theory was addictive and that, in its worst-case analysis, had now come to exert an independent force as ideology—as an *accelerator* for the nuclear arms race:

> There has never been a stationary state of mutual deterrence; instead there has been a ceaseless pursuit for advantage within that state. The operative pressures have come both from the regions of politics and ideology, and from the inertial thrust of research and development within the military-industrial complexes of the opposed powers. Deterrence theory did not give us Poseidon and Polaris, the SS-20, the cruise missiles, the neutron bomb. These were given to us by the 'alchemists' in the research laboratories, the arms lobbyists, the alarmist leader-writers and populist politicians, and by the inter-service competition of the military elites. Deterrence theory came in afterwards to excuse all these things.

The general case that I was arguing has received a notable confirmation from Lord Zuckerman who, as scientific adviser to successive governments, was actually there at the time. He wrote ('Nuclear Fantasies', *NY Review of Books*, June 14, 1984):

> During the twenty years or so that I myself was professionally involved in these matters, weapons came first and rationalizations and policies followed. Soon after the NATO alliance was formed, free-falling atomic bombs were introduced into the Western armory. Their addition to what was already there was not demanded by some new strategic theory. They were brought in because they were the most powerful destructive agents that were then available. . . First came the weapons; then they had to be fitted into a presumed tactical doctrine, which in turn had to be fitted into an illusory strategy, usually elaborated by armchair warriors.

And he goes on to say, a little later:

> In 1945 no one spoke about 'deterrent strategy'. . . I doubt if anyone in Whitehall had heard of Bernard Brodie, any more than it has been my experience that British political leaders religiously read the outpourings of American armchair strategists. To those who took the decisions, the atomic, and later the hydrogen, bombs were simply immensely powerful weapons which, if they had the means, nations just had to have.

These matters may be arguable, but it can be seen that the
analysis which I offered (an analysis which had been
influenced by Lord Zuckerman's earlier writings) was not the
'wildly inaccurate' chanting of a 'swami' but a sequence
confirmed by some evidence. Mr Theodore Draper does not,
in fact, usually write so wildly and inaccurately—he has made
telling criticisms of Pentagon policies, and within the
definitions imposed by deterrence theory he is one of the
doves. But his footnote dismissal is characteristic of a general
stance among American liberals. They dare not take one step
beyond the confines of deterrence theory and its premises
of an everlasting state of nuclear threat between the blocs.
Once outside that reassuring enclosure they would enter
an unknown and terrifying world, peopled by 'swamis' and
staring-eyed Greens and even ex-Communists, without well-
funded and prestigious conferences, and where the women
might make them sit in circles on the floor. Hence they
do not enter debate but curtly refuse it ('disgraceful', 'wildly
inaccurate'), putting up a set of concrete mind-blocks along
the outer edge of deterrence theory to mark the limits
between liberalism and the 'no go' regions. But in refusing
debate, they refuse also to engage with any real world of
politics, ideology, arms procurement. They must linger on
the liberal margins of the deterrence enclosure, elaborating
a discourse which is by turns techno-strategic (in which they
will always be amateurs) and scholastic—an extraordinary
abstracted speculation upon worst-cases, perceptions, bluffs
and hypothetical intentions. They refuse to acknowledge that
there could be alternatives, and, in doing so, they simply wall
out the discourse of the European and American peace
movements.

Mr George W. Ball, another 'moderate' of this kind,
acclaimed Wieseltier's book as 'an impressive tour de force',
and he especially commended the author for his 'disdain for
E.P. Thompson who, like Schell, "argues backward from the
apocalypse" to arrive at the "disgraceful" solution of unilateral disarmament' (*NY Review of Books*, February 2,
1984). Wieseltier follows the norm in drawing his readers'

particular attention to my former membership of the Communist Party. But he is kind enough to hasten on and add: 'Thompson's ideological biography does not discredit his ideas; they discredit themselves.' And in support of this discreditable operation, he pokes around with a stick among my writings of the past decades and pulls out a few sentences from their contexts to put on display.

Most of these sentences are from my 'Open Letter to Leszek Kolakowski', of 1973. This 'Open Letter' is my most extended reflection upon Communism and anti-Communism, it has been republished in *The Poverty of Theory*, and readers who wish to put Wieseltier's samples into their context may consult it. I would change very little in it today, and a part of my argument (as to the potential for democratisation repressed within Communist forms) has been vindicated by the phenomenon of Solidarnosc.

What puzzled me when I read Wieseltier was a sense of familiarity—not only that I had written those selected lines ten years before, but that I had read them more recently. Turning back to *Commentary* I found that every one of Wieseltier's five selected sentences were among those selected by Mr Scott McConnell in his identical operation. Whatever the explanation, this is a strange coincidence.

What this suggests to me is that Wieseltier has not consulted with a candid mind my pre-1980 writings at all, unless to thumb through one essay. He is, like Heseltine and Frost, just flashing signals. And what are these terrible signals? In one of these selected snippets I am quoted as saying (of the Soviet Union), 'Fifty years is too short a time to judge a new social system.' What I had written was that there is 'one consideration'—

Which is in a sense insulting to living and suffering people [which] is simply that, to a historian, fifty years is too short a time to judge a new social system, if such a system is arising. The comparison of course is with the protracted and contradictory events which signalled the arrival of capitalism-as-system onto the historical scene.

That is a philosophical consideration, which occupied half a paragraph in a 100-page essay, and which I readily agree offers no comfort to anyone living or dead. It does not take one far, and I did not follow it. But it is not an improper reflection to pass through a historian's head, nor to be placed on some Index of Impermissible Thoughts. It is made the occasion, by both authors, for paroxysms of polemic. Thus McConnell:

> Fifty years was ample time to consolidate the revolution, murder the socialist opposition, eliminate all freedoms of speech and publication, shut down the elected parliament, destroy the agricultural system, conquer and collectivize a dozen neighbouring countries, establish a gargantuan system of slave labour, commit political murders on a Hitlerian scale, and, finally, brandish a nuclear arsenal unprecedented in size at every nation in the world where people are free to elect their rulers.

And thus Wieseltier:

> Thompson is pretty serene. . . about the satanic statistics of Stalin's reign—fifty years may be too short a time to judge a new social system, but it was ample time to kill maybe a hundred million people. . .

If we leave aside the point that they are addressing a different question (I was asking whether, in the long historical perspective, the social system had a potential for evolution or self-transformation), these passages suggest authors for whom the display of self-righteous emotion is more important than reflection upon evidence. The USSR is not the only power which is brandishing an unprecedented nuclear arsenal, and Wieseltier's figures suggest that only a minority of the Soviet populace may ever be allowed to have died from natural causes. In a footnote he explains why he believes 'this almost unbelievable figure'. His total is totted up by including a figure of 32 millions who died in the Second World War—a figure well in excess of generally-accepted estimates. It is an offence, not only against truth, but also against any possible reconciliation of minds with the Soviet people, for Western writers to suggest that these '32 million' victims of Hitler's invasion were killed by Communism's own malice.

Wieseltier also asserts that I believe that 'there is an equivalence of evil between the superpowers', and he dances around contrasting Communist totalitarian tyranny with American rights. It is curious that the same accusation provokes the fury of ideologists in the Communist world. According to the Czech Communist daily, *Rude Pravo* (August 25, 1984), I am a 'notorious anti-communist' working on behalf of 'the US Information Agency' (CIA) to 'influence the peace movement according to Washington's ideas':

> Thompson demands that the peace movement should be non-political and non-aligned and professes a theory of equal responsibility of the two 'superpowers'. Equal responsibility, equal distance, equal guilt—this is rhetoric which deliberately ignores the facts as to who unleashes new rounds of the arms race, although the facts strike one right in the eyes.

As it happens I have not ever argued about 'equal' responsibility, as if this were some nicely-calibrated 'balance' of moral missiles. I was willing to debate with Caspar Weinberger that 'there is no moral difference in the *foreign* policies' of the superpowers, although the words of that motion were chosen by the Oxford Union. There is no moral difference in foreign policies because both superpowers pursue, not morality, but their own interests. What we said, in the END Appeal (1980) was:

> We do not wish to apportion guilt between the political and military leaders of East and West. Guilt lies squarely upon both parties. Both parties have adopted menacing postures and have committed aggressive actions in different parts of the world.

Guilt lies squarely upon both parties, but that does not mean that guilt lies equally upon both at all times and for all things. Now one, now the other is more awful, and the Americans are generally gold medallists in the arms race Olympics while the Russians take the medals in the ideological marathon.

What I have argued is that the superpowers, and their attendant blocs, stand in a *reciprocal* relationship to each other, mutually inciting each others' armourers and ideologists, feeding upon each others' hostilities. In proposing this as a direction commanding whole societies, and as a logic of process, I may have abstracted the pressure of this logic from the full social context, and suggested a determinism which would render the efforts of the peace movement futile. I have sought to correct this in 'Exterminism Reviewed' (*The Heavy Dancers*,* p. 135). But I have never at any time suggested an identity or an 'equivalence of evil' (Wieseltier) in the opposing societies. How did we get into such an absurd non-question?

We got into it, I think, because Wieseltier's kind of anti-Communism requires that emotion expend itself in repeated public displays of moral abhorrence of the Other, and that this is its own sufficient end. Yet even if all that McConnell and Wieseltier say about the past fifty years of Soviet history is true (and some part of it is, give or take 32 million lives), what is left unsaid is that the Soviet Union has changed in extensive ways since Stalin's death, the *gulags* have shrunk, the 'disappeared ones' are now few, there are even some fragile rules and norms of law, and the cultural potential is changing all the time. This might be a moment, not for strengthening 'deterrence', but for strategies to moderate the political relations between the blocs.

But the very notion of this throws Wieseltier into a new moral apoplexy, provoked, on this occasion, not by myself but by Mr George Kennan. For Kennan has offended by arguing that 'we have to put an end to the often systematic

---

* My notions were exposed to criticism by many authors in the collection *Exterminism and Cold War* (Verso/NLB, 1982). The discussion has now been carried forward vigorously by Ken Coates, 'The Peace Movement and Socialism', in *The Most Dangerous Decade* (Spokesman, 1984).

condemnation of another great people and its government—
a condemnation which if not stopped will really make war
inevitable by making it seem inevitable'. But (says Wieseltier) to 'put an end to the systematic condemnation' of the
Soviet Union 'is to put an end to the telling of the truth'.
He accuses Kennan of pleading that, 'Because of the
possibility of nuclear war, the United States may do nothing,
in words or in deeds, to express its profound philosophical
differences with the Soviet Union.' And if the United States
were to follow Kennan's advice and 'exercise restraint in
the tragic question of human rights', this would 'deprive
the victims. . . of their only hope'.

The key to this passage may be found in the last three
words, 'their only hope'. It has a self-congratulatory
resonance. It massages the American ego to know that they
are the 'only hope' of all those myriads without 'human
rights'. As Mr Wieseltier crosses the campus, or perhaps
walks back from his publisher, his breast must swell with
pride to know that he is 'the only hope' of countless victims.
But I do not know that he is. Nor even that America is. For
many 'victims' in the Communist world, American cold
war heroics are only a pain. They make their situation worse,
by identifying them as suspect sympathisers with the Other.
They offer no way, no way at all, of transforming the Communist world. With the exception of a few individuals, and
the major and important exception of the Jewish emigration,
these heroics have hindered the cause of 'human rights' more
then they have helped. And the Jewish emigration from the
Soviet Union, by draining out tens of thousands of gifted
and internationally-minded people (who certainly had the
right to live where they chose) did nothing to assist the
renewal of Soviet society. The only society that it may have
transformed is Brighton Beach in Brooklyn.

I do not wish American citizens to cease to be concerned
with human rights. I only wish that the United States *government* would shut up. From our standpoint, neither President
Reagan nor Mr Chernenko look like profound philosophers.
Mr Kennan is, of course, right; the business of governments
is to deal in a business-like way with their international

interests and relations, and not to pronounce each other
'evil empires' or 'sworn enemies' in the advance of a declaration of war. If American and Soviet philosophers wish to
argue about their profound differences, then let them do so
directly as philosophers and not as the catspaws of states.

A great deal of humbug is stirred up when states become
involved in philosophy, whether the universals of 'socialism'
or 'human rights'. I strongly support commitment to human
rights, when it comes from informed voluntary agencies,
like Amnesty International or Helsinki Watch, or from the
solidarity actions of citizens. But the NATO politicians who
engage in a *jihad* against Communists on grounds of human
rights are guilty of transparent hypocrisy, and on at least
four counts. First, for their double-standards which are
too notorious to merit discussion. (There are more political
prisoners today in Turkey, NATO's loyal ally, than in any
East European nation—and that is before we look into Latin
America or Asia.) Second, these politicians celebrate movements in Communist countries, such as the huge self-
management movements of Solidarnosc, which they would
put down with riot police in their own. (As Mrs Thatcher's
government has recently been demonstrating.) Third,
NATO's professed ardour is a bluff which has long been
called: Hungary (1956), Prague (1968), and so on. And
any 'dissidents' with any sense know it. Fourth, NATO's cold
warriors need the suffering of the victims and want it to go
on. It is the strongest card in the whole cold war pack. It is
good for war business and it is good for their own self-
image. 'Human rights' are for NATO politicians the 'last
refuge of the scoundrel'. They are good for the election of
Presidents.

The 'only hope' of the victims does not rest in Mr Wieseltier nor in President Reagan but *in themselves*. If the
Communist world is to be democratised or transformed,
this will be done, in their own time and in their own way,
by their own peoples. The help that can be brought from
outside is small, and it will not be brought by a self-
congratulatory Other with a Pershing II in his right hand
and Central American blood on his left. The damage that can

be brought from outside is immense. It is being brought by
cold warriors every day. It is here that the Western peace
movement has a different entitlement and might even be of
some small service. By initiating an alternative healing-
process it might loosen the bonds of security and open the
windows of communication. Human rights are a proper
concern of the peace movement, not as a precondition for
disarmament but as *part of the process of making peace.*

This alternative way, which is neither the addiction to
deterrence nor surrender, is one which Wieseltier's mind is
simply incapable of receiving. Anti-Communism blocks
entry to the ideas which many Europeans have been proposing, and he can only deal with us by beating up the
favourite straw man of the century, 'Better Red than Dead'.

> Neutralism—or, as Thompson prefers, 'internationalism' [There is
> a difference. E.P.T.]—is presented as a logical requirement of dis-
> armament. So, too, is 'better Red than dead'; or, as one of
> Thompson's lieutenants in European Nuclear Disarmament said,
> 'better Finnish than finished'. So, too, is the idea of unilateral
> disarmament. Unilateralism is a disgraceful notion, produced by
> people who think so little of themselves that they believe in nothing
> except life. Neutralism is an admission of philosophical exhaustion.
> Staying above the war of ideas is not a spiritual triumph; it is a
> spiritual collapse. It represents a loss of interest in the principles at
> stake in political systems. And 'better Red than dead' is an insult
> to those who believe 'better dead than Red'. . . It is not only a
> response to the threat of extinction; it is an attitude towards public
> life which affects the moral and psychological preparedness to resist
> totalitarianism at any time.

That is a mouthful, written by a very self-confident
moralist. But whose ideas is he writing about? What is he
writing against? There is one quotation, 'better Finnish than
finished' which is attributed in his footnotes to 'Jolyan
Howarth. . . in a conversation with the author'. When I
confronted Dr Jolyon Howorth with this passage he was
astonished, partly to find such a witticism (of which he had
no recollection) attributed to him, but much more to
discover that he was my 'lieutenant'. He could recall a
heated conversation one night at Harvard with someone who

did not listen and he supposed that this could have been
Wieseltier.

There are three distinct issues in this package: neutralism,
unilateralism and 'Better Red than Dead'. We will take them
in inverse order. Since the Western peace movement is such
a motley, diverse crowd it is probable that some persons
somewhere have been saying 'Better Red than Dead'.* I have
never seen it on a banner, or in the movement's literature,
nor heard it from a platform. Wieseltier knows, or could
know if he did any reading, that it is not an axiom supported by any responsible peace movement. He knows perfectly
well that he will find nothing like it in my own writings,
which is why he has recourse to the stratagem of attributing
a quite different witticism, without permission, to an un-
recorded private conversation with someone whom he
describes, in absurd military terminology, as my 'lieutenant'.
These are disreputable procedures.

I do not know who first invented the phrase. It was
around in the late Fifties in Britain, when it was employed
against CND by the peace movement's *opponents*.† And it
has been employed in this way ever since. To those who are
working for an alternative to both, it is of course a trick
question, very much like 'Have you stopped beating your
wife?', to which no answer is possible. It is also a question
which confuses the individual choice with the general case.
When in the late Fifties Professor A.J.P. Taylor, who was
then active in CND, was asked it by a hostile interviewer,
he is reported to have replied that he personally would opt

---

* Christa Wolf, in an entry dated April 1981, refers to 'Better Red
than Dead' as a 'West German catch phrase you often hear these
days': *Cassandra* (Virago, 1984).

† Bertrand Russell has sometimes been accused of originating the
phrase. Ken Coates, of the Russell Peace Foundation, has pointed
out to me, in a private communication, that Russell was at pains,
on several occasions, to refute the suggestion. Thus he wrote in
Unarmed Victory (1963, p. 50) of American attitudes of 'firmness'
against Communism: 'They had been indoctrinated with the
pernicious belief that only the American way of life can be tolerated.
The only other point of view that they saw lay in the attitude
"better red than dead"—a slogan which has been fathered upon
me, although it is not mine but a translation of the slogan of a
hostile German journalist. I believe in the possibility of co-existence.'

for death rather than surrender to a Communist occupation, but that neither he nor any government had the right to take this personal decision on behalf of a whole population, including the infants and the unborn.

It is an axiom, then, which lives as a taunt employed by polemicists *against* the peace movement, and the intention is to display us as defeatists or cowards and to close off any discussion of alternatives. There is also a trick of language here. In English the jaunty rhyme is clearly half-polemic, half-jest. But in French *(plutôt rouge que mort)* it has lost all taint of wit, and it can then be laid out with solemnity upon the shelves of *Paris Match* or *Art Press* as an example of the 'slogan' adopted by English (or American or German) *pacifistes*—a specimen to be dissected with elaborate philosophical disquisitions as to the subterfuges, liaisons and self-delusions of the human soul, and, in particular, as to the Anglo-Germanic threat to Parisian post-Maoist café culture. *Le pacifisme* is a disease against which France must be 'vaccinated', and M. André Glucksmann (who has suffered from most known ideological diseases in his time) is ready with the vaccine, culled from his own blood.

The present dissociation between French and other West European political cultures, and the misrecognitions between them, is indeed a problem, and one which must be overcome.* The Parisian intelligentsia has got into some complacent and provincial habits. In some directions it is deaf to any discourse which has not been approved by the priests of the local cults. In other directions it is sensitive, even to excess; it does indeed (if tardily) concern itself with human rights; it gave far more support to the Polish renewal (and its aftermath) than the British or German intelligentsia did; and it has remembered Afghanistan when others have forgotten. And for this reason the French language is a carrier of concepts (including *le pacifisme*) to some of our friends

---

* See the excellent discussions in Jolyon Howorth and Patricia Chilton (eds.), *Defence and Dissent in Contemporary France* (Croom Helm, 1984); Jolyon Howorth, *France: the Politics of Peace* (Merlin/END, 1984); and in Diana Johnstone, *The Politics of Euromissiles*, Chapter Three.

in East Europe, who naturally suppose that what the French tell them must be true and of good report.

There is a trick of language here also. *Le pacifisme, les pacifistes allemagnes*, confuse the concepts of pacifism and of the peace movement. I am told by another 'lieutenant' (that is, friend), Dr Paul Chilton, that *le pacifisme*,

> Appears to lump together the whole range of attitudes towards defence and security to be found in the peace movement and implies that they are all 'pacifist' in the strict sense that they reject all forms of defence through physical force. In contrast with most utilisations of the word *pacifism* in English, the French utilisation, however, has an invariably pejorative meaning. It is thus hard, for example, to predicate the word of oneself or one's group: to say 'je suis pacifiste' is as odd in many contexts as to say 'I am a treacherous coward'.

Because of the weight of a particular political and linguistic inheritance, *le pacifisme* can be employed pejoratively, to imply something a little more than 'surrender' and only a little less than 'quisling'. That is, the axiom 'better Red than Dead' appears to be already built in to it. And since the loudest peace movement in France, the *Mouvement de la paix*, is, unlike that in any other West European country, a Communist-dominated movement with a pro-Moscow inheritance, some of whose actors are certainly 'Red', this seems to confirm the linguistic shift. It is against all these problems that our friends in the non-aligned French movement, CODENE, must contend.

It is a tragic misrecognition that the complex political enterprise of the non-aligned peace movements should have been caricatured as 'Better Red than Dead'. This is perhaps because a vocal portion of the French intelligentsia has blindfolded its eyes with the words *le pacifisme* and has passed on this lazy libel to their friends in the East. But the same blindfold obscures the vision of the liberal apologists for 'deterrence theory' in the United States. These basic 'cold war assumptions' were long ago identified by Father Thomas Merton:

> The first and greatest of all commandments is that America shall not and must not be beaten in the Cold War, and the second is like

unto this if a hot war is necessary to prevent defeat in the Cold War then a hot war must be fought even if civilization is to be destroyed. . . The one great 'reality' is the threat of Communism, and all else is illusion, fantasy, speculation, theory or what you will. . . It amounts almost to an obsession and this is what really worries me most: so many good and reasonable and intelligent and well trained minds are held captive by this absolute principle which makes them unable to. . . take any other viewpoint than that of cold war military practicality.*

It is because of this 'obsession' that intelligent minds block out the consideration of any possible alternative, and when they encounter certain key-words, such as 'unilateral', they react with knee-jerks: 'disgraceful!' This is strange, since for thirty-odd years the multiplication of nuclear weaponry has been going on by unilateral additions on one side or the other. Among the intelligent minds which have recently contributed to nuclear debate are those of Mr Robert MacNamara and Mr George W. Ball. Both of course are convicted unilateralists, since they were in office—Mr Mac-Namara as Secretary for Defense and Mr Ball as US Under Secretary of State—during a period of unprecedented US nuclear armament, carried through unilaterally and justified by falsified estimates as to a 'missile gap'. It has been estimated that in the period 1960–1964 United States ICBMs increased from 18 to 834 (the Soviet Union's complement increasing, also unilaterally, from 4 to 200), while US tactical nuclear warheads in Europe increased from 2,500 to 7,000.† I do not point this out in order to disallow MacNamara and Ball's voices in the current debate (I find Mr Mac-Namara's recent confessions and second thoughts to be moving and honourable). But I do so in order to plead with them to show more humility towards those of us who, in those same years, were arguing that unilateral refusals or subtractions, rather than additions, might further the cause of peace.

---

*   Thomas Merton to W.H. Ferry, March 6, 1962, in *Letters from Tom*, ed. W.H. Ferry (Scarsdale, 1984).

†   A cogent summary of this period is in Robert Neild, *How to Make Up Your Mind about the Bomb* (1981), pp. 23–27.

Mr Ball, however, follows Mr Wieseltier in finding 'the idea of unilateral disarmament. . . a disgraceful notion'. And this is taken, unexamined. I cannot rebuke American commentators for supposing that the policy of the West European peace movement, and in particular of British CND as well as the British Labour Party, is that of 'unilateral disarmament', since this has frequently been reported as uncontested fact, not only by the American media, but also, to the British public (in particular during the General Election of 1983) by such agencies as the publicly-financed British Broadcasting Corporation (which has a pretence of being non-partisan).

But the policy of CND and of the British Labour Party is *not* 'unilateral disarmament'. It may help to clarify this point if I reproduce some passages of an article which I published in the *Observer* in November 1983 in response to a column by Mr Conor Cruise O'Brien.

CND's most famous doctrinal commitment ('unilateral nuclear disarmament') is a recommendation to *this* nation [i.e. Britain]. Like most doctrines it should be understood in its historical origin. It was the founding charter of CND, over 25 years ago, and was graven on tablets by Bertrand Russell, Canon Collins, A.J.P. Taylor, J.B. Priestley, Peggy Duff, James Cameron and the other founders.'

It was, in origin, the first demand to stop 'proliferation'. America and Russia had "the Bomb" (and it is interesting to recall that It used to be thought of in the singular). If Britain were to set an example by refusing the Bomb, then this might seal off further proliferation.* It is tragic for us—and perhaps for the world—that CND, first time around, did not win.

CND remains loyal to its founders' charter. It continues to argue, cogently, that nuclear weapons are a suicidal property upon this island; are obscene; and that a non-nuclear defence would greatly enhance our national security.

This policy is not 'unilateral disarmament' (as TV presenters snicker) but unilateral *nuclear* disarmament; and this, not for one

---

* The ineffable Mr Gerald Frost, who is still maundering on in *Encounter*, and who cannot write three words without getting one wrong, offers to correct an earlier folly (*Encounter*, 'Letters', Sept–Oct 1984) by saying: 'As for "all those marches to Aldermaston", most of them were not *to* the Aldermaston US Air Force base, but *from*. . .'. They were of course from the (British) Aldermaston Weapons Research Establishment, and they were in protest against the manufacture of British nuclear weapons.

bloc in the Cold War confrontation only (without reciprocation from the other bloc) but for *this* country—as an initiative to get the multilateral thing moving.

That ought to be clear, although the media make it as clear as mud.

It is also of interest that CND's policy is more radical, on this point, than many other sections of the Western peace movement. Few major European movements are 'unilateralist'—partly because they don't inhabit nuclear-weapons-owning nations. The majority Italian and Belgian movements agitate for 'balanced reductions'. The Dutch movement has a policy similar to CND ('let's get rid of nuclear weapons from the world, starting with Holland!') but the German movement is, essentially, united around the demand to stop Pershing II and cruise, while the United States majority movement works for a freeze.

That still seems to me to put the position plainly. Some imperfectly-informed observers suppose that 'the peace movement' has one single, abstract, universal platform (which is then sometimes described as 'unilateral*ism*', as if a tactic or national strategy could be presented as a philosophical '*ism*'!). But all that is universal in this multitude of movements, with their differing national accentuations, is the world-wide growth of peace consciousness, with its dimensions of fear, love and hope and its refusal of the means of genocide.

This globe is not going to get rid of nuclear weapons in one single move, like cutting a tape with scissors. It is entirely proper that different national movements will adopt differing policies: thus, Scandinavian and Balkan movements are concerned with regional nuclear-free zones; the Spanish movement is interested in moving Spain out of NATO to add her influence to the non-aligned nations such as Sweden, Yugoslavia and Austria; some of our friends in the East are more concerned with ideological disarmament (with 'dialogue' and the building of 'trust'); while the movements in West Germany are preoccupied with various proposals for healing the wound of Central Europe (demilitarised corridors? a new Rapacki-style zone? the neutralisation of both Germanies?). The largest British movement, CND, has long supported the refusal of all nuclear weapons on British soil and waters.

The reasons for CND's policy (which is now endorsed by the British Labour Party and by several smaller political parties) have been written out with patience and by many expert hands. British 'independent' nuclear weapons (which are not independent) are a nostalgic and expensive imperial status symbol, while American weapons on our territory subvert our independence and reduce us to cliency. Since there is now a grotesque surplus of weaponry in Europe this affords space for certain nations (Britain and Holland) to get rid of them, without endangering any notional 'balance' between the superpowers, in the hope of initiating an alternative (and reciprocal) process of multilateral disarmament. For decades the superpowers have ignored all other nations (even their dearest allies) and bored the world to death with 'negotiations' whose only outcome has been to legitimate the absurd increment of weapons. We envisage unilateral refusals (that is, unilateral subtractions instead of additions) as a means of negotiating directly by *actions*, and in the hope of calling forth some response.

CND's policy of unilateral refusal is a policy for Britain, and we have not set up an export agency to impose our policy on peace workers in other nations. It is true that from time to time we have recommended to both superpowers immediate unilateral initiatives (negotiation by actions) as a means of getting the reciprocal process going. Some of us approve of Charles Osgood's GRIT strategy (graduated reductions in tension) by which one power or another makes a substantial unilateral reduction in some weapons-system, holds the ratchet, and awaits a response. (There is abundant fat in every system to try these things.) If the majority of American peace workers consider that the freeze is the most viable strategy, then that is their affair and we will not interfere. So long as they understand that this is *their* strategy, and it does not therefore have to be *ours*. If the superpowers could only agree to STOP, and to hold the arms equilibrium steady, this might be precisely the time when intermediate lesser powers can run down their stocks and make a space of quiet between the giants.

It will be seen that what harmonises in this ill-conducted orchestra of European (and, increasingly, Asian, Australasian and Third World) movements is the mounting pressure to move out from under, and to resume some national autonomy. For decades the superpowers have glared at each other, eyeball to eyeball, over our heads. It now seems to be beyond the mental capacity of some Americans and some Russians to allow entry to the notion that there might be some other ball-game than their own. This mental prohibition affects the hawks and doves of both Establishments alike. The hawks shift their client states around, and deposit their nuclear stool on their territories (Britain, Sicily, both Germanies, Czechoslovakia) at will. The doves elaborate 'arms control' agendas, in which the clients remain unconsulted but controlled. They do not mind a little nonalignment, if it seems to tip the balance of things their own way: Romania is applauded by NATO for making faces at SS-20s, Greece is applauded by Soviet leaders for making faces at American bases. But authentic independent initiatives which call in question the whole ball-game draw down the anathemas of both houses.

I find that these anathemas are visited, with increasing frequency, upon my own white head. Week after week they plop through the letter-box, some from one side, some from the other. It is unnerving to find that I am a target for the ideological missiles of both blocs. When I am working in my Worcestershire garden and a helicopter hovers overhead, I am tempted to run and hide. It might be theirs or it might be theirs, but it cannot be one of ours because all we have are typewriters and marching feet.

The Soviet ideologists do not trouble with the niceties of argument but go straight into political hard-porn. Mr Yuri Zhukov, the President of the Soviet Peace Committee, has recently explained in *International Life* (June 1984) that 'having made a painful reappraisal of the current situation, U.S. and NATO psychological warfare units are attempting to sabotage some of the anti-nuclear movements from the inside, smuggling their own instructions and ideas into them'. I am singled out for attention by Mr Zhukov as a leader of one of these 'units', and Mr G. Lokshin, the Secretary of this same peace-loving Committee, adds the names of the Bertrand Russell Peace Foundation; the British END Committee; Mr Mient-Jan Faber, the general secretary of the Dutch Interchurch Peace Council (IKV); and, for good measure, the IPCC (International Peace Communications and Coordination Centre), an office in The Hague which brings into regular conferences nearly all the major European (as well as some American) non-aligned peace movements, including the Norwegian, Swedish, Danish, Italian, Spanish, West German, Belgian, Swiss, Finnish, Irish, French CODENE and British CND. (I am sorry about all these acronyms, but the European peace movement is now a complex beast.) I am simply pointing out that Mr Zhukov and Mr Lokshin have just 'unmasked' a quite extraordinary conspiracy in which the most powerful European peace movements turn out to be under the control of 'US and NATO psychological warfare units'.

Mr Lokshin's article gives more details as to how this has come about:

In NATO's arsenal of methods of subversion directed against the anti-war movement, an ever-greater place is being given to ideological warfare. This is carried out partly with the help of various front organizations and groups that insinuate themselves into the anti-war movement. . . E.P. Thompson, an English historian and sociologist, widely publicized of late, a former professor at Oxford University [not guilty. E.P.T.], is the noisiest mouthpiece of these anti-Soviet conceptions. As to the views of this Thompson concerning the internal political situation in the USSR—views which he strenuously advertises on any convenient occasion—these are simply a mixture of absolute ignorance with the basest of lies spread by Cold War professionals. (*International Life*, June 1984.)

I do not mind so much about this invective, which is the only language Soviet ideologists know how to employ. I have got used to it over the years. As long ago as 1958 a writer in *Novy Mir* unmasked me as a 'renegade', 'traitor', 'anarchist' and 'philosophising slanderer', and the file has been kept up-to-date ever since. But I will admit that I do somewhat resent the suggestion that I, and END, and the

Russell Foundation are 'agents of NATO and imperialism. . . infiltrated by Western Secret Services' into a movement which, in its present form, we helped to start.

As for myself, I was 'infiltrated' into the peace movement in 1945, when Britain intervened in the civil war in Greece, and have been there, in one capacity or another, through the times of Korea and German re-armament, the first wave of CND, and the Vietnam War. As I look back down those forty years I could even be bitter that wars and the threat of nuclear war have eaten half of the lives of myself, my family and my closest friends.

But I mean to go on. I am willing even—distasteful as it would be—to talk once again with Mr Zhukov and Mr Lokshin, if an occasion should arise when it might be productive of any good. This occasion may well not arise, since (Mr Lokshin explains to his Soviet readers) Mient-Jan Faber and I are currently preoccupying ourselves with attempts to pull the anti-war movement—

> into an authentic 'crusade' against the socialist fraternity, while cynically hiding themselves behind stolen banners of peace. E. Thompson incites his listeners by saying: 'We have to begin acting as if a unified, neutral and peaceful Europe already existed'.

So that we now know the full measure of my anti-Soviet incitements. As it happens this terrible phrase is not strictly mine (although I first drafted it) but is taken from the European Nuclear Disarmament Appeal of April 1980:

> We must commence to act as if a united, neutral and pacific Europe already exists. We must learn to be loyal, not to 'East' or 'West', but to each other, and we must disregard the prohibitions and limitations imposed by any national state.

I have already noted that this Appeal was signed by thousands across the continent (and also in Australia, Japan and the USA) and so far from being 'infiltrated' at a late stage was a major initiative setting the movement in motion.

This Appeal signalled that the signatories—and the movements which ensued—were no longer content to play on either side of the superpower ball-game. Nor were we even content to watch from the sidelines and say 'shush' to both parties. We were setting up a new game in a different place, in which we were going to attempt to make peace between citizens in contempt of the blocs and their ideologies; and we explicitly declared that 'we must defend and extend the right of all citizens, East or West, to take part in this common movement and to engage in every kind of exchange'. As for the political stance of a peaceful Europe, I would today prefer the term 'non-aligned' to 'neutral', since it signifies an active, peace-making diplomacy, a third way, rather than a passive opting-out in the hope of self-preservation.

It is here that we must return (I must hope for the last time) to the Little Blue Book of Chairman Wieseltier. For Wieseltier is quite as scandalised by me as are Comrades Zhukov and Lokshin. He indicts me as an advocate of European 'neutralism', which he takes to mean that 'there is no need to take sides in the struggle between the United States and the Soviet Union if it makes no difference who wins'. This is a remarkably silly statement. If there is a 'struggle' between the US and the USSR, which must be fought out to some 'winning' finish, then this is a disaster for both parties; and if either side were to 'win' it would be a total disaster for Europe, culturally, spiritually, materially, and politically. It is a no-win situation. Europeans are bored by this Pretend War, and are increasingly alarmed by it (since it might at any moment become real). They wish neither the USA nor the USSR to 'win' it, and they are forming some notion of mediating between these overmighty strugglers and of asking them both to go home.

But 'neutralism', for Wieseltier, 'is an admission of philosophical exhaustion. Staying above the war of ideas is not a spiritual triumph; it is a spiritual collapse. It represents a loss of interest in the principles at stake in political systems'. No, Mr Wieseltier: you are a specimen case of the 'obsession' against which Father Thomas Merton has warned us. You project your American ego upon the world, just as Zhukov projects the ego of Soviet man, and presume to impose upon it a 'struggle' in which there may be only two 'sides': the Other and your own. You have the presumption to impose this same stunted binary definition of 'the principles at stake in political systems' upon the intellectual and spiritual world: once again, there can be only two 'sides', the Other and your own, and 'the war of ideas' must be a war between only such ideas as will pass muster with the sidesmen. Has it never occurred to you, Mr Wieseltier, that there might be three sides, or four, or five? Is there some binary determinism in the human mind which breeds this Soviet-American arrogance? How did the great globe, in all its historical diversity, shrivel (in the minds of Soviet and American ideologists) into the two halves of a Manichean walnut?

It is perhaps true that there is a certain 'loss of interest in the principles at stake in political systems', if the only systems admitted to view are those of the United States and the Soviet Union. This 'loss of interest' may be felt, not only in Europe, but throughout the world, and not least among the publics of these nations. Yet it is arrogant in Wieseltier to conclude that this signals 'a spiritual collapse' among the lesser breeds without the law. What makes for anxiety is the sense that we are witnessing, in very different ways, the spiritual collapse of *both* systems under the weight of their obsessional confrontation—a collapse which will drag us all down together.

The obsession which may destroy the world is precisely this: that there may be only two 'sides'. This is to enforce a closure upon all alternative lines of political and spiritual growth, and to lock the blocs onto an inexorable collision-course. American and Soviet ideologists, who ceaselessly strive to conscript all human resources to one side or the other, are genuinely unaware that in doing so they may be writing the death-warrant of their own civilizations. For their own future, as well as that of Europe and the Third World, may depend upon new forces and new spaces entering in between the adversaries, pressing them gently apart, and enabling them to unlock from their death-wishing struggling.

That is what we suppose that we are attempting, in the European peace movements. As the ideological missiles of both sides plop through our postboxes it scarcely seems that we are 'staying above the war of ideas'. We appear to have touched that war at such a sensitive place that both Mr Zhukov and Mr Wieseltier forget to 'struggle' with each other and combine their forces to struggle against us.

Both of these mighty strugglers reveal the imperial mentality of the superpowers. Mr Zhukov considers that the European peace movements ought to be auxiliaries of Soviet diplomacy and, indeed, pay deference to his leadership. He is scandalised, and the entire official Communist and World Peace Council apparatus is scandalised, by the suggestion that there could be co-responsibility by both superpowers for the world's predicament. Mr Wieseltier is no less scandalised. He announces, as a theorem which admits of no discussion, that 'for moral ends the United States has made an extraordinary commitment to Europe'. This 'commitment' is witnessed by the nuclear excreta which the United States had deposited on the lands and seas of Western Europe. These represent a commitment to 'extended' deterrence, which locks West Europe and America together in the war of Two Camps.

And so indeed it does. I will not follow Mr Wieseltier into his chapter on 'The Case of Europe', since it is spectacularly ill-informed. Several of his assertions are so misleading that they rival certain press conferences of President Reagan (in which he asserted that on 'their' side there were umpteen hundred SS-20s and on 'our' side there was—nothing!), and it is difficult to see how anyone pretending to intellectual credentials could descend lower than that.* What I wish to note, once again, is Wieseltier's self-congratulatory tone.

---

* Wieseltier says (of 1983) that 'the intermediate-range missiles of the Russians are met only by the long-range missiles of the Americans' bringing Western Europe into 'a single-hostage relationship' to the Soviet Union. He pretends not to have heard of Poseidon nor of several air and sea-based systems nor of the British and French systems, nor of the multitude of 'tactical' systems. He could have enlightened himself by consulting several of the works cited in his own notes, including my own *Protest and Survive*.

He is becoming 'bitter' with all Europeans: with the peace movements because they show ingratitude to the 'moral ends' of the U.S. of A., and with West European governments because they will not jump to the orders of General Bernard Rogers and engage in a massive build-up of their conventional forces. West Europe has to have cruise and Pershing 'because Europe is not prepared to take responsibility for its fate on its own'; Europeans 'prefer the nuclear peril to higher taxes'. They are willing to 'sacrifice' America 'for the sake of their standard of living'.

This is a difficult argument because there are at least three parties to it and not two: the United States, West European governments, and the peace movements both in America and Europe. These parties do not share the same interests nor the same 'moral ends'. Mr Wieseltier is right to insist that the pro-Atlanticist governments of West Europe (and notably those of Chancellors Schmidt and Kohl, Mrs Thatcher and Mr Craxi) have been accomplices before, during, and after the act of NATO 'modernisation'. It does not follow that their interests are identical. As Lord Zuckerman has noted, those who are 'immediately informed about political and strategic issues' need not necessarily share 'what seems to be the official American view of the danger of the threat that the USSR poses to their security'. For the official American view appears to come out of the heads of arms promoters, populist politicians and intrepid ideologists but not from the heads of informed observers. Living closer to the Soviet Union than Washington does, and with more opportunities to observe the symptoms of Soviet weakness and the cruel mess which is developing in Eastern Europe, common sense as well as respect for their taxes may suggest to European governments that this is not the moment to engage in a huge and provocative build-up of conventional armaments.

It is an odd situation when those who are most strident about the threat of the Other are the ideologues and politicians most remote from each other, not only in miles but in culture; whereas those supposed 'enemies' who are immediate neighbours have learned to sleep easily at night. It suggests that the Threat is continually reproduced and

amplified within American and Soviet ideology. That is not
to say that there is *no* threat, but that the threat is one which
increments of missiles and ideological incitements only feed
and make worse. As for the third party to this argument, the
peace movement, Zuckerman is surely right to say that
'while most of the protesters are not sympathetic to communism they also do not give a hoot about the *jihad* against
communism President Reagan has proclaimed. What worries
them is the picture of trigger-happy Americans'. And they
are also working on their *own* 'moral ends'.

Mr Wieseltier is a confident moralist. He is very confident
about America's moral ends, and the radiance of this
morality is reflected in his own self-approbation. I do not
wish to undermine his moral ego. I am sure that he is a true
believer in the principles of the Free World, and, for all that
I know, his fellow-moralist, Mr Yuri Zhukov, is a true
believer in the moral ends of Soviet Socialism.

I wish only to note the signs of an imperial mentality. It is
one thing for a nation to cherish moral ends; it is another to
seek to export them. To become insensitive to the moral
ends of other nations, to hector them when they will not
comply, to seek to impose upon other peoples one's own
moral ends—this is immorality.

I cannot, as an Englishman and a historian, get into
a lather about this. British imperial history is littered with
moral ends. In Victorian and Edwardian times every British
interest was vested in moralistic rhetoric as to our civilizing
mission, every Gatling gun in the Transvaal and every British-
held fleapit East of Suez was a 'moral end'. Nor was it all self-
interested rhetoric: many of the moral missionaries were true
believers, and a few of them dealt out honest coin. There was
even, perhaps, a little 'civilizing' done. Both the imperial
rulers and most of their domestic critics (the Liberals,
Radicals and Fabians—I had almost added Democrats) shared
in the same infection. The rulers taught the lesser breeds to
obey and the reformers taught them how (in civilized and
constitutional ways) they might press for reform. What was
wrong was that it was our own 'moral ends' and not the ends
opted for by other peoples which were consulted. Since we

possessed the power, we imposed our own definition of legitimate ends upon others.

It is inevitable that American and Soviet rulers, and their missionary apologists, should fall victim to the same imperial mentality. Commanding unprecedented military power, reaching far into every part of the globe, United States rulers assume that the globe should be brought into compliance with their own ends. It is not a matter about which the British should show surprise. But the precedent should be borne in mind. It is the easiest thing in the world to dress up self-interest as a moral end. The Kissinger Commission's report on Central America lists as the first goal of United States policy in that tormented zone:

> To preserve the moral authority of the United States.
> To be perceived by others as a nation that does what is right *because* it is right is one of this country's principal assets.

However 'others' may perceive the United States, this self-perception is certainly a source of national self-approbation. It was one of the loudest themes of President Reagan's loud election: 'America will never give up its great mission, never.' And, invoking America's 'manifest destiny', he offered himself as Vice-Regent of 'the God who made us and who has blessed us as no other people on earth'. A few months before, Mr Caspar Weinberger conceded that 'there is no corner of the world so remote no nation so insignificant, that it does not represent a vital interest of the United States'. The claim is one which would have brought a blush to the cheek of Cecil Rhodes. It is a chilling claim, when made by the War Minister of the most powerful nation ever known, fully capable of incinerating the earth.

Yet how is it possible that Mr Weinberger can assume this licence to intervene anywhere, by America's manifest right, unless he is, like his President, stupefied beyond recall by the axiom that whatever America may do it must be for the 'moral end'? He is, like Mr Wieseltier, punch-drunk with imperial hubris, to the point that he does not know that the rest of the world is watching him in an odd way. And the world is right to be watchful. Imperial arrogance of this order is more vicious and more dangerous than racism, sexism and all other isms which honourable Americans so consciously resist, since it compounds them all.

It was in 1965 that Father Thomas Merton warned that 'the American illusion of innocence and universal messianism is now about to unleash THE worst war that ever happened, maybe the final one'. Thomas Merton got the timing wrong but the bearings right, and American messianism is still on course. Towards 'USS Messiah' there steams, on opposing course, the imperial supertanker of Soviet socialist teleology. At present in Europe we are contemplating the 'moral ends' jettisoned in the wake of these two generous superpowers. In the churned-up waters the cruise and Pershing missiles are now copulating with the SS-21s and SS-23s, and breeding on each others' vile bodies the next generations of missiles which will burn our children. There will follow, blessed by the moralists of both sides, the moral end of the world.

▲ 'ACTING AS FREE PERSONS' ▲

The Soviet ideologues are quite as zealous only-two-sidesmen as are the most zealous apologists of NATO. They will not delay us long in argument, because argument is not their chosen medium. Confronted by the least suggestion of a third way, or of a third or fourth side, they resort instantly to slander or to political hard-porn ('CIA agents', 'NATO psychological warfare agencies', etc.). The most subtle variant of which they are capable is that of suggesting that well-meaning persons have been misled into positions which 'objectively serve the interests of. . .' (NATO, President Reagan, etc.) and which have 'nothing in common with' the positions of true 'peace champions'.

Thus Mr Lokshin, the Secretary of the Soviet Peace Committee, lamented the fact that some people were confused at CND's Annual Conference in Sheffield (December 1983) and others (identified with END) argued against the logic of 'balance' and 'persistently tried to convince us that the retaliatory measures of the Soviet Union [i.e. SS-21s and 23s on GDR and Czechoslovak territory] were allegedly unwarranted and even harmful':

> In the conditions of the unbridled anti-Soviet campaign conducted by the powerful propaganda machine of NATO countries, with the extremely limited possibilities to get truthful and objective information, the ranks of the peace champions are infiltrated with false ideas of the 'equal responsibility' of the USSR and USA. . . This is greatly influenced by all sorts of 'experts' who disguised under the

mask of 'objectivity' skilfully confuse not very experienced and misinformed people. . .

Of course, such pseudo-theoretical exercises, which fill pages of the publications issued for the anti-war activists, and which, under the guise of objectivity and so-called non-alignment, repeat the elements of NATO's official propaganda, inflict great damage on many sincere opponents of the arms race by confusing and disorienting them.

> *(Twentieth Century and Peace*—the Organ of the
> Soviet Peace Committee—2/1984.)

It is extraordinary—and a sign of its obsolescence—that Soviet ideological polemic has reduced the rich Russian language to these predictable and stagnant routines. It would be easy to say that it represents the mental reflexes of persons habituated to operating within a culture where arguments are settled by police measures or slander, rather than intellectual means; and if the vocabulary of 'masks' and 'disguises' and 'infiltration' is an indication of their own techniques of operation (perhaps within the Western peace movements?) then one must draw the most pessimistic conclusions.

Yet the curious thing is that the further one gets from public situations and official noises, the more flexible discussion may become. It is even possible to flush out from among the diplomats and officials of the 'peace' apparatus the occasional dove who (off-the-record, of course) allows a little reality to break in.

Hence this polemic is a language of public policy and of propaganda. It is not internalised. It is not a language of belief. It is a business pursued with failing conviction. The polemicists of 'peace' do not pretend to credibility, but they continue with their weary slanders because they fear that they could not control the consequences if an honest dialogue were to be thrown open between East and West. The tone of their exchanges becomes increasingly bitter, but also more brittle.

It may help readers if I outline, not so much the course of this polemic, as the events which occasioned it—the quarrelsome dialectic between alternative notions of the peace movement.

I have already described some of the ways in which the West European movement built itself up from non-aligned bases in 1980-1. Among the first few hundreds of international signatories to the European Nuclear Disarmament Appeal (April 1980) there was one solitary Soviet name: that of the courageous, independent-minded historian, Roy Medvedev. (His brother, Dr Zhores Medvedev, an involuntary exile in London, spoke at the Appeal's launching conference.) To borrow the language of our opponents, 'it is no accident that' this was the case. For an Appeal which laid guilt upon both parties, which not only called for the cancellation of NATO 'modernisation' (cruise and Pershing II) but also called on the Soviet Union to halt production of the SS-20 at its then total (of some 140 missiles), and which proclaimed that 'we must defend and extend the right of all citizens, East or West, to take part in this common movement and to engage in every kind of exchange', was unlikely to win the approval of the Soviet 'peace' apparatus.

But, as I have already noted, there has been some pro-Moscow influence in the Western peace movement, and it has been damaging and time-wasting. Some of this has come from the World Peace Council which, ever since early 1980, has been panting after the non-aligned movement, 'trying to catch hold of its coat-tails and to claim it as its own'. This Council was founded in the last years of Stalin, and has sought to impose its hegemony upon all peace movements ever since; it has offices in Helsinki, carbon-copy 'peace' committees in Communist countries, some influential affiliates in the Third World, two or three affiliates of influence in the West (including the French *Mouvement de la paix*) and a number of small unrepresentative committees without real grass-roots support (such as the British Peace Assembly and the American Peace Council).

The World Peace Council has been an organ of Soviet diplomacy for thirty years and there has never been any serious attempt to pretend that it is not. Indeed, this stance is justified on the grounds that the Soviet government's policies and proposals are in every respect the most peace-loving possible, and therefore the peace-loving masses of the world should rally to these. Neither the Council nor its Warsaw bloc affiliates have ever criticised in public any military measure or procurement on their own side, with the instructive exception of the Czechoslovak Peace Committee in 1968 which was at once disbanded. According to the tactics of the moment, the WPC may arrange international conferences which are more or less flexible in their appeal to 'all men and women of goodwill'. (The conferences promoted in Sofia, 1980, and Prague, 1983, may be examples.) But it has always been utterly inflexible in seeking to slander, contain or destroy any international peace initiative which offered alternative non-aligned perspectives.

A few authentically independent movements in the West have always sought to remain on good-neighbourly talking terms with the WPC, on the grounds that if the world is divided into two halves, someone must seek to keep open bridges of communication, however frail. These have included the International Fellowship of Reconciliation; the West German ASZ (Aktion Sühnezeichen); Western Christians co-operating with the Prague-based CPC (Christian Peace Conference). and of course the Quakers, notably the American Friends Service Committee and the British Quaker Peace and Service. (Lord Noel-Baker and Lord Brockway's World Disarmament Campaign entered into similar relations.) I make no objection to attempts at bridge-building if they are done with clear eyes and dignity, in the old Quaker spirit of 'speaking truth to power'. But sentimental efforts at East–West brokerage can be manipulated in damaging ways.

My favourite Quaker is the sturdy one who, when on shipboard in the early 19th century, found that his vessel was being boarded by pirates. Since his faith forbade him to take up arms he witnessed the scene with mounting impatience. At length, when one ruffian with a cutlass in his teeth swarmed over the side directly in front of him, he held out his hands with the quiet remark: 'Friend, thee hath no business here,' and pressed him gently back into the sea. I sometimes wish that today's Quakers would show the same courtesy to the World Peace Council ruffians who swarm up the sides of the good ship 'Peace'.

The unexpected emergence in 1980–1 of a Western peace movement from independent bases and with growing mass support was viewed by the East bloc establishment with perplexity. On the one hand, a surge of public opinion which was chiefly directed against NATO modernisation was clearly a bonus, and its supporters were not to be snubbed; on the other hand, the establishment viewed with acute suspicion a movement whose proponents included individuals and organisations committed to human rights (such as the Russell Peace Foundation and the West German 'Greens'), which made demands on Soviet militarism also, which sought to reach citizen opinion in the East, and whose members, at their demonstrations, wore the badge of Solidarnosc alongside the badges of peace. Attempts to bring the movement under World Peace Council leadership proved futile—almost no-one (except Bukovsky) was interested in that WPC event in Sofia—and open opposition would have been inopportune. The supporters of the WPC settled down to more quiet attempts to influence or manipulate the Western movement from within.

In this they met with a novel difficulty. Before 1968 it was usually possible to gain a major influence in Western peace movements by the dedication of committed Communist cadres in organising roles. But since the repression of the Prague Spring there has been a growth in Eurocommunism, one of whose leading principles has been the resistance to such kinds of Soviet manipulation. Hence the Eastern bloc establishment found that their attempts at influence were often resisted, not only by Greens and social-democrats and liberals, but also by Communists. In particular, the powerful Italian Communist Party threw its weight on the side of the non-aligned movement, as did many Eurocommunists in Spain, Finland, Britain and other countries. In certain countries the picture remained confused (for example, in West Germany where the pro-Soviet DKP long had an influence in the movement greater than its actual strength), whereas in Portugal and France, where pro-Moscow parties attempted an old-fashioned 'peace' operation, the result was to weaken the peace movement itself.

I will not waste time on the skirmishes of 1980-1. During that time the Soviet Union was steadily putting down more SS-20s, month by month. The litmus test between peace movements and 'peace' movements came to be between those which called publicly and in earnest for the halting or dismantling of SS-20s and those which forgot to mention them. Those of us who mentioned SS-20s, rather sharply, began to receive missives from the Soviet Peace Committee's office in Moscow, in language addressed to deaf children, patiently explaining that SS-20s were wholly defensive weapons developed 'in response to actions of the imperialist circles which aspire for world domination'.

On Hiroshima Day, 1981, the Dutch IKV and British END Committee issued an Appeal to all parties to cancel NATO modernisation and (to the Soviet government) to halt and commence reductions in SS-20s. We drew this Appeal to the attention of the Soviet Peace Committee and courteously invited their support: 'It is a frequent argument of our opponents. . . that peace organisations in the Soviet Union and in Eastern Europe direct their propaganda *only* against the military measures in the West and do nothing to make the same demands upon governments in the Warsaw alliance.' After a long silence END received a heavy response from Mr Oleg Kharkhardin, Vice-President of the SPC (December 11, 1981):

> Unlike anti-war public movements in the West, the Soviet peace movement exists in a country which has made the struggle for peace the basis of its foreign policy. . . No Soviet government would be able to conduct any policy other than one aimed at the security of our country and the strengthening of universal peace.

As for our Appeal in the matter of SS-20s, 'the Soviet people and their government will not agree to unilateral disarmament'.

Looking back, it is now possible to see October and November 1981 as the highest tide (until now) of the West European peace movement. Demonstrations took on epidemic proportions. There was a significant shift, an opening towards reconciliation with the East, in middle opinion. Polish Solidarity was still overground, giving rise to a hazy euphoria in which it seemed that Eastern societies were on the verge of great transitions. The defeat of NATO modernisation (then still two years ahead) seemed a practical political possibility—indeed, President Reagan sought to contain, not the SS-20s but the peace movement, with his 'zero option' in late November. A thaw in the cold war seemed to be almost within reach.

Euphoria ended on December 13th, 1981, with the hammer blow of martial law in Poland. A few months later Britain disappeared into the black hole of the Falklands War. By contrast with 1981, 1982 was a bitter and complex year. It ended with the first overt attempt by the Communist establishment to split the Western peace movement and bring a part of it within their control.

The attempt was signalled in a letter from Yuri Zhukov, President of the Soviet Peace Committee (December 2, 1982) which came through the postboxes of dozens of Western peace organisations and individuals. In July 1982, largely as a result of the energetic initiatives of the Russell Peace Foundation, there had been held in Brussels a successful European Nuclear Disarmament Convention. Full rights of participation had been limited to those organisations and individuals which were signatories to the END Appeal of April 1980; but others were welcomed as observers, including representatives from the Hungarian and Romanian Peace Committees. The Soviet Peace Committee had pretended to immense insult at this procedure. How dare anyone presume to convene an anti-war conference without inviting them onto the rostrum as full plenary participants? (It was never explained why it was legitimate for the World Peace Council to convene its own affiliates and invited guests at Sofia, or at Moscow or Helsinki, but illegitimate for the supporters of the END Appeal to do the same.)

Arising from the Brussels Convention an international END Liaison Committee was established (comprising major Western peace movements) to prepare for a Second END

Convention in 1983, and an invitation was accepted from a working-group (of Greens, Social-Democrats and 'Alternative List') in West Berlin. Both CND and the British END Committee were at first unhappy about the choice of Berlin as venue, since we knew that it might arouse the Russians' susceptibilities and be regarded as a 'provocation'; but our doubts were silenced, we (and most major Western peace organisations) gave our support, and, in the event, no terrible 'provocations' took place (apart from Petra Kelly and some Greens sallying into East Berlin with 'Swords into Ploughshares' badges and 'Make Love not War' T-shirts!).

Possessed by his ideological fantasies, Mr Zhukov was determined to be thoroughly provoked, many months before the event. The choice of Berlin as venue was intended (he said) to 'resuscitate revanchist sentiments', and the very discussion of 'the German question' would 'challenge the inviolability of the post-war European frontiers'. But Zhukov's polemic took in the whole non-aligned movement. The 'true objective' of the Convention's sponsors, and of 'so-called' END, was to 'split the anti-war movement', 'infiltrate cold war elements into it', and 'push the anti-war movement off the right way': i.e. a 'united universal anti-war movement' in which the official peace committees of Warsaw bloc nations should be equal participants. No less than his fellow only-two-sidesmen, Messrs Frost and Wieseltier, Mr Zhukov was driven into a frenzy by the notion of superpower co-responsibility. The leaders of the Russell Foundation and END—

> Keep foisting on others their concept of 'equal responsibility'. We are firmly convinced that this concept is aimed at the disorientation, demobilisation and undermining of the anti-war movement, and is called upon to conceal and justify an aggressive militarist policy of the USA and NATO. . .
>
> It is a truly monstrous design to try and use the banner of peace in order to draw the anti-war movement into what is to all intents and purposes a 'cold war' against the public in socialist countries. . .

The British END Committee responded to this vitriol with a long and carefully-reasoned reply, published by END's

Secretary, Meg Beresford, in the *New Statesman*, January 21, 1983. END reassured Mr Zhukov as to Berlin 'provocations', clarified its views as to superpower co-responsibility, and discussed in detail the steady increment in SS-20s:

> We invite you to reconsider your basic premise, which is that Western weapons must be aggressive and bad whereas Soviet weapons must be defensive and good. And we invite you to turn your backs upon the futile arguments of 'balance' (which are questions for military advisors and not for peace workers) and put your faith instead in a transcontinental movement of peoples. . . It is the first responsibility of peace activists in every nation to watch and to criticise the military policies of their own nation first of all.

END went on to explain its views on the bloc division of Europe:

> Barbed wire divides not only the territories of the two blocs, there is also barbed wire in peoples' minds and hearts. The change which we work for can only come about after a preparatory process in which people on both sides come into closer communication with each other, modify their perceptions of each other, learn to tolerate differences and establish mutual trust. There can be no 'victory' of one side over the other without war. Instead, there must be a healing process. . . This cannot be done by the directives of governments (which harbour, for historical reasons, deep suspicions of each other) but only, in the first place, by direct citizens' exchanges. . .
>
> If all those whom you regard as 'anti-Soviet elements' were to be purged from the Western peace movement, then that movement would be reduced in numbers from hundreds of thousands to mere hundreds. It would be reduced to a handful of small pro-Soviet committees, without influence or independence.

END also suggested that the exchange of letters might be circulated, not only in the West, but also to supporters of the Soviet Peace Committee in the Soviet Union. After two years END is still awaiting Mr Zhukov's reply. On enquiry, it turned out that the publication of END's letter in the *New Statesman* was a 'breach of protocol', making any reply 'impossible'. (It was not explained under what protocol Mr Zhukov had circulated his own bitterly-divisive letter in the Western movement.) If NATO's missiles will be sent on their way in support of 'moral ends', the SS-20s will be sent in defence of 'protocol'.

There was, however, one novel theme in Zhukov's letter, whose significance has been growing ever since. Zhukov complained bitterly about the presence at Brussels (and expected at Berlin) of a small number of émigréés or exiles from Communist countries who had given support to the non-aligned Western movement. Ironically, Zhukov's fury was most aroused by the presence at Brussels of Dr Zhores Medvedev who, with his brother Roy, had published by far the most convincing apology for Soviet militarism in terms of reaction/response to pace-setting American innovations (see *Exterminism and Cold War*, pp. 153-174). Such exiles Zhukov described as—

> A group of people who have left their countries and have nothing in common with the struggle for peace and who, while representing nobody, are busy disseminating hostile slanderous fabrications about the foreign and home policies of their former motherland.

It is clear that this was the most sensitive issue. The END Appeal had envisaged a transcontinental movement, 'a European-wide campaign, in which every kind of exchange takes place', not only between organisations but also between individuals. We knew from the outset that this would be difficult work (when Dorothy and I visited Prague in the summer of 1980 we met with little support in those critical circles who had come to view 'peace', in the aftermath of the invasion of Afghanistan, as cynical Communist rhetoric). We also knew that unofficial citizen exchanges would be resisted woodenly by the Communist apparatus. Nevertheless, we hoped that a Western peace movement, which was un-conditionally opposing additions to NATO's nuclear armoury, might succeed in opening some doors to unofficial East-West dialogue. And a few East European and Soviet citizens in exile—at first a very small number—shared our perspective and gave us their valued support.

Nothing in END's perspectives drew down upon us more scepticism or ridicule than this. At first the Western media

laughed us out of court: of course no independent expressions of peace would appear in the East. Then, when such
expressions did appear, we were told that these were tiny
and unrepresentative (as a *Times* leader wrote, a 'barely
audible echo'), and the media reported them only in terms
of the harassment which they suffered and never in terms of
the ideas which they promoted. In Britain the public media
simply repressed all discussion of this part of our perspective
—for example, my proposed Dimbleby Lecture, 'Beyond
the Cold War', was cancelled—since it contradicted the
'one-sided' image which opponents of the peace movement
were busily promoting. Even now (November 1984), when
there are many answering voices from the East, general
discussion of the perspective in the Western media remains
desultory and misinformed.

My intention here is not to offer an abridged history of
the independent peace movements in the East. Even though
these movements are still only in their early stages, their
history is complex and I have no competence as their
historian.* They have not been organised or single-issue
movements of the Western kind, and sometimes we are
considering brief episodes (like petitions against Soviet
missiles in Czechoslovakia) or the voices of individuals (such
as György Konrád's *Antipolitics*). All that I can do here is
illustrate the problems from examples within my own
experience.

The question of independent peace expressions in the
Communist states is directly related to the space which
exists in these states for *any* independent expressions. This

---

* END has published several special reports: *Moscow Independent
Peace Group* (1982); *The New Hungarian Peace Movement* (1982);
and John Sandford, *The Sword and the Ploughshare: Autonomous
Peace Initiatives in East Germany* (1983). The first two are now
dated and new publications are in preparation. Also Jan Kavan and
Zdena Tomin (eds.), *Voices from Prague* (Palach Press/END, 1983).
The best regular coverage will be found in *END Journal* (from END,
Southbank House, 12 Black Prince Road, London SE1). In the
United States regular reports appear in *Nuclear Times* and *Mother
Jones,* and especially in *Peace & Democracy News* and *Across
Frontiers.* Christian initiatives in the East are reported regularly in
the *Churches Register* (END).

lies at the heart of the world peace movement's problem. There could only be a truly two-sided movement if there were some parity of rights of expression and organisation on both sides. Which there is not. Hence we are led directly into questions of civil rights, which are the necessary precedent condition for any independent peace movement's existence. It may be possible to argue that differing social systems can peacefully co-exist; but if we are to move from this increasingly-tense condition of uneasy co-existence to a condition of active peace-*making* (or healing-process) then it is no longer possible to pretend that 'peace' and 'human rights' are not inter-related. If some Eastern 'dissidents' perceive the Western peace movement as being one-sided, it is no good our retorting that they could set this right by getting a movement going on their side also. For this could simply be to offer them a ticket to prison. Which none of us has any right to do.

But the position is not as unrelieved as this. A little space for citizen dialogue can be found, and it is our business to press more open. Professional groups, writers, Christians, physicians, cities engaged in twinning—all these have found ways to enlarge a dialogue, if not to escape from controls. And spaces have been found for some independent peace actions. In the German Democratic Republic the space was afforded by the protection of the Lutheran churches, around which the youthful 'Swords into Ploughshares' manifestations grew up. In Hungary the space for 'Dialogue' groups was found in colleges and schools, in apartments and coffee-bars. In Czechoslovakia jazz and popular music clubs have shared the aspirations of the peace movement, but the most significant space has been that which the network of civil rights supporters, Charter 77, have held open, often at the cost of their liberty or livelihood.

In 1982 these spaces began to be occupied, in direct response to the Western movement. This was perhaps the year in which 'Swords into Ploughshares' had their largest manifestations. In Czechoslovakia Charter 77 commenced a public correspondence with elements of the Western movement, a cautious exploration of views; one of their three spokespersons in that year was Ladislav Lis, who had in 1968 organised in a Prague factory an underground Communist Congress in defiance of the occupation and under the gun-barrels of Soviet tanks. Fragmentary reports began to come through of the formation of the independent Moscow Group for the Establishment of Trust between the USSR and USA. And from Hungary came a steady correspondence, much of it initiated by a history graduate, Ferenc Koszegi, a founder of the 'Dialogue' Group.

At the end of September, 1982, in response to pressing invitations, Andrew White and I went to Budapest to visit 'Dialogue'. Whatever I do I am fated to bring down on my head the abuse of the only-two-sidesmen of both sides. On this occasion I have subsequently been abused by the official Hungarian Peace Council, which put around the story that I had been offered by them the use of a public lecture-hall with every facility, but that I had rudely refused. Whereas our old acquaintance, Scott McConnell in *Commentary*, writes that 'Thompson. . . spoke before the Communist party's official peace committee, and also, at his insistence, gave the same speech to private Hungarian citizens.' Both stories are false, although Mr McConnell's is the purest fabrication. It is worth teasing out the truth of this small episode, since it reveals in miniature the difficulties of direct East/West dialogue.

At Budapest airport, and before we came through customs, we were welcomed by an affable official of the Peace Council which had only got wind of our visit a few days before. I was pressed to give a talk, in the next two or three days, in a room on the Hungarian Council's premises; I replied that I hoped that this would be possible, but that I must first consult with our hosts (the 'Dialogue' group) to find out what schedule they had arranged. It was agreed that I would call at the Council's offices the next day.

At the barrier we were met by our host, Ferenc Koszegi; and also by a friend of mine, Miklos Haraszti, a prominent 'dissident' (or constructive oppositionist), author of *A Worker in a Worker's State*. Haraszti (who was not a member of 'Dialogue') drove us to the city centre, where he left us to meet our hosts. It turned out at once that we had walked into a sensitive situation. 'Dialogue' existed to further not only direct Hungary/West communication on questions of peace, but also internal dialogue within the country: they sought to bring around the same round-table people from the official Council and the constructive opposition. They did not see themselves as 'dissidents', and were hoping to pressurise the authorities into allowing them a little legal space: perhaps a meeting-room or some share in editing a regular Bulletin.

The members and supporters of the Peace Group for Dialogue were nearly all under 25 and support extended to the 15- and 16-year-olds in the school. They had, at that time, no formal programme. They were closely informed about the Western peace movement (and monitored its publications) and the thrust of 'Dialogue' was against the ideological and security structures of the cold war: they were impatient of the formal bureaucratic structure of the official Peace Council, and wished to mount their own spontaneous actions and enter direct relations with Western peace activists. They represented a cultural or sub-political generational shift as much as a political 'position': a shift away from the apathy, materialism and cynical conformism of the post-'56 (Kadar) generation, together with a rejection of bloc thinking. The mood was that of a search for a third way among the younger European generations.

But they occupied a precarious and contested space on the edge between 'semi-legality' and 'semi-illegality'. Hungary was (and remains) the most flexible of the East European states, with a degree of toleration which her neighbours envy. An oppositional friend described the situation as one of 'civilised repression'; a more optimistic friend suggested 'incipient pluralism'. It was a fine-tuned adjustment, in which the space between legality and illegality was marked by un-spoken (but well-understood) taboos. We found at once that one of the most frequent terms of political discourse was 'provocation'. A 'provocation' might be a word or action designed to push people further across the border of illegality than they wished to go. There are also certain ideological limits which may not be transgressed without 'provocation'. An important one (for peace workers) was explicit criticism of the Soviet Union (although such criticisms are nourished in most Hungarian hearts) and of the Soviet military presence in Hungary. We attended one meeting of young people where, towards the end, an older man suddenly launched into a vehement speech demanding, as a priority, the withdrawal of Soviet forces from Hungary. The young 'Dialogue' supporters at once started chatting with each other, then stood up and turned their backs on the speaker, talking to each other in groups and ignoring him. A few left the room. It was explained to us afterwards that this had been a 'provocation'. A more charitable friend suggested that the man was not a real provocateur, but one of the 'wounded' of 1956, traumatised by the experience. Yes, it was possible to discuss Soviet military withdrawal in Hungary; but only in the context of a transcontinental peace movement, making equal demands upon both sides.

The presence of these taboos can be felt as an invisible but palpable element in every discourse, defining the limits of the possible. Indeed, the ruling authorities are well aware of this, and use it as a means of intellectual and social control. Even in discussions with official persons one may be told, in a man-to-man, 'off-the-record' sort of way, that Hungary is a small and weak country with powerful neighbours, and regrettably the limits of any autonomy are strictly confined. The legacy of 1956 still hangs over all discourse.

At certain points the space between legality and illegality is more clearly defined. Two limitations are of particular importance: (1) the prohibition of illegal publishing, or *samizdat;* (2) the prohibition of unauthorised but publicly advertised open political meetings. Even here there are nuances. A good deal of *samizdat* is in wide circulation. Carbons circulate normally among friends. (By contrast, in Romania typewriters must be registered with the authorities as if they were hand-guns). There was even, in 1982, a *samizdat* 'bookshop' open every Tuesday evening in the centre of Budapest. The shop was in fact the apartment of Laszlo Rajk, an architect, whose father (also Laszlo) was a

leader of the Hungarian Communist Party who had been
executed after World War II after one of the notorious
Stalinist show-trials. When Andrew and I visited the 'shop'
we found that a new *samizdat* pamphlet was being published
that day—a translation of my own not-the-Dimbleby-lecture,
'Beyond the Cold War'. It seems that the lecture was no more
acceptable to the Communist authorities than it had been
to the BBC.

Of course, visitors to the 'bookshop' were noticed: there
was a plain-clothes man at the foot of the apartment stairs.
Every now and then the shop would be raided and some
samizdat confiscated. But it was a harassment which stopped
short of serious repression. There were similar nuances with
respect to meetings. Small discussion groups in private homes
were going on all the time, and they still are. They are a
normal mode of discourse and not the cloak-and-dagger
affairs of Western imagination. We attended such local
meetings of Dialogue supporters, where a dozen or so students
and senior school pupils discussed international questions
without inhibition or anxiety. Such meetings would cross
the line to semi-illegality only if they were conducted
'provocatively' or raised 'provocative' questions. Those who
crossed this line were rarely subjected to direct repressive
measures. The authorities employed the stick and the carrot
in more subtle ways. People could lose their jobs or job
opportunities or their right to travel. Their post could be
interfered with, although not by the brutal confiscations
frequent in Czechoslovakia and the USSR. This was already
going on around us. One 'Dialogue' member had unexpectedly
been called up for military service; the homes of secondary
school students active in Dialogue had been visited by
security officers, to the consternation of their parents; teachers had issued warnings. In 1983 all this was to increase.

But in September 1982 Dialogue occupied a semi-legal
space. Their activities were completely open ('we insist on
acting as free persons', one of the founders, Ferenc Ruzsa,
said), and they were in open negotiation with the Peace
Council. But they could not hire public rooms, nor advertise
meetings in the press, nor publish any literature. Even the

beautiful badge which they designed, the CND sign in the form of clasped hands holding a rose, in the Hungarian colours, could not be manufactured in Hungary. (Andrew and I brought the design back, END manufactured them, and subsequent visitors took badges across—until the authorities denounced this as 'foreign intervention' and Dialogue replaced them with paper stick-ons of their own manufacture.) They could run off a couple of dozen typed carbon copies of their own internal bulletin, but they refused to cross the legality border to real *samizdat*. The art students could use silk screens and designed beautiful posters. This, and the telephone, and the word-of-mouth message, comprised their resources.

It was into this narrow space that we blundered, bringing messages of goodwill from END and from branches of CND. We were among the earlier visitors to Dialogue and very many were to follow. We found at once that the question of my 'lecture' had acquired symbolic significance. Permission had been given to Dialogue to use a lecture-theatre at Budapest University, but a day or two before my arrival permission had been withdrawn. It was 'known', but could not be proved, that pressure had been brought to bear from outside the University, perhaps because such a lecture, under Dialogue auspices, was felt to be offensive to the Peace Council whose prerogative it was to be the sole conduit for Western peace visitors.

My hosts were, not surprisingly, angry that the lecture-theatre had been cancelled. They saw the invitation to me to speak on Peace Council premises as an attempt to co-opt me into that operation. Publicity for this in the press or on television would be a defeat for Dialogue; the average TV viewer, in any case, would turn the telly off with a yawn, saying: 'Oh, someone else getting a free trip!' In Dialogue's view, my agreement to take part in a round-table or meeting on Peace Council premises should be conditional upon my obtaining permission to lecture also in public, hosted by Dialogue. It was explained to me that not many young people would dream of going to a meeting at the Peace Council anyway, since the whole set-up was so stuffy.

There commenced two days of strenuous negotiations with the Peace Council. I had no objection to speaking on Council premises, provided that the other condition could be met. END, like CND, has always been in favour of plural exchanges: that is, we should speak with whomsoever, official or unofficial, is willing to speak with us, whether in the East or West. Critics of the peace movement have strange double-standards: when Mrs Thatcher speaks at an official banquet in Budapest, she is hailed as a far-sighted proponent of. . . 'dialogue' (a term which the young Dialogue group first brought back into political discourse): when a peace worker speaks on the other side, s/he is written off as a 'useful idiot' or pro-Soviet toad. However, I do consider it important when we visit the other side that we should speak firmly and explicitly in criticism of the militarism of both blocs, and should insist on speaking with whomsoever we choose.

My negotiations in this case culminated in a meeting in a cafe with several officials of the Peace Council. It was a discussion conducted with courtesy and over several beers. I was warmly invited to give my lecture on the Peace Council's premises, before an invited audience with representatives of the churches, scientists and youth. Perhaps a larger room could be found, and more youth could be invited. Some members of Dialogue would be invited too. I explained, frankly and courteously, the principles of a non-aligned movement: I would be happy to give the lecture, but I must also lecture publicly under the auspices of my hosts in Dialogue. Why not in the University? But (it turned out) the university authorities were 'autonomous' and it would be improper for the Peace Council to seek to influence them. Perhaps (I suggested) the Ministry of the Interior might have influenced the University? But the Ministry of the Interior (it turned out) was 'autonomous' also, and the Peace Council could not influence it. It transpired that the Secretary of the Council had been trying all day to book a public meeting-hall for me, perhaps a trade-union hall; but (surprise) every hall in Budapest was booked that night. After all, it was not usual that foreign tourists should arrive one day and demand a lecture-hall the next—how would we feel if they were to arrive in London with such a demand? More beer. Every now and then the conversation would shift to other matters—general peace policy—and I would find that it was somehow assumed that I had agreed to their proposals. When I dug in my heels, the offers went up. The lecture, on their premises, would be publicly advertised: the text would be published: I might have a slot on Hungarian peak television and address 10 million Hungarians, direct and uncensored. What I could not do was hold a public meeting under the auspices of Dialogue. In the end they realised that I could not change this condition. They were good and courteous losers, and invited me to lunch the next day. The lunch was excellent and the discussion frank.

Our hosts in Dialogue had therefore to accept the cancellation of the lecture or look for alternative private premises. Several sympathisers with large apartments were approached but without success. Finally, on two hours' notice, an invitation was received from György Konrád, one of Hungary's leading novelists, of the hospitality of his apartment. The invitation was accepted, perhaps a little grudgingly, because Konrád is known as a constructive oppositionist. In some miraculous ways the news of the venue was passed from mouth to mouth, and when we arrived some eighty young people were packed into two adjoining rooms. It was a deeply-serious, positive and responsive audience.

I have written out this small episode in such detail because it illustrates the complexities and tensions of opening direct dialogue on the other side. Very many other Western peace workers have had similar experiences, not only in Hungary but also (in different conditions) in Poland or the GDR or even the USSR. Always there is the polarisation between the official structures legitimated by the Party, on one hand, and 'dissidents' on the other, and always there is the difficulty of speaking with both (e.g. with the Soviet Peace Committee and the Moscow Trust Group) or of finding intermediate spaces in the tug-of-war between. For a brief period Hungarian Dialogue and the GDR 'Swords into Ploughshares' were remarkable in opening up a hitherto

impossible space for semi-legal political autonomy from the
'leading role' of the Communist Party. They were able to do
so, perhaps, because their function (as a peace movement)
was not seen to be threatening, and because the Western
peace movement afforded some small protection. It may
also be that Dialogue was protected by 'doves' in the Party
itself, who favoured a little pluralism; while the Hungarian
Peace Council is the most flexible and well-informed of any
in the Warsaw bloc.

The space opened up by Dialogue was an uneasy one. I
noted two contrasting comments made at the time. The first
was from a 'dissident' or democratic oppositionist:

> The Western peace movements make a great mistake when they
> enter into relations with official Peace Committees in the attempt
> to influence them or to use them as a channel to reach the public.
> In fact, these official bodies stand in the space where, otherwise,
> an independent peace movement would spring up. Their function
> is that of inhibiting the development of an independent movement,
> or of controlling it if it should begin to arise. Every Western visit to,
> or acknowledgement of, the official committees in fact legitimises
> their function of the repression of true peace movements.

The other comment came from a leading member of Dialogue:

> The official Peace Council wishes to do one or the other of two
> things. It wishes either to co-opt us (while allowing us a little space,
> a little flexibility within their control) or, if it cannot do that, then
> it wishes to drive us into 'opposition'. They are afraid of our in-
> fluence so long as we are 'semi-legal': we can then reach a wide
> public, especially in the schools. But if we are driven into 'semi-
> illegality' (with the use of *samizdat*, etc.) then we may remain a
> small intellectual force: but they can isolate us from the general
> public. The teachers and (even more) the parents will bring pressure
> on the school students. Our problem is this: the oppositionists want
> to provoke us into opposition, and the authorities (if they cannot
> control us) want to do the same.

For many months the 'semi-legal' space was held open—
and it rapidly enlarged. Dialogue soon had thousands of
supporters and groups grew up in the provinces. Many
Western peace activists were received with unfailing generosity

by Dialogue hosts. The Hungarian authorities then, and (with several sad exceptions) since, have treated these visitors with propriety and courtesy, and have let us talk with whom we wished. The Peace Council, while sometimes grumpy, has maintained formal courtesies, and has made an in-put into END Conventions. On several occasions Western peace visitors—Mary Kaldor, the editor of *END Journal*, Mient-Jan Faber and others from the Dutch IKV, Stephen Tunnicliffe, the editor of *END Churches Register*—were able to engage in 'trialogues', in which they discussed with both 'officials' and 'independents' around the same table.

But the tension expressed in the two contrasting comments above exerted itself relentlessly and, in the end, it pulled Dialogue apart. By the summer of 1983 the 'semi-legal' space had almost closed. For the young actors in these disputes it seemed that the splits in Dialogue were the result of their own internal dissensions; there have been (alas!) accusations and counter-accusations of bad faith. Yet as is so often the case, internal dissension was the product of external pressures which, at the time, they could not clearly see. A major pressure was that, from the first days of 1983, to re-establish 'the leading role of the Party' throughout the Warsaw bloc; not only Solidarnosc but also the spread of the Western peace infection into the East was to be controlled. Eager cold warriors in the West, in Radio Free Europe etc., acted as 'mixers' by issuing selective and sensational reports in which Dialogue was assimilated to 'dissidents'. Perhaps one or two Western free-lance peace visitors (but not, I think, from Britain) helped this confusion on. Mr Zhukov's letter (above p. 261) and the argument surrounding the rival Berlin and Prague conferences intro-duced new tensions. It is probable that 'the Russians' leaned on the Hungarian authorities. It is now known (for documents fall off the back of lorries in Budapest as well as Whitehall) that the Politbureau of the Hungarian Socialist Workers (Communist) Party accepted a report, at its meeting on March 29th, 1983, which signalled that it would no longer tolerate the semi-legal status of Dialogue.

This report spells out very clearly the mentalities and

methods of Party authoritarianism and deserves careful attention. Those who do not understand these methods of social regulation and intellectual control will always be innocents in their relations with official Peace Councils. The report was drawn up by the Central Committee Section for Party and Mass Organisations. It commenced by commenting on the 'new phenomenon' of 'efforts towards spontaneous peace movements', and upon the need to 'develop united political behaviour' in relation to this phenomenon. The influence upon Hungarian opinion of the 'large and multi-coloured mass actions' of Western peace movements, with their opposition to the 'superpowers', was noted. This influence had been felt especially among Hungarian youth, who were attracted by 'more colourful and lively forms' of action. As a result, several spontaneous initiatives had taken place, culminating in the Dialogue groups:

> The group does not have any significant mass support, but its influence is growing. At the present moment Dialogue groups are operating in Budapest, Szeged, Debrecen and Pécs. Their ideas are in equal measure mixed, immature and self-contradictory, even giving rise to controversy in their own circles. . . Pacifist efforts. . . in church and religious circles are also on the increase.

While the National Peace Council had tried to monitor and maintain contacts with such groups, 'a united standpoint' had not yet been formed as to how to handle them. 'The Party organs have not everywhere paid sufficient attention to directing and supervising the peace movement,' and the Peace Council had 'not been able to integrate the spontaneous peace initiatives within the bounds of their own framework.' Moreover, oppositional groups had sought to make use of these groups in order to strengthen their own influence and to encourage 'so-called independent forces outside the Party and state'. The demand for a nuclear-free Europe could also be a form of disguised 'anti-Sovietism'.

While the report noted that Dialogue had held itself distinct from oppositional groups, nevertheless 'their activities are not free from oppositional influences'.

In the name of the 'independent Hungarian peace movement' they build up foreign connections, invite foreign guests, and organise forums for them. They popularise their viewpoints in duplicated publications. According to these, they place equal responsibility for the intensification of the arms race on the United States of America and the Soviet Union. They do not believe in the possibility of success in disarmament negotiations carried on between governments. It is their belief that only the building up of a broad popular movement and the exercise of pressure on governments can lead to results.

They support the aims of END, and END 'supports them materially as well*. . .' This causes problems for the foreign contacts of the National Peace Council. The report concluded that it was necessary to enliven the routine and stereotyped forms of agitation available to the youth, and raise the level of their political understanding.

The Political Committee of the Communist Party, having frowned for a while over this report, came up with a series of Resolutions. It was decreed that where any form of peace group (clubs, debating forums, youth committees) came into existence, measures should be taken to 'ensure that they are brought into connection with the united movement directed by the National Peace Council'. It was also advised that 'their operations be tied to the places of work and institutions of education' (i.e. they should not function without supervision in apartments, coffee-bars and clubs). 'The responsible and orderly political orientation of these groups—by their activists—is the task of the Party and social organs and organisations in the workplace.'

At the same time, Party activists 'should expose and isolate in open debate' all those using the peace movement 'as a pretext for questioning the peace policies of our Party and Government, our commitments to our allies, and the initiatives for peace of the Soviet Union'. And—

If the activities of the groups comes into conflict with the law, if they offend against the fundamental principles of our state, then

---

* i.e. in making the first Dialogue badges—the only material aid that END ever gave!

administrative methods should also be used. . . The Hungarian peace movement must be kept united under the direction of the National Peace Council. Movements standing outside the Peace Council cannot be legalised.

For the rest, the Political Committee supported more colourful efforts to organise demonstrations, marches, debating forums, etc., 'appropriate to political needs, and. . . serving the social base of the foreign policy decisions of our government'. On these occasions 'it considers it necessary' that the Peace Council and the Communist Youth League (KISZ) 'should provide the badges, placards and other symbols. . . for youth peace actions'. Nothing, absolutely nothing, could be left unprovided-for by the all-wise guidance of the Party Central Committee and its handmaiden, the Peace Council. The brief era of spontaneity must be brought to a close.*

Under such pressures Dialogue came apart. The authorities withdrew the carrot and made more use of the stick. A crisis was reached in late July 1983 when a number of Western visitors arrived to take part in a summer peace camp arranged by Dialogue; at the last moment camp-sites were refused, and after some tense and confused discussions in Budapest, the police arrested many visitors (including four women from the Greenham Peace Camp) and ushered them roughly across the border. (Dr Lynne Jones wrote a lucid account of the whole episode in the *Guardian*, August 4th, 1983.) This introduced a heavier climate of somewhat less civilised repression; harassments, detentions, a few fines. In a separate incident the *samizdat* publisher, Gabor Demszky, was beaten up by plain-clothes police, and then charged with assault. Although the trial ended in a suspended sentence, it was the first trial of an opposition figure for some years. I mention it here, because Dr Demszky had published the *samizdat* of my own 'Beyond the Cold War'. Laszlo Rajk's *samizdat* 'bookshop' has also been closed down.

This is only a small part of a much fuller history, which is continuing and will be continued, since the Hungarian peace

---

* These documents were first published in *Alulnézet Kiadó* (Bottom-View Publishers), a *samizdat* publishing-house in Budapest, 1984.

movement is only in its earlier stages.* What used to be Dialogue split into two wings; those who, with Koszegi, chose legality at the cost of some independence, founding a new club in semi-detached relation to the Peace Council; and those who opted for *samizdat* and semi-illegality, which brought them into closer relations with those democratic oppositionists (such as Haraszti, Rajk and others) who also wish to be in dialogue with the Western peace movement. In between, fragments of semi-legal Dialogue continue to meet, and to welcome Western visitors; although some lost heart and dropped into inactivity.†

A similar account might be given of the complexities of dialogue with the independent peace forces in the GDR. What needs to be stressed, in both cases, is that while there have been great difficulties in maintaining autonomous organisational identities, the general *peace culture* (especially among young people) continues to grow. It is inevitable that new forms of expression will be found. And the search for these forms must be carried out by the citizens of these nations alone. It is no business of Western activists to interfere in any way in these internal affairs, or to seek to import their own prescriptions. Any such attempts will, anyway, be counter-productive. Since there is a small percentage of individualists, know-alls and nutters among Western visitors, some of them have tried and, no doubt, will continue to try to interfere.

It is also always possible (and in some future situations might even become probable) that other, more noisome, agents might try to play a hand in the same game. Just as Mr Zhukov and his friends view the Western peace movement in terms of an opportunity to exploit a 'weakness' within

---

* In the foregoing account I am much indebted to END's Hungary working group, to Hugh Baldwin's monitoring of the Hungarian press, and to information from friends in Hungary.

† An important example of the space still held open for 'third way' peace initiatives has been the informal seminar, 'Towards a Theology of Peace', held in Budapest in September 1984, jointly organised by Bishop Karoly Tóth of the Hungarian Reformed Church and Stephen Tunnicliffe, coordinator of END Churches Lateral Committee, and attended by Christians from thirty countries, East, West and Third World: see *END Churches Register*, Autumn 1984.

NATO to the advantage of the Warsaw bloc, so their *alter egos* in the Western war movement will view independent peace expressions in the East as opportunities to 'de-stabilise' the other side to Western advantage.

Mr George Urban, from his position of influence as Director of Radio Free Europe, has recently argued—

> Let us look at the chances of weakening the Soviet system in peaceable ways. . . Don't you think we could export, or re-export, this propagandist obsession with 'peace' to the Soviet Union and its client states in Eastern Europe? Couldn't we tell the Ukrainians, for example, that the deployment of so many Russian missiles on their soil would do nothing for their survival in a nuclear war— exactly as the Soviet Marshals are telling West Germany? Can you envisage Ukrainian 'peace'-marchers parading in the streets of Kiev under posters reading 'Ukrainian mothers will not allow their sons to die for Andropov's war', or 'KGB cooks books to exaggerate US nuclear arsenal'?. . . Couldn't we gently remind them through our information services: 'You may find yourselves in extreme danger if a nuclear war should break out. . . Show your national independence by demanding the removal of foreign rockets—and stay alive'? (*Encounter*, May 1984.)

These are interesting questions when posed by a director of one of 'our information services'. It reminds one that not everything that Mr Zhukov says about NATO's psychological war agencies is rubbish. How much of this is now being done? Which of us, in the Western peace movement, monitor Radio Free Europe, Radio Liberty, and the Voice of America? Or even the BBC Russian Service? It is for reasons such as this that some in the West have come to view with extreme caution independent expressions from the East. Are they genuine? Might they not be one of Mr Urban's 'plants'?

I can offer no easy answers. There may be 'plants', on that side as on this. There may also be cases where authentic centres of 'dissidence' employ the rhetoric of 'peace' as a cover for the pursuit of other oppositional objectives. Our amateur movement, with its slender resources, must find its way to friends in the East blindfold and tapping a white stick. We can only act as Dialogue commenced to act, as 'free persons', accepting dialogue when it is offered, refusing any methods of conspiracy, arguing the issues openly, making our judgments as we go along. Sometimes we may find that we must risk an act of faith—or trust.

This was, exactly, the case with the Moscow Trust Group. Some circumstances surrounding the group's origin seemed curious. Its existence was first announced at the time that the Scandinavian Women's Peacemarch was about to enter the Soviet Union. Could a small 'dissident' peace group be an exercise in cold war propaganda? Reports and the group's early statements came mainly through Western correspondents in Moscow. But, then, how else were they to get any messages out? Then Danielle Grünberg, a West Country member of CND of Danish extraction (the only Briton on the Scandinavian march) took her trust in her hands and (with Jean Stead of the *Guardian*) visited the Trust Group—she was the only marcher to do so, and she deserves our thanks. Danielle's and Jean's reports were positive; so also were reports from other American and British peace workers who visited the group, and who came to know the members' views and circumstances. One remarkable American visitor even managed to visit the group's founder, the young artist Sergei Batovrin, when he was placed in a psychiatric hospital. Meanwhile news of the group's harassment became worse and worse. They were accused by the Soviet authorities (and the Soviet Peace Committee) of being 'hooligans' and 'drunkards' and 'Zionists' (some of them are Jews) or 'refuseniks' seeking tickets to the West (some of the group's founders had filed applications to emigrate, but, on the foundation of the group, several had withdrawn their applications).

END decided to trust the Trust Group: that is, we decided, not that the group was a like-minded group which shared our strategies, but that it was a group of independent-minded and courageous persons, deeply-concerned about peace, in a situation of extreme exposure which demanded some solidarity from the Western movement. We therefore published an *END Special Report* which included press reports, some statements of the group, and the accounts of Danielle Grünberg and Jean Stead. It was the first substantial English-language publicity for the group's existence, and it carried the information widely into Europe and the USA. This pamphlet, and supporting representations and letters in the press, may have done a little to offer protection to the group, and even to get Batovrin out of psychiatric detention. It was an action which drew upon END the particular hostility of the Soviet Peace Committee, which found its legitimacy to be challenged by the group's existence.

It was an action which also met with some scepticism in the peace movement, and among our own supporters. Although we made it clear that we did not (and do not) regard the Trust Group as the only locus for dialogue with Soviet citizens—and continue to favour an extensive plural dialogue—we were accused of identifying with a small group of unrepresentative 'dissidents', who might even have been 'set up' to embarrass the Soviet authorities.

It was at this time, when some of us in END and CND were making representations on behalf of the group—in the face of much scepticism—that we were hit amidships by the Popov missile. To our astonishment there surfaced briefly in London a Dr Oleg Popov, who pronounced himself to be the authorised 'spokesman' of the group in the West, who gave interviews in several national newspapers, had instant access to the news programmes of the BBC, and who signed a letter (drafted by other hands) in *The Times*. In these Dr Popov said nothing about the policies of the Trust Group, nothing about its activities but much about its harassment and repression, and delivered his condemnation (in the name of the Trust Group) of any 'unilateral' measures and especially of the policies of END, CND and the Labour Party. His views of the prospects for the Trust Group were profoundly pessimistic ('under the existing power structure in the Soviet Union' there was almost no hope of building an independent peace movement, and the support of Western 'unilateralist groups has proved to be in vain', *Times*, November 8, 1982), and he wrote (or someone wrote and he signed) that 'we do not want our existence to be exploited by bodies of unilateralists who do not share our aims'.

This was a most damaging attack, and its ill effects can be felt in the British peace movement to this day. They may also have been felt in Moscow. As Dorothy and I wrote, in a response in *The Times* (November 17th): 'Does Dr Popov not know that he has given a licence to the KGB to portray the Moscow Group as nothing but a Western intelligence "plant", drawing in a few innocent persons, whose ulterior aim was to discomfort Western peace movements?' There are some in the Western peace movement who still feel that, having burnt their fingers trying to support the Moscow Trust Group, they will never risk burning their fingers with independent movements in the East again.

Who was Dr Oleg Popov? He was not a member of the Trust Group, but he was friendly with several members, was one among several score of signatories to the group's first Appeal (June 2nd, 1982), and gave the group some advice as to its legal status. He was not its official 'spokesman' in the West, but when he received emigration papers from the Soviet Union a few weeks after the Group's foundation (in July) he was asked to take messages out. He came by way of Vienna to Italy, and in early November was flown for three or four days to London to consult with Amnesty International on matters concerning the persecution of the Moscow Helsinki Group. By then he was completely out of touch with the Trust Group, and at that time some of us in the British and American peace movements were in more direct communication. He knew nothing about Britain, nor about the representations made on the Trust Group's behalf by END and CND (Bruce Kent had spoken out publicly in Moscow in its defence).

At the time there were deep suspicions about Popov; but I now consider that his offence was weakness—he blundered into a situation he did not understand and allowed himself to be made use of by others. This view is the charitable one taken by members of the Moscow Trust Group itself. Several members wrote to me next February apologising for

our friend Oleg Popov. There is no doubt that he acted with insufficient tact, publicly expressing his views about END without meeting you first. . . It can only be justified by explaining that the psychological strain connected with emigration, adapting to sharply different conditions of life and finally, a lack of knowledge of the

traditions and ways of life in the West placed him in a very difficult
position. . .

They add that if they had agreed with Dr Popov's assertion
that 'under the existing power structure in the Soviet Union'
there could be no hope of independent peace initiatives,
then 'it goes without saying that we would never have
entered the Trust Group'.

Oleg Popov, having unloosed his missile, flew back to
Italy, and thence onward to the United States, where he has
been rather quiet about Trust Group matters. He does not
appear on the editorial board of *Return Address: Moscow*,
the English-language bulletin of Group members in exile. If
we wished to tease out the true details of this operation we
would have to examine certain little offices in London to
which Dr Popov was introduced, as the supposed offices of
multilateral 'disarmament' movements: the Coalition for
Peace through Security, which specialises in dirty tricks
against CND, and the office in Golden Square which houses
(surprise, surprise!) the pretentiously-named Institute for
European Defence and Strategic Studies of Mr Gerald Frost
(above p. 3). At this same address were then to be found a
number of peace-loving organisations, including the Institute
for the Study of Conflict, Alliance Publishers, the Anglo-
Russian Peace Movement and the Association for a Free
Russia. This well-funded operation (END could not dream of
renting premises in Golden Square nor employing telex and
half-a-dozen typists) is not—as one visitor remarked—exactly
a hole in the wall. It appears to have the best of connections
with like-minded organisations, including the Coalition for
Peace through Security, some services of the BBC, and
Encounter. Its credentials as the office of mass movements
are less secure: the 'Anglo-Russian Peace Movement', set up
after Dr Popov's visit and perhaps now defunct, is supposed
to have had three members, two of whom were Young
Conservatives who had distinguished themselves in a heroic
operation running up and down a Moscow underground
distributing leaflets hidden in their socks.

It was to this honeypot that Oleg Popov was directed, and

there are other such honeypots in the West. I will be frank and admit that, when Sergei Batovrin and his family were (in effect) expelled from the Soviet Union at the end of May 1983, Dorothy and I flew to Vienna not only to welcome them with flowers but also to forestall another Popov operation. We need not have worried, since Sergei already had some notion of what to expect in the West. The Batovrins moved on to New York, where they continue to work for Trust, produce a journal, and are in continuous discussions with the American peace movement. The egregious Gerald Frost, of Golden Square, keeps jumping up and down in *Encounter* (May 1984 and 'Letters', July/August 1984) proclaiming that I have misrepresented Sergei Batovrin's views for malign purposes. He wishes to persuade readers of *Encounter* that Batovrin is (like Dr Popov) contemptuous of the Western peace movement and has lost interest in conducting any dialogue or joint actions with its members.

This is far from the truth. Batovrin and a small group of his fellow-exiles in New York are now very active in publicising the cause of the Trust Group in the Western peace movement. Their journal (*Return Address: Moscow*) is sharp in tone, and may be criticised for giving more publicity to KGB harassment than to the positive work and proposals of the group. And it has been so criticised. No doubt there may be differences of view in Trust Group circles (both in Moscow and abroad), as are commonly found in such situations. But it is, most emphatically, Batovrin's intention to strengthen direct East-West citizen communication, even if at the painful cost of destroying some Western illusions.

In any case, Batovrin has never asked Frost to be his amanuensis, nor has he invited me. He is perfectly capable of correcting either one of us if he so wishes. When he came through England in October 1984 to do a series of meetings with the peace movement (some of them hosted by END) he made none of the complaints which Mr Frost seeks to put into his mouth. It is also instructive to note that—although a press release was put out by END in good time—the only national paper to notice his visit was the *Guardian*, while both BBC and ITV turned down opportunities for interviews. It seems that most of the media are interested in Russian peaceniks only if they come, like Oleg Popov, with missiles to launch at CND and END.

Dr Popov's complaint was against 'unilateralists' who do not share the Trust Group's aims. Of course, no-one ever has supposed or said that the group supported 'unilateralism'. Their position on nuclear weapons is similar to that of many in the American movement: they support a freeze and mutual balanced reductions. They do not criticise Soviet armaments policies (such criticism would anyway be a legal offence). This being so, they do not assume the right to criticise the armaments policies of other nations either. As a point of principle, their proposals are always framed as positive suggestions rather than as criticisms. Several of them have written to us privately, expressing courteous doubts as to the advisability of a British policy of unilateral nuclear disarmament. But we have never been able to have a thorough discussion of these questions, simply because the Soviet security authorities have always made the exchange of letters, books and documents so difficult.

However, the question of 'unilateralism' is beside the point. We never supported the rights of the Trust Group on the grounds that they endorsed our policies, nor have they asked us to endorse theirs. We simply supported their right to exist and to do their own thing, and to contribute in this way to the common dialogue. This is also the way in which Professor Yuri Medvedkov saw it, in an early letter to END (December 29, 1982):

It is up to us (participants of the independent peace movements) to provide alternative forms of constructive East-West dialogue. . . There is some division of labour among various peace movements. . . For the public of Western nations it is permitted to object to budget-ary appropriations and to political alliances of certain kinds. As for the Trust-Building Group, the field of vision plus the field of possibilities both dictate the emphasis on steps for healthier detente, with our conviction that it's not weapons but people with hatred who do the killing.

(*END Journal*, 2, Feb.-March 1983).

This has always been the emphasis of the Trust Group's work, and it is this which the Western movement has learned from them and should go on learning. While the Western activists have been preoccupied with the build-up of nuclear weapons (and the West's prior responsibility in this), the Trust Group has been preoccupied with distrust and ideological confrontation (and their own authorities' responsibility in this), and they have issued proposal after proposal for greater citizen exchange. In this they have shown astonishing courage. As Yuri Medvedkov wrote: 'We risk our liberty and even our lives every day, but to be outside the peace movement is impossible for us. It's the point of honour, the point of being humans.'

In the past two years I have accumulated enough files on the Moscow Trust Group to write a fat book. These include letters and proposals from the group, furious attacks from the Soviet Peace Committee, the records of disputes in the Western movement, and reports of the growing number of Western peace visitors to the group—the important visits of Women for Life on Earth (who took Olga Medvedkova with them into the innermost sanctum of the Soviet Peace Committee), of the American Friends Service Committee, of members of CND and European peace organisations. But even if I were to write this book, I do not know what I would say in the conclusion. Perhaps this may be because the story is not yet concluded.

What I have learned is something of the complexity of attempting an independent initiative in the capital city of the Soviet Union; the fierce loyalty of the group's members to each other, but also their fierce disputes and divisions. Although I have never visited Russia, I have come to know the members as neighbours and friends. I have known of their moments of despair and also of renewed hope. I have also learned of the impossible pressures placed upon them—not only the surveillance, the house arrests, the telephones cut, the interrogations, the exhibitions and paintings confiscated, the slanders in the press, the arrests and emigration of members, the suspicion of neighbours—but also the repeated confusions as to direction, the suspicion of penetra-

tion (might someone be an informer? and to the KGB or to
Western intelligence?), the succession of Western visitors
expecting immediate attention—many of them true-hearted
and welcome, but a few false-hearted ones trying to trick
them into 'provocations' on one side or the other in the Cold
War. And, on the bottom line, moments of black pessimism
when members of the group have come to doubt the very
purpose of their work. Might it not be that, by becoming
the occasion for a 'cold war' within the peace movements,
they might actually be worsening 'trust'? 'We appeal to you'
(one of them wrote to me in September 1984) 'not to make
any actions with the goal of helping us, if such actions could
seriously deteriorate international relations. Peace is more
important than our lives. . .'

Not once but several hundred times I have been told that
the group may be very 'sincere' but that they are a tiny
group of unrepresentative intellectuals (or Jews or refuseniks) who are a distraction to the business of making peace
with Soviet people. Not once but a dozen times something
odd has happened which has made me wonder if there was
not some cold war joker in the Trust Group pack. Not once
but twenty times it would have been easy to throw all the
papers in the air and to walk out of the room. But I am glad
that many of us—and now an increasing number—answered
the group with our own trust. If we had not stood by those
beleaguered people it would have been an act of such deep
dishonour that it would have called the whole project of the
Western peace movement in question.

If the independent peace movement in the GDR and in
Hungary has acted always in a narrow and precarious space,
any independent group in the USSR acts in no space at all.
Its space is a small apartment under surveillance, and even
the visitors may only be wearing masks of goodwill. The
two 'sides' press almost physically upon them, and any third
way of peace is disallowed by the rules of state. The very act
of existence is construed as a 'provocation', which is regarded
with particular fury by the official Peace Committee since it
feels that its own legitimacy is called in question. However
much the group proclaims that it is not 'dissident', the KGB

uses every means to try and drive it into dissident mentalities.

The Trust Group took the sharpest action possible, by just existing, by publicly proclaiming its own existence, and by entering into open communication with Westerners. Was it wise to do so? Were there intermediate ways, which others have been quietly taking? I do not know. But in doing so, it broke, not this specific law or that (for the group has always sought to assert only its legal rights), but the dominant taboo of the Soviet state: the leading role of the Party—and this in the most sensitive ideological area. We can illustrate this by examining some extraordinary documents which dropped off the back of a lorry in Siberia.*

The documents refer to Alexander Shatravka, a supporter of the Trust Group with a 'dissident' record: he had suffered previous imprisonment for attempting to cross the border into Finland. He was an early signatory to the group's Appeal of June 4, 1982, and he took the Appeal with him on a trip into Siberia, collecting signatures in villages and at a saw-mill. He was arrested, tried, and sentenced to three years in a Siberian labour camp. He succeeded in appealing, and the case was referred to the Procuracy of the city of Tyumen.

I have before me an incomplete record of the examination. The case turned on the question of the Trust Group's founding Appeal, and whether this was or was not an infringement of Soviet law. This document was examined by several learned Thebans, and their opinions were given. First, Dr Woldemar Alekseyevich Danilov, assistant professor of history and dean of the History Faculty of Tyumen State University, found that the document was of an 'anti-Soviet, anti-Socialist character', bearing 'a pacifist character'. Among its offences were that 'it posits equality between the positions and aims of the USSR and USA', 'there is an attempt to underestimate the significance of contemporary forms of the movement of peace champions', and 'the idea is expressed of the formation of some kind of public force, standing above governments', an idea which reflects 'cosmo-

---

* I am indebted to Sergei Batovrin for copies, and to Gerard Holden for the translations which follow, as well as for advice on other points in this essay.

politan ideas'. The Trust Group's Appeal 'could give rise
to incorrect ideas, especially among that part of the population which is not well-prepared politically'. Thus the learned
Dr Danilov. His colleague, Gennady Filippovich Kutsev,
Rector of the same University, concurred: the document
expressed 'the well-known thesis of Western propaganda
concerning the equal responsibility of imperialist and socialist countries for the cold war. . .' Dr Kutsev noted that
appropriate scientific specialists were already handling Soviet
disarmament negotiations: 'it should however be noted that
modern weapons systems are so complex that in practice it is
impossible and even unwise to bring unprepared people into
the consideration of these problems'.

Reinforced by these expert legal opinions, the Procuracy
got down to a formal judicial examination before a Commission comprised of Professor G.B. Ignatenko, head of
the Law Department at the R.D. Rudenko Institute; Professor K.N. Lyubishin, Ph.D., head of the History and
Philosophy Department at the Ural State University; and
Professor G.P. Orlov, Ph.D., head of 'historical materialism'
at the same University. This Commission 'established' a
number of points. The Appeal of the Trust Group was
'naive', 'utopian' and 'slanderous'. It was also 'directly
opposed to the essence of Marxist–Leninist ideology'. After
much rehearsal of these themes the Commission came to
judgment. According to article 62 of the Soviet Constitution
citizens 'are obliged to defend the interests of the Soviet
state, to assist the strengthening of its power and authority'.
Those who drew up the Appeal had broken this 'constitutional norm'. And in accordance with article 190 of the criminal
code of the Russian Soviet Federal Socialist Republic 'it is
not necessary to establish actual consequences'. Intention
or 'purpose' was decisive. And the Appeal had two such
hostile purposes. First, internally, it attempted to set society
in opposition to the Soviet state and Party and 'place them
in a position of mutual antagonism', by setting up
spontaneous national groups with international contacts.

'The call to unite international social groups* is nothing other than a call for the formation of a group of "initiators" outsite the framework of our state.' Second, externally,

> The outward orientation is a weakening of the position of Soviet diplomacy in the negotiations in progress, to the detriment of the authority of the Soviet leadership in the eyes of *those international forces which are considered by us, and can practically be used as, an effective reserve in the anti-imperialist and anti-militarist struggle*. . . [My italics—E.P.T.]

Finally, the Appeal's 'call for the provision of "free" information about disarmament on both sides about the deployment of armaments† is equivalent to an intention to reveal Soviet defence capabilities to a potential aggressor'.

Thus refreshed, these learned Thebans no doubt returned to their rigorous academic studies of law and historical materialism. Alexander Shatravka returned to his labour camp. Sergei Batovrin has reported that early in 1983 at the Sverdlovsk Transfer Prison Shatravka was discovered by guards to have addressed a letter to Western peace activists: he was taken into the prison yard, stripped, and beaten with clubs and rubber hoses. He has subsequently suffered severe illness, been on hunger strike, and, in the summer of 1984, exhausted by repeated beatings, attempted to take his own life. It was after hearing such reports that Bruce Kent held a vigil, in August 1984, on behalf of Shatravka and also Dr Dikerdem, President of the Turkish Peace Association.+

---

* The Appeal called upon the general public of the USA and USSR 'to create integrated, international public groups based on the principles of independence, whose functions would be to accept and analyze individual proposals for disarmament and the establishment of trust between countries'.

† The Appeal had called for the governments of the USA and USSR to create an international bulletin in which both sides entered into open dialogue, and which carried information on disarmament negotiations, and 'an exchange of information about the possible consequences of using nuclear weaponry'.

+ There is good news for once (November 1984). Dr Dikerdem has been released from prison, although several of his colleagues in the

It will be seen that this Commission reached much the same conclusion as our own learned Lord Chief Justice Lane, that 'national security' is whatever the government says it is, and that all citizens must defer to this 'constitutional norm'. But the Soviet authorities, especially in distant Tyumen, have a great many more teeth than our own authorities are yet provided with; and they use them. If Lord Chief Justice Lane, and Mrs Thatcher, or President Reagan sometimes drive some of us into dissident mentalities, then how much more bitter must be the dissident mentality of Soviet citizens who have bumped against rabid ideology masked as law. Before Western peace activists start calling such reactions 'anti-Soviet' they should reflect that Batovrin and Shatravka are 'Soviet' also, just as both Tolstoy and Lenin are part of the Russian inheritance; and that if they had been confined to psychiatric institutes or beaten up with rubber hoses for their peace activities, then they might now be more 'anti-British' or 'anti-American' than they are.

If some potential friends in Communist states have been driven into dissident mentalities, the credit should be given to the KGB which intends to drive them there. It wishes to isolate and alienate critics from that large sector of middle opinion which recalls the horrors of World War II, which justly finds Western militarism menacing, which has no taste for any actions which would lead them into a life of harassment and yet which yearns for democratic changes and a human opening to the West. The dissident mentality, while fully understandable and indeed inevitable, cannot offer any strategy for healing the Cold War so long as it is a simple inversion of 'only-two-sides'—a sort of flip-over from one 'side' to the other. (Such flip-overs happen sometimes in the West as in the East). The Moscow Trust Group has had the temptation of this inversion pressed upon it again and again, and the record of harassment in Sergei Batovrin's *Return*

Turkish Peace Association remain in prison awaiting a fresh trial. Also recent accounts suggest that Alexander Shatravka's treatment in his prison-camp has much improved in the past few months. In both cases publicity and the representations of the peace movement appear to have had some effect.

Address: Moscow makes painful reading; yet what is most remarkable is the way in which the group has risen above its persecution again and again, and has continued, with restraint, to search for a third way.

I do not know if the Trust Group will succeed in its courageous project. In the most optimistic view it may have opened the door a crack, through which an increasing informal traffic of trust will flow, until the Party's taboo upon unlicensed citizen exchanges with Western peace activists has to give way. At that stage one would expect that much more widespread informal channels for international exchanges would come into being, which would manage to disengage from confrontations with the authorities. But for this to take place, the authorities also would have to modify their sacred rule (the 'leading role of the Party'), and the Soviet Peace Committee itself would have to learn to tolerate peaceful co-existence within the USSR with other kinds of citizen peace initiatives.

▲ 'DECAYING IDEOLOGICAL RUBBISH' ▲

I must now return from a long digression. I was explaining why Soviet ideologists commenced to lampoon END and substantial sections of the Western peace movement, and why Yuri Zhukov, of the Soviet Peace Committee, sent out his divisive letter in December 1982. This led me to our relations with independent peace groups in the East, and I have tried to explain their complexity by sketching two examples: Hungary, where there has been a little space for independence, and the USSR, where there has been no space at all. The cases of the GDR, Czechoslovakia and Poland would reveal equal complexities. From the first moment of martial law in Poland it was apparent that our strategy of resisting Western nuclear arms while at the same time seeking for human openings to the East would encounter heavy resistance. By the winter of 1982-3 this evidence was accumulating: the harassment of 'Swords into Ploughshares' in the GDR, the arrest of Ladislav Lis of Charter 77, the unceasing pressure on the Trust Group, and a Warsaw Pact summit (January 5, 1983) which combined a series of disarmament proposals addressed to Western opinion with more private discussions on re-establishing the 'leading role of the Party'. It was in these circumstances that I published, in late February 1983, my article on the 'Soviet "Peace Offensive" ' in the *Guardian* and the *Nation*.

It was not well liked. It made some people angry in both the British and American peace movements. The British

movement, especially CND, was flexing its muscles in the
year which was expected to 'refuse cruise'. The American
movement was resisting MX and the B-1 and was getting
ready to help with Pershing II and cruise. Both were standing
up against a growing torrent of anti-Communist invective,
and were seeking to discount the aggressive enemy image that
was being projected (by aggressive ideologists) upon the
Soviet Union. The disarmament proposals of the Warsaw
Pact summit (several of which were good) had been
welcomed. And in any case, what could possibly be wrong
with a Soviet 'peace offensive'?

Very possibly I pitched my article in the wrong tone. I
commenced by warning the Western peace movement that
it was 'sleepwalking into a situation of extraordinary
complexity'. This caused offence; no-one could accept that
they had been sleepwalking. And yet I think that we all had
nodded off on our marching feet once or twice. We had not
noticed the shift in the terms of political argument in the
previous year which had come with Reagan's 'zero option'.
In terms of 'balance' and 'arms control' Reagan's proposal
was clearly specious: in offering that the Russians should
take out, not only all their SS-20s but all their SS-4s and
SS-5s, he was generously offering that the Soviet Union
should reduce its European nuclear arsenal to the level of
1960 while not one reduction was made on NATO's side.
It is now generally acknowledged that the 'zero option'—

> Could not provide the basis for serious negotiation and was not
> meant to do so. It was a position constructed purely for show, one
> designed to make the administration look generous in offering to
> give up any deployment of missiles, while at the same time assuring
> that the negotiations got nowhere.
>   (George W. Ball, *NY Review of Books*, November 8, 1984.)

This is to say that the 'zero option' was intended not to
disarm any nuclear weapons but to disarm the Western peace
movement. Sensing that this was so, the peace movement
confronted the 'zero option' with ridicule and refusal; and in
doing so, it fell, not into a Soviet, but into a Reagan trap. In
1980 and 1981 the swelling movement had united behind

the positive demand: for a nuclear-free Europe! After the
'zero option', in 1982 and 1983, the argument had been
subtly tipped, so that the peace movement appeared to be
arguing on the side of the Soviet negotiating position—that is
in favour of the retention of x number of SS-20s. But a non-
aligned movement ought not to have allowed itself to have
been manoeuvred into the position of seeming to defend any
nuclear weapons whatsoever.

Was there an alternative? Reagan's public relations staff
did not intend us to find one. Within ten minutes of Reagan's
'zero option' speech I was rung on transatlantic phone to
demand my instant reactions. So was Bruce Kent, and so, no
doubt, were a score of 'spokespersons' of the European peace
movement. We were supposed, instantly, to say 'yes' or
'no'. If 'yes', then that was a victory for Reagan; if 'no', then
we were exposed as pro-Soviet which was another victory for
Reagan. With our slender resources no instant conference of
European movements was possible. In the next few days I
was with Daniel Ellsberg in West Germany. Ellsberg was
convinced that the hawks in the Pentagon were shaking on
their talons, for fear that the Soviet Union might go a long
way to *accept* the 'zero option'. He suggested that the peace
movement should say 'yes' if (but only if) the 'zero option'
was combined with an across-the-board nuclear weapons
freeze. I suggested a different response: we should say 'yes,
but more', and demand that more be thrown in on the
Western side—for example, Polaris and Pershing IA—as a
sweetener. (Bruce Kent suggested much the same in a letter
to the *Guardian.*) The West German peace movement leaders
(including Greens) were not even interested in sitting down
at a table with our British and American delegation and
discussing it. The Krefeld Appeal had never mentioned
SS-20s. The West German movement at that time was
reluctant to direct any criticism at Soviet militarism, in part
through the understandable historical legacy of guilt for
World War II and the vast Soviet losses of that war. When
Ellsberg and I raised the issue at a meeting in West Berlin
our reception was stormy. Reagan's offer was a 'trick' (it
was), and in the German view it should be confronted and

'exposed', whereas in our view it should be trumped by an even more far-reaching demand.

I suppose that the outcome was inevitable. Mass protest movements cannot engage in subtle diplomacy. They are 'yes' and 'no' movements, and the more nuanced proposals of Ellsberg, Bruce Kent or myself—given fleeting media exposure or none at all—could not become visible within the high-visibility shouting-match on every media channel of the opposed superpowers and their allies.

The ensuing Geneva 'negotiations' which dragged through 1982 and 1983 were negotiations not to control arms but to control public opinion. Reagan and Caspar Weinberger, and their conspiratorial advisers, Richard Perle and Richard Burt—as is documented abundantly in Strobe Talbott's *Deadly Gambits*—never desired the negotiations to reach a resolution, were determined to put down the new missiles in Europe, and were (and still are) reaching for clear nuclear superiority in every field (whatever that may mean). As the *Wall Street Journal* remarked candidly (October 7th, 1983) United States postures of negotiating 'flexibility' were—

Perhaps the most important element of a multifaceted West European strategy aimed at countering peace movements and getting ready for the likely deployment of 572 US medium-range missiles.

As for the Soviet Union, in 1982 and the first months of 1983 it was also playing to Western public opinion, hoping to pick apart NATO 'modernisation' (and also perhaps NATO) with the help of peace movements and the German and British elections. Only in the last months of 1983, when Andropov was dying, did it come up with hard and, in arms control terms, acceptable proposals. At that stage Mrs Thatcher and Mr Heseltine helped on their American backers by putting the boot in; they rushed in the first flight of cruise missiles to Greenham Common, a month in advance of the date announced by NATO, in order to foreclose any further negotiations or public discussion. It had been throughout a negotiation between two con-men with public opinion as the patsy.

In these circumstances it was necessary and honourable in the Western peace movement to expose the spoof of the 'zero option'. And any peace movement deserving the name had to assert its unconditional and implacable refusal of cruise and Pershing II. (The well-intentioned 'multilateralists' were being conned even more dishonestly than were the 'unilateralists'.) Yet mere opposition, without a large and imaginative transcontinental alternative, of necessity appeared to cast the peace movement in the role of auxiliary to Soviet negotiators—a casting which Western media and politicians did all in their power to enforce. This perception was also transmitted to a wide public in Eastern Europe, where an unholy alliance of Communist media and Western 'free radio' operations projected the Western movement as pro-Soviet and one-sided, and suppressed all mention of the reciprocal demands made on the Warsaw powers.

That is why I wrote 'The Soviet "Peace Offensive" ' in February 1983. It seemed to me at that time that it was more necessary than ever, if we were to hold onto middle opinion in Europe and America, that we should enforce our non-aligned perspective, repudiate the role of auxiliary to either side, and even attempt to extract concessions (whether cuts in SS-20s or more fluent citizen exchanges with the East) from the Soviet Union. If we could not do this then I foresaw defeat; and it gives me no satisfaction that this defeat (with the return to power of Kohl and Thatcher) took place as I foretold.

What happened in 1983–4 was that the ideological confrontation *between* the blocs was displaced, in an extraordinary way, by an internal ideological civil war *within* each bloc. Thus in Britain the traditional Right fought it out, not with the Russians, but with CND, the Greenham Women and with the traditional domestic Left (the Labour Party). In the Warsaw bloc the Communist hard-liners reestablished their disciplinary rule over Solidarnosc, Charter 77, all 'dissidents', and over their own Party. And, in a final episode, the Republicans in the United States in November 1984 wreaked their vengeance in a Massacre of the Democratic Innocents. The extent of the defeat of 1983-4 is expressed, not only in the nuclear excreta strewn on the territory of Europe, East and West, and increasingly washing around in the Atlantic, Pacific, Mediterranean and Indian oceans, but also in the fact that in the twin succession-crises in both superpowers the armourers and ideologists pushed their own hard-liner to the top. The hawks had fed the Other's hawks.

The argument of which this article was a part has trickled on ever since. It arose simultaneously in many places and languages; from Holland (Mient-Jan Faber and the Dutch IKV), from both Germanies (notably the Greens), from Britain (Mary Kaldor and others in *END Journal*), from France, Italy and the United States, but also—commencing from different perceptions—from Eastern Europe and the Soviet Union. The growing confluence of East/West public opinion, the 'peace-and-freedom' mood of 1981-2, was reversed in 1983-4 as the blocs hardened against each other. It seemed to some, as it had seemed in the first cold war, that one must either be for a (pro-Soviet) 'peace' or for a (pro-Western) 'freedom': one could not be for a non-aligned *both*. In the Western peace movement some viewed the issue as a distracting debate about 'human rights'; and I debated it in these terms in the *Nation* ('The Wisdom of Solomon', in *The Heavy Dancers*). Yet I regard this debate as itself a diversion. Human rights are being violated in every part of the globe. But if we consider the problems of peace-making, not only with respect to the instruments and symbols of bloc confrontation (nuclear weapons), but in a full political and cultural perspective, then it becomes obvious that any healing of the blocs entails greater rights of citizen communication and expression, not as a precondition to disarmament ('linkage') nor as a wished-for consequence of disarmament, but as an integral part of the process of making peace.

The political problem is neither armaments (alone) nor human rights (alone) but the very condition out of which confrontations, new weapons-systems, and the repression of rights continually arise. This condition is the bloc-division of the world itself, and specifically the division of Europe, and it is this which we must address if civilization is to survive. It is of the first importance that voices have been answering us from the East in similar terms. The most significant have come from Central Europe where, in Czechoslovakia, the GDR and Hungary, there are cultural resources derived from both the Communist and the Western democratic traditions. It was the Czechoslovak civil rights organisation, Charter 77, which (at risk to itself) initiated a long and searching dialogue with the Western peace movement; and the most luminous essay on the whole problem of making 'a democratic peace' has come from Dr Jaroslav Šabata, a veteran first of the Communist Party (until 1968) and then of the human rights movement (for which he has suffered years of imprisonment), now in retirement at Brno. (See *Voices from Prague*, Palach Press/END, 1983.) It is a discussion which continues.

Official ideologists of the Communist bloc have not tried to join the discourse but to close it down altogether, either by police measures or by political hard-porn. Shortly before the World Peace Council's 'Assembly for Peace and Life' in Prague in June 1983 (which itself was organised as a reply to the non-aligned European Nuclear Disarmament Convention in Berlin the month before), a private Czech Communist Party security briefing for its activists was disclosed (perhaps by a cousin of Sarah Tisdall in Prague?). This noted that 'imperialism' was trying to weaken the peace movement 'by infiltrating it with ideas, persons and whole organisations whose clear aim is to break the peace movement, to prevent its unification, etc.' These wicked groups 'are apparently conducted and financed directly from the centre of CIA and similar agencies', and END was the first of such organisations listed ('with explicit anti-Communist and anti-Soviet function'), whose 'best-known personality is Professor Thompson', along with 'numerous exiles from socialist countries'. I have already noted examples of this porn which is now being manufactured by the metre, and which is too repetitious to merit further attention.

It is curious that argument has not been joined, since the ideologists on the other side could mount a plausible case against our strategy of a 'thaw' or 'healing-process' between the citizenry of the blocs. They could mount *two* cases: a (thin) public case, and a private, or *sotto voce*, case which is stronger. It has been left to an American polemicist, Professor Mark Solomon,* to argue the public case, in a polemic, *Death Waltz to Armageddon: E.P. Thompson and the Peace Movement*, which has been dutifully extracted and translated, in several languages, in the organ-of-export of the Soviet Peace Committee, *Twentieth Century and Peace*.

Mark Solomon is a zealous pro-Soviet only-two-sidesman, and an example of that process of 'inversion' or dissident mentality which I have already discussed. He does not write badly, and the best way of describing his *Death Waltz* is to say that it is like a tract in which the right-hand page only is printed and the left-hand is left blank. On the right-hand page we have a record of the sins of successive United States governments in driving forward the nuclear arms race; much of this is true, it is relevant, and it should be remembered. On the left-hand page (where we might expect some corresponding record of Soviet behaviour) there is nothing: a sweet blank: no discussion of Soviet conventional armaments, of the division of Europe, of the occupation of Czechoslovakia by Warsaw Pact forces in 1968, a dismissive reference to my 'reflexive' views on Afghanistan. Where the Soviet Union does appear is on the right-hand page, as ecstatic points of light to throw into even deeper shadow the murky acts and intentions of the USA. Solomon's mythic descriptions of Soviet society ('the absence of a basic antagonism between government and public', 'consistent, mutually supportive relationship between the majority of the Soviet public and the government's diplomatic and defense policies') and of the 'independence' of the Soviet Peace Committee with its '130 million' members would be hilarious if it were not that the realities are so sad and anxious.

* I am told that Mark Solomon, who is an officer of the small U.S. Peace Council (affiliated to the World Peace Council), is not to be confused with Norman Solomon. It seems that 'Solomon' is a sobriquet (like 'General Ludd', etc.) which is employed by pro-Soviet polemicists in the United States to signal their surpassing wisdom.

I will take one sample of Mark Solomon's polemic:

> Thompson regularly ignites the combustible materials that inflame the Cold War. He has stated, for example, that the Soviet Union is untrustworthy because 'the information available to its citizens is strictly controlled and. . . public opinion can scarcely influence the rulers'. But Thompson does not indicate what information is withheld from Soviet citizens. Widely distributed literature on the nature of nuclear war, publicized television programs featuring US and Soviet physicians discussing the medical effects of a nuclear holocaust, the public contributions of Soviet scientists on 'nuclear winter', even graveyard humour about nuclear war, are all known aspects of Soviet life.

Unlike Professor Solomon I am not an authority on the Soviet media and information services. But I have discussed these matters with authorities (and with Soviet citizens) and have been given different accounts. I have been told that there is, indeed, a great deal of daily information (or propaganda) about nuclear weapons. But 95% of this is about *Western* nuclear weapons, and the aggressive designs of imperialism; and perhaps 5% gives reassurance that the Soviet military are also preparing those weapons which are essential for the Soviet people's 'defence'. This is to say that the information available to the Soviet public might be fairly compared with that available to the British public if they had been reduced, in 1983, to abject dependency on such brochures as the Ministry of Defence prepared under the strong guidance of Mr Heseltine—comprised of charts of SS-20s and the Soviet military build-up, together with a recommendation of cruise missiles as an 'insurance policy' for peace.

There is, in addition, much media coverage of manifestations by the Western peace movement, Greenham Common and so forth. What is absent is (a) any hard information about Soviet weaponry, etc. (Even the code-names for Soviet missiles are those used by Western intelligence, as are the estimates of their numbers.) (b) Any publication of any Western peace movement programmes and policies, appeals or books, which contain any whisper of criticism of any

Soviet military or ideological posture. (c) Objective scientific works on nuclear questions are not available, unless in certain restricted specialist libraries—even the SIPRI (Stockholm Peace Research) annual handbook must be taken in by Western visitors—and may be impounded at customs. (d) As a matter of course, publications which raise questions critical of Soviet military and diplomatic policies are disallowed, so that if it is true (as Professor Solomon insists) that the Soviet public support all their government's policies, this might perhaps be because they are not permitted to read about or discuss any others.

During 1983 some scientists associated with the Moscow Trust Group, who had been influenced by the pioneering work in peace research of the British Quaker mathematician, Professor L.F. Richardson, commenced econometric researches and attempted to elaborate an index of international tension by measuring the centimetres in the press devoted to hostile commentary on the Other. I do not know whether this is a valid approach or not. In any event, in the aftermath of the shooting-down of the Korean airliner, KAL 007, Professor Yuri Medvedkov wrote to me in the greatest alarm. Their index had suddenly sky-rocketed through the roof.

Yuri Medvedkov added: 'The most horrible rhetoric each day can be heard over the TV or radio. . . The man in the street gets lots of hatred propaganda.' He added that as a result he expected the Geneva talks to fail, and the efforts to secure a freeze would be indefinitely delayed. The Soviet public were filled with fears that there were 'plans in the West to start any night a preventive nuclear strike against Russia'. He urged upon Western peace activists every possible measure 'to keep channels open for constant dialogue'.

A count of the column inches of anti-Soviet material in the New York or London *Times* in that period would be equally alarming. It will be recalled that President Reagan used the incident to shoot down, not the Russians, but the US peace movement, forcing through a shattered Congress budgetary appropriations for the MX missile and for binary nerve-gas facilities. Whether centralised and censored or private and 'free' the major media did their own sensational thing on both sides and piled tension upon tension.

But we have strayed from the main point, which is Professor Solomon's confidence that the Soviet public is well-informed on all nuclear and international matters, that it has studied these matters with care and on every issue has freely decided to support government policies, and that, unlike us anarchistic Westerners, it stands in no need of any independent organisations or any area of uncontrolled press which might offer alternative information or even criticism of Soviet military and diplomatic policies in Soviet public life simply because (unless in the minds of a handful of embittered 'dissidents') there are no criticisms which an open-minded Soviet citizen could possibly sustain.

As it happens I have in front of me an 'Open Letter' to Professor Solomon which discusses these points in passing. It is written by Dr Mark Reitman, a member of the Moscow Trust Group, who is a mathematician, now invalided from work as a result of Parkinson's disease and diabetes. Dr Reitman writes that the fact that the information available to Soviet citizens is strictly controlled 'is not challenged by the Soviet government. . . and we are, unfortunately, obliged to confirm it':

You say that television broadcasts in which Soviet and American physicians discussed the medical consequences of nuclear catastrophe were widely publicised in the USSR. True, these broadcasts were widely publicised, especially in the West. But why do you refer to them in the plural? Such a programme occurred only once, although its participants announced that it would become a regular feature. Evidently some powerful forces interfered with this. . .

A citizen of the USSR, even if he were highly committed to the cause of peace, would find it difficult to obtain detailed and balanced information other than from the mouth of Yuri Zhukov. In particular, information about the possible calamities to come, about all aspects of a nuclear death, about the 'nuclear winter', about 'conversion': a simple survey or opinion-poll of the Muscovite intelligentsia shows that they know virtually nothing about it—in fact I myself quite recently confused 'the nuclear winter' with 'the freeze'!

I do not make this argument because I view the situation to be hopeless. On the contrary, the higher regions of Soviet administration may now be occupied by tensions between the old hard forces of control and forces looking for 'modernisation' or even democratic openings. There has been one good TV discussion between Soviet and American physicians, and with pressure from the Soviet public and the Western peace movement there might well be more. There has been one Scandinavian Women's Peacemarch through Soviet cities, and with pressure such manifestations by Western peace activists might be permitted more often. With determined pressure we might even see some centimetres of *Izvestia*'s columns given over to faithful reporting of the policies of non-aligned Western movements. What I wish to do is to rubbish the sentimental mythology promoted by Mark Solomon and others, which is damaging and counter-productive. So long as Western peace workers doze over Noddy books like his, they will be helplessly unprepared to meet events, and they will not press steadily, with self-respect and without provocation, for the human openings essential for the making of peace.*

There is in fact a more plausible case to be found within Solomon's polemic, and it is one which appeals to Western peace workers who honourably desire to redress the anti-Soviet rhetoric of their own societies by coming to a better understanding of Soviet perceptions. This case has three leading propositions.

First, it is asserted that at every stage the United States has led in the nuclear arms race, and that the Soviet Union has been in an 'arms chase' from behind, reacting defensively to Western initiatives. Therefore it follows that the onus is upon the United States, or NATO, to be the first to stop. And the Soviet Union will then follow, to a halt or a freeze.

This is a strong and significant argument. The United States has an atrocious record as pace-setter in nuclear

---

* A companion volume to Mark Solomon's *Death Waltz to Armageddon* has now been published in Britain: this is Professor V.L. Allen's *Images and Reality in the Soviet Union: or Professor Noddy's Trip to Utopia.*

weaponry, and the record of France and Britain is little better. Caspar Weinberger and his advisers are now clearly going for across-the-board superiority. Inevitably this nourishes fears among their Soviet analogues of Western nuclear blackmail or a decapitating strike. The Western peace movement is right to call 'stop!', and if need be unilaterally. The nuclear arms race has long been in part about 'face'. In Wilfred Owen's parable of the Old Man and the Young, Abram prepares Isaac for sacrifice when an angel appears and offers the Ram of Pride as substitute—

> But the old man would not so, but slew his son,
> And half the seed of Europe, one by one.

If the nuclear arms race cannot be stopped without the sacrifice of the Ram of Pride by one side or the other, then it is in the West, where the pace has usually been set and where public opinion can be brought to bear upon power, that the sacrifice must first be made.

It is also probably true that the Soviet government is now, and has been for several years, more anxious to put a cork on the nuclear arms race than the Americans. It has no taste to follow the United States into scenarios of space wars; it knows very well that in most areas the United States has the technological edge on the Soviet Union; and the diversion of skills and resources to armaments inflicts great damage on the Soviet economy and society. As a Soviet colonel has said, in an off-the-record interview:

> We do have internal problems: we need an economic reform, we need to expand human rights in our country and further to develop Soviet democracy. And we can only make headway in tackling our problems under conditions of prolonged detente. We need detente, lots and lots of detente.
>
> (*Detente*, October 1984.)

This is not to say that there are no Soviet hawks (whom Western hawks are doing their best to strengthen), nor that Soviet negotiators will not be as hard-nosed as those of the United States. It is to say that the main thrust of the nuclear

arms race is now from the USA (with Britain), and that
Soviet professions of a desire for a freeze and for extensive
measures of arms control are a good deal less spurious than
professions of Western leaders.

This argument is good. But it has limits. It narrows the
question down to that of nuclear weapons only. It is silent
about conventional weapons; it is silent about the political
and ideological components of bloc confrontation; and it
confuses historical origins with present consequences. (Such
writers as the two Solomons are strangely silent as to the
means by which the USSR made the prodigious stretch
forward to nuclear 'parity', and as to the consequences of
this assertion of 'balance'.) The argument has been presented
most ably by Roy and Zhores Medvedev, and I have criticised
its limitations in 'Exterminism Reviewed'

Second, we are enjoined—in the pursuit of peace—to set
aside all considerations which do not bear directly upon
nuclear weapons and their control. It is said that an 'anti-
war movement' must narrow its focus, not to the occasions
of war and the causes of tension, but to the nuclear instruments only, and that any other matter is extraneous and
divisive. This is a bad argument. It offers to disinfect our
cruel historical experience of all political and ideological
content. It can drag the peace movement into the tit-for-tat
rituals of 'balance'. At worst, it leaves us like the spectators
at Wimbledon, craning our necks as the ball goes to and fro
between the superpowers, cheering on one side. Much of my
writing in the past three years presents a counter-argument,
and I will leave it at that.

Third, we are enjoined to recall the Soviet people's
prodigious losses in World War II (and, indeed, in the earlier
wars of intervention) and to understand their deeply defensive mentality. This is also a good and significant argument.
But its significance must be examined with some care.

The figure which is customarily used to indicate Soviet
losses in World War II is some twenty million lives. This is
approximate only, and to this must be added the wholesale
destruction of towns and villages, of industrial and agri-
cultural plant, of schools, of livestock, and the 'scorched

earth' of the western and southern regions (including the
most productive and populous regions) of the Soviet Union.
It is as if the whole of New England, New York State and
some of the Mid-West of the USA, together with a large part
of its population, had been 'taken out'. There is no way in
which such an experience will not have traumatised the
Soviet historical memory.

Critics of Soviet policies sometimes offer qualifications,
but certain of these are beside the point. It is true that other
European nations suffered comparable *pro rata* losses (for
example, Poland and Yugoslavia). But this does not lessen
Soviet losses by one digit; at the most it suggests that the
Soviet memory of the 'Great Patriotic War' is selective and
ungenerous to the losses of others, as is the way of all nations.
(Americans, whose folk-and-media memory of World War II
is absurdly US-centric, should be the last to complain.) It is
also true that umpteen million lives were lost in the previous
two decades by the self-inflicted savagery of Stalinist purges,
the liquidation of the kulaks, and so on. But this also is
beside the point. These losses have inflicted their own
traumas, but the healing of those wounds (if they can be
healed) is a matter which the Soviet people must resolve
amongst themselves. Whereas the losses inflicted by Hitler's
armies are remembered as an unprovoked act of aggression,
delivered without warning, and inflicted from 'the West'.
This laid down a ground in Soviet popular expectation
which is easily stirred into anxiety: may there not be 'plans
in the West to start any night a preventive nuclear strike
against Russia'?

It is necessary to bear these perceptions in mind also when
considering the difficult questions of 'Yalta' and the division
of Europe. I argue repeatedly in *The Heavy Dancers* that
these are proper and central questions for the peace movement, and that we must place them on the agenda. But this
cannot be done in a way which offends against what is just
in Soviet historical experience. Glib cold warriors today
imply that the entry of Soviet armies into Central and
Eastern Europe in 1944-5 was done with premeditated and
aggressive intent, which 'Yalta' then condoned. But this is

not how men and women of my own generation remember
the event. We recall a Europe totally subordinated to Nazi
and Fascist militarism; and then Soviet armies (fighting
sometimes, as in the suburbs of Stalingrad, with petrol-
bottles and their bare hands) forcing that invincible and
implacable military machine backwards, long before the
Western Allies had launched their long-trumpeted Second
Front. Soviet armies entered Central Europe and advanced
to the Elbe in pursuit of Hitler's armies, and they were at
that stage no more engaged in actions of expansion than
were the armies of the Western Allies in Italy, Holland or
France. If Soviet armies remained in East Germany, so also
do American, British and French armies remain in West
Germany to this day. And it was the Western Allies who
tore up their treaty obligations by initiating West German
rearmament.

I apologise for rehearsing this brutal historical ABC, but
I find that in some discussions of 'Yalta' it is forgotten, even
by sections of the peace movement. The historical origins
of the division of Europe condone nothing that followed;
and (in the East) they do not condone the betrayal of
Poland, the twice-repeated betrayal of Czechoslovak democracy, and the Stalinist rigours throughout the whole region.
These are the traumas which we now have to heal. But we
cannot heal them if we offend the historical memory of the
Soviet public, if we suppress the record of Soviet suffering
and valour, and view 'Yalta' only from the Western side.*

---

* A brochure prepared by 'Solidarity' (the Solidarność Information
Office in London) refers to 'the infamous Yalta Conference which
resulted in the enslavement of more than 150 million people in
Central and Eastern Europe [and which] made the Soviet Union the
greatest threat to world peace since the demise of Hitler's Third
Reich'. It calls on the British government to 'renounce Yalta',
advertising a public meeting in support of this demand (February
4th, 1985) to be addressed by Winston Churchill, M.P. President
Reagan, during his election campaign, gratified a section of his
Polish-American constituents with a similar rhetorical repudiation of
'Yalta', while Zbigniew Brzezinski has called in the *New York
Times* for a 'well-funded French–British–West German-Italian
consortium to aid Eastern European efforts to emancipate peacefully', in supplement to American aid in support of dissident 'subversion'. Such bald incitements, which revive the rhetoric of John

The Soviet popular memory of the losses of war is just and to be respected. Yet we still have to enquire whether this is an influence which, in every circumstance, is making for peace. And the evidence here is contradictory. It does not necessarily follow that great suffering disposes a nation to peace: there are historical examples on the other side. We may take it that, in the Soviet case, it has enforced a desire for peace. Yet this finds expression in a willingness to concede to the Soviet rulers extraordinary authority over every matter concerned with Soviet 'defence', to ensure that the experience of 1941–44 shall never be repeated. In the name of 'defence' the Soviet public has seemed to be willing to accept the diversion of vast resources to military expenditure, restrictions upon civil rights, and restraints upon living standards. It is precisely in their highly-advertised role as defenders of 'peace' against Western (or Chinese) imperialist aggression that the old-guard post-Stalinist leadership legitimises its rule and resists long-overdue reforms.

We have, then, a paradox: the Soviet public has a peaceful disposition, and Western visitors to the USSR are overwhelmed with peaceful assurances which are heartfelt and sincere. Yet the USSR is a society in which the visibility of the military is higher than in any Western democracy. Great events of state, parades in Red Square, solemn state funerals, have the highest military symbolism. They signal that this is a nation which feels itself to be threatened and besieged in which the prime function of the rulers is to build up the nation's defences, and in which all else must be subordinated to these priorities.

The traumas of World War II also left numb the Soviet internationalist conscience. In popular memory the USSR is seen as the victim of external invasion, and the memory imposes itself on the perception of the present. I am told that the ordinary man or woman in a Moscow queue concern themselves little about the policies of their rulers towards

Foster Dulles, do nothing to advance the causes of civil rights or of Polish autonomy, destroy the chances of a healing-process between the blocs, and should be repudiated by independent peace forces in West or East. We can never permit the ideologists and agencies of the cold war to set our own citizens agenda.

Czechoslovakia or Afghanistan; if they grumble, it may be about supporting lazy and ungrateful Poles, or subsidising indigent Third World nations at the expense of their own standard of living. They do, however, believe in the reality of the threat of the Other, just as the majority of the British and American public have proved themselves to be true believers; and, like our own publics, they endorse 'defence'.

I became, a year or two ago, a little vexed by the Simple Solomons who repeatedly assure us that, because the Soviet people suffered grievously forty years ago, their rulers could not possibly, in any circumstances, take an unpeaceful action today. And I wrote, inadvisedly, in February 1983 about Soviet 'paranoia', and added:

> Those weeping Soviet grandmothers who still deck with flowers the graves of the last war have dry eyes for Afghanistan, as they had, in 1968, for Czechoslovakia. The Soviet people will support their rulers in preparations for any war that is 'in defence of peace'.

No sentences which I have written gave more offence to some in the peace movement. And I am convinced that they truly offended some Soviet readers, not only in form but in reality. A year later, at a conference in Athens, Mr Yuri Zhukov quoted these lines and proclaimed them to be an insult to the entire Soviet people which unmasked my pretences to be any kind of advocate of peace. Mr Zhukov is a great showman, who has a regular slot on prime-time Soviet TV in which he 'answers' letters about war and peace, but on this occasion I think he spoke from his heart. My words seemed to him, when set against the remembered suffering of World War II, to be obscene.

I have been asked: why did I write these lines? I did not write them to mock the grief of Soviet grandmothers, and if it seems otherwise then the words were ill-written. I was vexed with the Soviet apologists (especially in the West) who increasingly invoked these grandmothers in order to deflect us into sentiment and away from any analysis of Soviet policies. There are, after all, some grandmothers and grandfathers in the West, who still cherish graves of the last war, but who do not for that reason remain silent about their own governments' sins. I wrote those lines simply because I think that they are true. The Soviet public, like great sections of the Western public, will support all military preparations in the name of 'defence'; and perhaps will support them even more readily because of its historical memories of the horrors of war. A war 'in defence of peace' has been going on now for five years in Afghanistan, and the Soviet public (which may approve of it less than it did) has not yet been able to find any means to call its course in question.

Yet the argument which enforces Soviet war experiences remains a sound and important argument. Undoubtedly the Soviet people are of a peaceful disposition; the very notion of war fills them with nausea; and this may be contrasted with the disposition of a section of the American public which, never having suffered such experiences on American territory, can be whipped up into shallow and braggart clamour to 'stand up to the Commies' everywhere, so long as this can be done by space-age technological marvels and on some other nation's territory and without risk to one drop of sacred American blood. If the Soviet public is encouraged to perpetuate World War II memories with familial rituals—for example, the newly-weds visiting the graves of their kin on their wedding-day—then this may cement Soviet patriotism but it is not a source of braggart adventurism. Such ceremonial pieties merit Western respect, and not least from that other part of the American public which is seeking to understand this combination of Soviet defensiveness and pride.

But the peaceful disposition of a people who have no means to inform themselves on military questions, and who cannot voice criticisms nor discuss alternative policies, does not take us very far. It has taken a good number of Soviet citizens, in 1983 and 1984, into a number of actions and demonstrations organised on their behalf by the Soviet Peace Committee, in response to the Western peace movement. On these occasions the slogans are usually determined (and the placards are manufactured) by the organisers, and it is satisfactory to note that more even-handed slogans have now appeared than the old denunciations of Western imperialism. In particular the slogan has now appeared: 'No Nuclear Weapons in Europe, West or East! No nuclear weapons anywhere in the world!' I take this to be an advance, even though no slogans critical of Soviet weaponry are permitted, and the speeches and demands continue to be directed against the West.

I have no doubt that many of the demonstrators in Moscow and other cities genuinely wished to further the cause of peace. There is some kind of stirring in public opinion going on. In the summer of 1984 some members of the Moscow Trust Group sallied out into Moscow streets with an unauthorised petition calling on the leaders of the USSR and USA to hold a summit meeting. They also met with a ready response, from a random selection of the public who knew that the petition was not 'official'. Dr Mark Reitman, who shares the view of myself (and Mark Solomon) that the Soviet people are disposed to peace, described the incident in his 'Open Letter':

> We saw how unanimously Soviet people spoke out on behalf of peace when we gathered signatures. . . We saw close up the faces of women, stooping heavily under the load of their shopping bags when they read the short text of the appeal and signed it, not without difficulty freeing the right hand from its burden. These were impressive faces. Like the faces of three men from a kvas queue, who at first stood indifferent and motionless, but who hastily added their signatures onto the disappearing sheet when the militia and the police dragged one of us off into a car. These are the people Thompson refers to as 'the third force'.
>
> You, comrade Solomon, are enraptured by 'columns of quietly determined marchers carrying signs demanding that weapons of mass destruction be banished everywhere'. But I would venture to point out that marching under banners and slogans is not very difficult when you have been specially released from work or lectures for this purpose, and the boss has instructed you as to which column you are to join. Far more striking is the determination to stand up for peace under extraordinary conditions. . .

We are all agreed, then—myself, Dr Reitman, and the Venerable Solomon—that the Soviet people want peace. This strengthens the case of the Western peace movement. We can all agree that this is a time for Western governments, not to pile up new weapons, but to strengthen this peaceful disposition by offering reconciliation and concession. It is also the time (but here Professor Solomon does not agree) for Western peace workers to try to break through the rigid controls set up by the deeply-defensive (and sometimes offensive) security and ideological establishments, and to effect multiple direct contacts with Soviet citizens. This direct communication will also be welcomed by most Soviet citizens, who are yearning for a 'thaw'. In short, our independent friends in East Europe and in Moscow have made the right diagnosis. What we need most of all now is the establishment of trust, and of dialogue, between peoples, without which, whatever the peoples of both sides may 'want', they will not get it. If wishes were horses, beggars would be riders. In a climate of deepening distrust they will get not peace but more weapons and eventually terminal war.

It can be seen that the pro-Soviet only-two-sidesmen have two strong arguments: the United States (with Britain and NATO) are driving forward the nuclear arms race: and there is no evidence that Soviet popular culture nourishes aggressive and expansionist urges. It might seem to follow that this is a moment when the Communist authorities would welcome our strategies for a thaw between peoples and a healing of bloc divisions. Yet some of them have shown themselves to be implacably opposed, to the extent of lampooning non-aligned peace movements as NATO agencies, denying peace activists visas, in certain cases arresting them and throwing them out of their countries, confiscating Western peace materials at the border and intercepting post.

What this suggests is that the public case of pro-Soviet apologists is concealing a private case, which may only be expressed *sotto voce*, if at all. The *sotto voce* case is a strong one, and one which the peace movement should understand and take into account. But by its very nature it is not one which Mr Zhukov or Professor Solomon, or any pro-Soviet apologist, can argue aloud. It is that the Soviet Union after

decades of civil war, purges, war and cold war, repression
and censorship, finds itself now without any mechanisms
of self-reform, and its political and intellectual life has got
snarled up into so many knots that the authorities fear any
external influences as 'de-stabilising'. If the infection of
peace were to pass from West to East, in self-activating
forms which exposed the Communist authorities themselves
to criticism, then there is no way of estimating into what
recesses of Communist society the epidemic might reach.

Mark Solomon could not possibly argue this case, since
he has assured his readers that Soviet society is the most
stable known to time. There is no antagonism between
government and public, and there are 'consistent, mutually
supportive' relations between government and public in all
matters of defence and foreign policy. That being so, it must
puzzle Solomon's readers to know why government takes
such careful measures to channel and invigilate relations
between Soviet and Western publics, and why a few score of
independent-minded peaceniks have been persecuted by the
KGB. One would have supposed that if Mark Reitman or
Olga Medvedkova had got hold of some mistaken views, then
this should be a matter beneath the notice of the state, and it
could safely be left to sturdy-minded Soviet citizens to
dissuade them or to laugh them out of court. And one
would have supposed that if Mient-Jan Faber or Randall
Forsberg, Daniel Ellsberg or Mary Kaldor were to hold
public lectures and seminars in Leningrad or Moscow, in
which they made some even-handed criticisms of both US
and Soviet nuclear policies, then it could be left to the good
sense of the audience to decide on the merits of the case.

Both suppositions would have been wrong. The Soviet
authorities—or at least the old guard among them—are
frightened of the least action derogatory to the 'leading role
of the Party'. They are fearful of allowing their 'mutually
supportive' citizens to stray on their own any further than
the end of the Party street. And (at the risk of being called
'anti-Soviet' once again) I will say that I am in turn frightened by a government which places so little trust in its own
citizens, and which is one of the world's two great ranchers

of nuclear weapons. I cannot see how the peaceful disposition of these citizens can be, in any emergency, an effective restraint upon government.

This is the political bind we are in, and it explains some of the divisions between movements for peace and for 'peace' which have become apparent in 1983 and 1984. So long as it seemed possible that the non-aligned Western movement— German Greens and Social-Democrats, Dutch churches, British CND and Greenham women, American freeze, Italian Eurocommunists—might actually stop cruise and Pershing II deployments, the Soviet ideologists confined themselves to grumbling polemic, slander upon a few individuals, and low-profile attempts at manipulation. Once deployment had taken place, the non-aligned elements (with their suspect independent contacts in the East) became—in orthodox Communist perception—expendable. As Stalin once asked: 'How many divisions has the Pope?' All those untidy myriads of Western marchers had been unable to topple one citadel of Western power. Hard-nosed Communist leaders put the peace movement in a 'pending' file, tried to stub out the sparks of independent groups in the East, and squared up to their real antagonists: Reagan, Thatcher, Kohl. If one takes an only-two-sidesman view, then one can see their point.

But the growing apparatus of Warsaw bloc official peace institutions still had to be found employment. As it seems to me, they were given a new brief. This was to 'unite' the Western and Eastern peace and 'peace' movements behind a common anti-war programme, and, insofar as possible, bring Western movements under the hegemony of the Helsinki-based World Peace Council. In doing so they should be willing to cut their losses. Certain articulate non-aligned spokespersons should be lampooned and driven out (with the help of such materials as those provided by Mark Solomon and Professor V.L. Allen). They should be willing to induce splits in the Western movement, and to tie it up in internecine divisions. The majority Western peace movements were becoming an ill-disciplined nuisance and even making raids into the East. It might now be scattered, and a part of it (even if a minority) should be firmly brought within World Peace Council leadership so that it might still have nuisance-value as auxiliary to Soviet diplomacy.

I take this to have been (and still to be) the brief of the Soviet Peace Committee, which is run by some of the toughest hard-line ideologists in the Warsaw bloc. Its President, Yuri Zhukov, earned his spurs as a *Pravda* columnist (a sort of Soviet Bernard Levin or William Buckley) during the Warsaw Pact 'fraternal' occupation of Czechoslovakia in 1968, and he has recently been sent on a Soviet Party delegation to split the Spanish Communists. To be just, I think the operation has critics among doves even within the Soviet apparatus, and it has never been followed wholeheartedly by the more flexible Hungarian Peace Council.

The operation has not succeeded, although it continues. At Athens in February 1984 there was a conference, hosted by the peace committee of the governing party, PASOK, at which Eastern 'officials' and Western movements met together. I there set out openly the difficulties of comparing like and unlike as if both were 'peace movements'; if Western voluntary organisations, confronting Western militarism, were asked to 'unite' with state-endorsed organisations in the East which were also confronting Western militarism, then we could not regard this as 'a fair swap'. I appealed for a thaw and citizen communication between the blocs ('What Kind of Partnership?' in *The Heavy Dancers*). Professor Hylke Tromp, a leading Dutch peace researcher, Andräs Zumach from West Germany, Chiara Ingrao from Italy, and many others made similar appeals. The conference broke up inconclusively, with some embitterment. In the Soviet hissing that followed, blame was placed upon myself and Mient-Jan Faber (General Secretary of the Dutch IKV), who were alleged, in a Soviet foreign-language hand-out, *News from the USSR*, to have issued exhortations to 'change the socialist system' in the East. In an interview with CND's monthly, *Sanity*, Zhukov used the hospitality of its columns to accuse me of wishing to 'bury the peace movement'.

Throughout the year the weary skirmishing has gone on. In the GDR independent women peace activists, Barbel Bohley and Ulrike Poppe, were arrested after meeting

Barbara Einhorn, an END and CND activist, who was roughly detained, interrogated, and thrown out of the country. Representatives of the IKV and of French CODENE who tried to hold a seminar with members of Charter 77 were thrown out of Czechoslovakia. British, Dutch and West German peace workers have been refused visas to the GDR. Attempts to engage in discussion of the bloc division of Europe, and of means of healing it, have been repudiated indignantly by the Soviet Peace Committee as 'interference in internal affairs' or have been caricatured as 'revanchist, unrealizable dreams of changing the post-war European territorial and political arrangement'. Any attempt to place on the agenda the sensitive 'German question' in any form whatsoever—for example, in Rapacki terms or in terms of the demilitarisation of both Germanies within some loose associative structure—has been denounced without discussion as 'neo-fascist revanchism'. Criticisms by Western peace movements of Soviet missile deployments in Czechoslovakia and the GDR have been repudiated with indignation as products of NATO propaganda. ('The nerves of the Soviet people are strong,' says Zhukov.) The network of campaigning non-aligned Western peace organisations, the IPCC (p. 40), which grew up from its own resources to meet Western needs of consultation and co-ordination is denounced as if it were a trespass upon the World Peace Council's proprietorial cabbage-patch—a Council which lays claim to some superordinate authority over all to do with 'peace'. Yuri Zhukov writes:

Attempts are being made to isolate the anti-war movements in the West, to place them under a new leadership which would stand in opposition to the World Peace Council.

(*International Life*, June 1984.)

After months of painful and time-taking negotiation, delegations from several Warsaw bloc peace committees (including the Soviet) attended at the European Nuclear Disarmament Convention in Perugia. In nearly every case independents from the East were prevented from coming,

unless they were already in the West. It was scarcely a dialogue of open minds, and there were discourtesies on both
sides which have been sufficiently reported in the peace
movements' press. But perhaps dialogue was not what the
hard-liners of the Soviet Peace Committee had in mind?
Early in October 1984 there was summoned (mostly by
give-away air tickets) by the World Peace Council at Helsinki
a select private conference of 'Representatives of Peace,
Disarmament and Anti-War Movements from Europe and
America'. The United States delegation was headed by
(surprise!) Professor Mark Solomon, Co-Chair of the US
Peace Council. Mr Yuri Zhukov entertained the delegates on
the first day with his now-predictable litany of abuse of
myself, Mient-Jan Faber, Mary Kaldor and (for novelty)
two Finnish Eurocommunists:

> It is not difficult to guess who is interested in forming a bloc of a
> definite group of organizations acting under the flag of the struggle
> for peace—a bloc which would abandon the anti-nuclear struggle
> and devote itself to the struggle aimed at undermining the state
> system of the socialist countries.

And Zhukov, in the name of 'unity' (!), exerted every effort
to drive off the non-aligned movement and to drill the ragged
remnants into one united anti-war movement, Peace Councils
East and West, behind the demands prescribed by the Bureau
of the World Peace Council. According to the TASS report,
the conference at Helsinki concluded with a unanimous
resolution that:

> The enemies of peace are using extremely subtle methods to under-
> mine the peace movements. Above all they are striving to lead
> these movements astray from the line of continued struggle against
> nuclear war and convert them to that other line, the aim of which is
> a revision of the boundaries formed after the Second World War
> and intervention in the affairs of the socialist countries. (*Népsza-
> badság*, 9 October 1984.)

This kind of attempt at splitting has no chance of success.
Anyone who knows anything about the Scandinavian, British,

Dutch, German, Spanish and Italian movements will know this. As for the American movement, its multitudinous amoeboid formations can be split (unless in a few central offices) no more than a knife can split water. But the movements can be confused, diverted into time-wasting ill-tempered arguments, even a little demoralised. In my own view, which is not a majority view, these games of diplomatic footsie between utterly unlike organisations with opposed functions should be brought to an end. We do not have the time or resources for large, inconclusive, snarling conferences. If we wish to attempt dialogue with the 'officials' (which we should) we should opt for smaller and more private fora. If President Reagan is to be serious about arms control he will show it by sacking Richard Perle, and if the Soviet Peace Committee is to be serious about dialogue it will pension off Mr Yuri Zhukov.

The revelation of all this sweet billing and cooing in the dove-cotes of international 'peace' may come as a surprise to some readers, since some of it has been known only to those circles which attend conferences or monitor the Eastern press. Yet it raises issues which should be in the public peace domain. And what the record of the past three years suggests to me is uncertainty. The Communist authorities reveal an extraordinary sense of insecurity in the face of the Western peace movement. It even seems that a certain kind of old-style Communist ideologist feels *more* secure when confronting his old-style mirror-opposite—some Western warrior embattled like the heroic Mr Heseltine across the Berlin Wall. All that has the comfort of the familiar: the script is known by rote. But the Western peace movement proposes unknown and sensitive problems and is received with a deep sense of threat.

I said a few pages back that pro-Soviet apologists might have a strong case, but one which may only be expressed *sotto voce*, if at all. The situation on the other side has become so screwed up, and in several different ways, that the infection of peace, in certain circumstances, actually could be de-stabilising. And, in the present posture of NATO, any 'de-stabilisation' to the East would be seized upon as a sign of Communist 'weakness', and would be exploited to NATO's advantage. This would probably induce the hardest-line reactions from the insecure Communist apparatus, and could lead on to enhanced bloc confrontation and enhanced internal repression. In short, any meddlesome attempts by Western peace movements to export the 'third way' to the East could blow up in their own faces; they could set in motion a chain of events which led to the opposite outcome.

This is not a stupid argument. In the politics of peace it is the most sensitive place of all, and in the coming years the most critical problems of both strategy and theory will lie in this area. No-one can foresee how things will work out, no-one has the expertise to foretell internal developments. But certain general observations may be offered.

First, some caution should be exercised before we accept this threatening term, 'de-stabilisation'. For the reigning incumbents of power any challenge to their authority will be perceived as 'de-stabilising'. Mrs Thatcher might find her authority 'de-stabilised' by a Freedom of Information Act or by a reproof from her bishops. Some experts on Soviet affairs (including Soviet citizens) advise that no extensive reforms are likely unless they are initiated from within the Party and from above. Even so, the mechanisms of reform are obscure, and will involve intense faction-fighting between interest-groups. And if reforms promise to be extensive as, for example, in the first years of Khrushchev, a great many powerful and comfortable people might find their positions to be threatened: not only hawks in the Politbureau and officials of the KGB, but also their deferential subordinates such as the learned Thebans of the State University of Tyumen. All these people will set up a great squawking that not only their jobs and patronage but also the Soviet state itself is being 'de-stabilised', and laid open to the aggressive designs of Western imperialism. What this emphasises is that the clipping of the wings of power is a necessary and normal objective of the peace movement, in the East as in the West, and that an outcry about 'de-stabilisation' could be the last refuge of the cold war scoundrels on both sides.

There could be, in the Soviet Union, a very much more untidy political scenario. This is a society which is, by any reckoning, long overdue for rationalisation and reform and most of the Soviet public knows it. Soviet life is tied up into dozens of knots, in part (but only in part) because of the protraction through decades of the cold war. The incumbent Soviet rulers need the cold war, and the siege mentality that goes with it, to hold their own ramshackle rule together. But in Russian history—way back into time, and before the Soviet Union was invented—'Westernising' influences have often been a precipitant of change. It is not impossible that the influence of the Western peace movement (which cannot plausibly be seen as the threatening Other) could precipitate an extensive thaw in culture and ideology, especially among the younger generation.

I will not attempt to foretell what contradictory ideological and political events might follow. But one thing is very clear. This will not be the moment for President Reagan (or his successor) to hurry forward new instalments of weaponry, nor for Western warriors to seek to take advantage of Soviet confusion by poking around in Soviet affairs and by beaming advice on Radio Liberty. They will of course attempt to meddle, and that is why it will be the first duty of the Western peace movement—not to meddle on its own accord—but to exert all its influence upon Western governments to meet a Soviet thaw with concession, reconciliation and measures of disarmament. If that could be done, then what might be 'de-stabilised' would be the cold war itself.

There is, secondly, a more serious possibility of 'de-stabilisation'. While this is improbable in the Soviet Union, successive episodes of 'instability' and 'normalisation' appear to be the norm in Eastern and Central Europe. And however clearly we may set out, as a theoretical proposition, the 'third way' of peace, in the real political world all social and intellectual forces are subject to the gravitational pull of the 'two sides'. As soon as any element detaches itself from one pole, it senses the tug of the other. The cold war, like a patrolling involuntary moon, pulls the tides of politics now to the West, now to the East.

All this was clear in the case of Poland. If the strategy of dialogue and of 'recognition' between the Western peace movement and autonomous social movements in the East was to be tested, surely the huge spaces forced open by Solidarity afforded abundant opportunity? Yet Poland has seemed to be, in the matter of peace, the lemon in the basket of oranges. It is not even true that the strategy was attempted and failed. It was never put to serious trial.

One comment on this record will be found in my exchange with Timothy Garton Ash in 1982 in the *Spectator*. Mr Ash has now returned to his criticisms in the final chapter of his study, *The Polish Revolution* (1983), which is a serious essay in political analysis. His challenge to the peace movement, and more especially to END and to myself, is not unfair. Yet it involves misunderstandings and misrecognitions which must take us into parish-pump matters.

Ash notes the remarkable simultaneity of the emergence of Solidarity and of peace movements in 1980-1. Yet 'these two apparently parallel movements showed remarkably *little* interest in each other. Most western peace campaigners did not see their struggle against cruise and Pershing II missiles as being linked to, let alone conditional upon, Solidarity's struggle'. A 'rare exception' was British END. Yet he implies that END's interest was largely rhetorical and for the record. A 'leading member of the international relations department attached to the National Commission of Solidarnosc in Gdansk' has informed him that END never formally approached Solidarity's leadership, and 'there had been almost no approaches from any of the western peace movements'. And she added: 'I think they were afraid of what they might find.'

But Mr Ash is trying to have his argument both ways. On the one hand, he explains (correctly) that Solidarity 'deliberately kept the whole area of defence and foreign policy off the agenda' because any intervention into such sensitive issues would have damaged the possibilities of a 'peaceful compromise' with the Polish regime. Solidarity was not a peace movement and it did not (until its final Congress) express any views on armaments. On the other hand, western peace movements are chided for not entering into some kind of formal diplomatic relations with the Hotel Morski in Gdansk—relations which, as we knew very well both from Solidarity's public positions and our own private enquiries, had not been invited and might be unwelcome.

The formality of Ash's language disguises the incoherence of organisations and the pace of events. For most of the time the 'international relations department attached to the National Commission' at Gdansk was a small group of translators working amidst hubbub and with little experience of the West; when a letter arrived belatedly, in a pile of post, from Len Murray, the General Secretary of the British TUC, 'the first reaction was: "Who's he? What's that?" ' (John Taylor, *Five Months with Solidarity*, p. 6). And of course: how could it have been otherwise? And, on the other side, 'western peace movements', which could bring out 'millions' onto the streets, sound like very heavy pieces of furniture, whereas they were movements made up of five parts of mood and of consciousness and one part of organisation. None of them had the resources to send formal delegations on speculative visits, nor to send ambassadors to present their credentials at Solidarity's Court of St. James. In Britain, CND, which is certainly open to criticism for insularity, did not appoint an international worker until the end of 1984; and END, in 1981, had 1½ full-time workers, deluged with work, and the most slender resources for travel. Moreover—and this is of general importance—END, as a point of principle, does not offer to intervene or to 'organise' on the other side. Dialogue, yes; interference, no.

In the early days of Solidarity the Institute for Workers Control (which is closely associated with the Russell Peace Foundation) attempted to send a formal delegation which would have included members of END Committee. The attempt was perhaps too high-profile, and visas were refused. In the next year several distinct attempts were made to interest pro-Solidarnosc weeklies or presses in publishing the END Appeal. The suggestions were always turned down. The message that came back to us, loud and clear, was that Solidarity did not wish to enter into relations with peace

movements and might indeed find these compromising. In
these circumstances British and other western peace activists
visited Poland low-profile and on their own free enterprise—
not as ambassadors to the Hotel Morski but simply as
supporters of peace, trade unionism and civil rights. They
always met with a ready welcome; but they also discovered,
to their dismay, that—in Mr Ash's words—'a great many
Solidarity supporters privately thought the western peace
movement was a bad thing, because it tended to weaken the
West's resistance to Soviet imperialism'.

It is a record of non-communication and misrecognition.
In our view, Solidarity had proclaimed that it was a trade-
union movement *only*, and therefore it was the first responsibility of Western trades-union and Labour movements to
make a response. Some of us did our best to press forward
this mutual recognition, but the British response was sluggish
and inadequate and (but this is another story) the advisors
of Solidarity and KOR in exile did not always appear to wish
that this recognition should take place. Meanwhile it became
daily more clear that the Polish renewal *was* a peace question.
On the one hand, it signalled an opening towards the East
and a crumblihg of the blocs, and Solidarnosc badges multi-
plied at western peace demonstrations. On the other hand,
the ominous preparations for Soviet or Warsaw Pact intervention threatened the entire peace project. It was
emphatically a time when Solidarity (and KOR) and the
peace movements should have found time for dialogue with
each other.

I am certainly willing to accept that the Western peace
movement merits some of Solidarity's and Mr Ash's criticisms.
But I cannot accept that misrecognitions were only on the
western side, nor can I accept the argument as presented
in Ash's terms. For he writes (of Solidarity's leadership):

At first, they recognised as western 'allies' almost anyone who
declared themselves as 'allies'. Later, they became more discriminat-
ing about their western supporters. They did not particularly
recognise the western peace movement as an ally because the western peace movement did not particularly distinguish itself as an
ally, by vocal or practical support where it mattered. They were

more inclined to recognise in the initials NATO an ally, because the voice of NATO was actually heard loud and clear, for example in December 1980, warning the Soviet Union against armed intervention. If 300,000 people had marched through the streets of Bonn to warn the Soviets against intervention, as they did in October 1981 to protest against NATO's new Pershing II and cruise missiles, then Solidarity members might have begun to think seriously about their nearest western counterparts.

There is something right in this passage and there is something wrong. If I attend to what is wrong, it is because this illustrates how misrecognitions arise (which still continue and will recur). I take it that Mr Ash is saying that 'at first' (1980?) Solidarity was open to any kind of alliances with the West, but that 'later' (by 1981?) the leadership was tipping in its interests towards NATO. He does not explain what 'practical support' Solidarity hoped to obtain from peace movements whose approaches it did not wish to receive. So far as 'vocal support', Solidarity was very probably not in any position to know what support it had. The West German peace movement could not have mounted 300,000 people in the streets of Bonn in December 1980, because, as we have seen (p. 219), as a mass movement it did not arrive on the scene until October 1981. At that great Bonn demonstration, the question of peace and Poland very certainly found vocal expression. I was present at that huge meeting, and perhaps no speaker met with a warmer reception than Erhard Eppler, who declared, to immense applause, 'Any Soviet intervention in Poland affects us all.'*

Two weeks later I was a speaker at CND's rally of some quarter-of-a-million in Hyde Park, and declared: 'We must demand upon both NATO and the Warsaw powers—no intervention in either Greece or Poland. Let Poland be Polish and let Greece be Greek!' Once again the huge crowd responded with applause. Similar messages went out from the great

* 'Wir feiern hierzulande den Mut der Polen, die sich nicht mehr vorschreiben lassen wollen, wie sie zu leben haben. Ist es so schlimm, wenn wir uns nicht vorschreiben lassen wollen, wie wir zu sterben haben? Die Europäiserung Europas findet nicht nur an der Weichsel statt, sondern auch am Rhein. Das bedeutet auch: Eine sowjetische Intervention in Polen träfe uns alle.' (*Bonn 10.10.81*, p. 114.)

Amsterdam demonstration a week later, and no doubt from
other capitals, and it is difficult to know how we could have
been more 'vocal' than that.

This was very late in the day. The Kremlin may not have
been impressed by these vocal offerings, nor by the many
that had preceded them. But the *Daily Telegraph* was, and it
editorialised (October 26, 1981): 'Mr Brezhnev would long
since have sent in the Red Army to crush Solidarity had he
not feared that the gruesome spectacle would stop the now,
for him, almost unbelievably promising European "Peace"
movement in its tracks.' It is conceivable that Western peace
voices were among the field of political forces which enforced a 'Polish' solution instead of a far more terrible re-
enactment of Hungarian and Czechoslovak experience. But,
if so, how was Solidarity to know that our voices were
raised? Do they know now? The official Communist media
in Poland will certainly have suppressed this part of our
message (while enlarging all parts critical of NATO). And
neither Radio Free Europe nor the Voice of America will
have gone out of their way to correct them.

By October 1981 the movements may have been within
reach of mutual recognition. But it was already too late.
Influential hands had been extended from the West to
Solidarity, but (in my own experience) we never received
any firm hand-clasp in return. This was not only because
Solidarity wished to keep its hands out of sensitive areas.
It was also because Solidarity, in its foreign relations, had
become sucked within the tidal tug of that patrolling moon,
the cold war, and had come, as Ash says, to 'recognise in
the initials NATO an ally'. Moreover, all the resources for
ready communication lay on that side. The 'voice of NATO'
could be heard 'loud and clear', even through the Polish
static, because it could be projected by multiple loud-hailers.
The peace movement had no 'Radio Peace', few foreign
correspondents or expense-account emissaries who could flit
to and fro. And in many Western nations the role of spokespersons and prime defenders of Solidarity had been taken
over by first and second generation émigré Poles, deeply
embittered by prior experiences of betrayal, fiercely hostile

to 'the Left', and in some cases actual advocates of the 'roll back' of 'Yalta', by military force. The substantial Solidarity headquarters in the expensive heart of Washington proclaims not only the loyalty of the vast American-Polish community, but also the assimilation of this loyalty to a Reaganish view of the world.

A few days after the proclamation of martial law I attended the most mournful political event of my life: a demonstration of protest called in Hyde Park. It was a day as bitter and cold as were our hearts. I felt shame at the small numbers —a few thousand only—picking their way through the ice and turning up their collars against the wind. The scene seemed to symbolise the return of the cold war, just as the scene of CND's great demonstration in the same place only eight weeks before had symbolised the promise of thaw. There was a good scattering of CND badges: not nearly enough, but at least the peace activists turned out better than the multitude of our critics, who in the warmth of their homes had become Solidarity supporters overnight and were laughing at us through their lace curtains.

I think that the meeting had been set up in the wrong way, although the organisers were doing their best. Surely, on the declaration of martial law against Solidarnosc, the immediate mass protest should have been called by the British trade unions, with political parties and the peace movement giving support? I do not know what mixture of lethargy or factionalism, insularity or timidity, had deprived Solidarity of its obvious partner's support. But it was one more sign that the tide, both within Poland and without, was swinging to the West. The meeting had a cross-party platform, and one or two speakers made scarcely-veiled incitements to war against the Soviet Union. I spoke (as requested) on the peace movement's behalf, and at the first mention of 'peace' incurred the barracking and abuse of the ethnic Poles who pressed around the platform. We then formed ourselves into a melancholy crocodile, with the Poles singing again and again and again, as if it were a lament over the dead, Żeby Polska, and we trooped off to the Polish Embassy. It had become a Polish, and not a British, protest.

It was now the turn of President Reagan to say, 'Let Poland be Poland', not at Hyde Park, but on prime-time TV. Solidarity's pinioned body was laved by Western rhetorical tides. No doubt some of Solidarity's supporters accepted the NATO basket of bluster, bluff and boycott in the instrumental spirit in which it was intended. It was not for their own but for Russian consumption. (As British officers used to say in World War II, in the privacy of the officers' mess, of the alliance with the Soviet Union against Hitler: 'Any stick will do to beat a dirty dog.') But, as Mr Ash himself has testified, Mr Reagan became popular with many in Warsaw and remains so to this day. This is more than a matter of misrecognition, and it is absurd to suppose that it does not present difficulties to the Western peace movement. The difficulties have extended into the domestic political life of some nations, where support for Solidarity has become a football kicked between small leftist sects and the conservative Right. In the extensive opinion in the middle (which includes much of the Labour, trade union and peace movements, and especially the young) a deep respect for Solidarity is nourished which has never found effective expression; people feel that the radical young Solidarity activists 'blew it' in the final months (but they were driven into a corner), that they never responded to the voices of the peace movement (but they may never have heard these), but that it is a movement of hope and honour which must arise again.

I spoke again, on the peace movement's behalf, at another demonstration in Hyde Park in August 1982. The attendance was even smaller, with no winter weather as excuse. There were few CND flashes to be seen. This time the hostility of those around the platform stood up against me like a wall. For some, the mere mention of 'peace' was an obscenity. I learned that the very invitation of a speaker from the peace movement onto the platform almost provoked a split in the organising committee. But, as a gentle sign that some communication was still possible, one elderly Pole separated himself from his fellows and came to shake my hand: 'I do not agree with what you are saying, but I thank you for coming.'

I remember this because it has not been often in the past few years that a Pole has shaken my hand. The personal experiences which I have sketched are perhaps not unrepresentative. In the past three years (1982-4) a little dialogue has developed; offices of Solidarnosc in exile have signed common statements with sections of the peace movement; their representatives have spoken at END Conventions; individual Solidarity exiles have found (perhaps to their surprise) that they have met with a warm welcome as speakers with the Greens, the Italian Communists, at CND branches, at CND's annual Glastonbury Festival. In Poland itself we have passed through a most melancholy period of failed communication. The majority of Poles who, for deep historical reasons, love the Russians rather less than the Irish love the British, retired within the stockade of their national and Catholic culture: any enemy of the Russians was a friend of theirs. Since the peace movement was presented to them by their media as pro-Soviet—or at least 'soft' on the Soviets —then it must be their enemy.

As a criticism of a lopsidedness in some parts of the Western movements this had some validity—most notably in regard to the silence of some West Germans. But it was not a criticism which took rational or constructive forms. I have learned from published and from private accounts that in the aftermath of martial law extraordinary fantasies of war or 'liberation' disturbed the public mind. Lawrence Weschler reports (of the last months of 1981),

> The scenario I was frequently offered conjured up a Russian army bogged down in Poland for months, maybe years, of bloody guerrilla fighting, while one by one the other Warsaw Pact countries—whose armies, incidentally, would likewise be detailed on Polish soil—would become engulfed in working class rebellions of their own, rebellions that would eventually spread into the Soviet Union itself, leading to the collapse of the Kremlin regime.
>
> (*Solidarity*, 1982, p. 220.)

Mr Ash also acknowledges the spread of messianic visions, as in the aftermath of other thwarted revolutionary impulses:

the chiliasm of despair. Returning to Poland in late 1982, Weschler found such fantasies endemic. Talking with a village priest and longtime 'activist', he asked:

> 'So what do you think is going to happen?' He leaned forward and quietly said, 'A miracle,' rolling his eyes toward Heaven and smiling. I . . . leaned forward and asked, 'Like what?' He leaned even closer, his face now a mixture of anticipation and serenity, and whispered, confidentially, 'The Third World War'.
>
> (*The Passion of Poland*, Pantheon, 1984, p. 170.)

With extraordinary and self-disciplined non-violence the masses who were Solidarnosc had attempted a Polish renewal until they confronted the limits of the possible. The response had been martial law. In their bitterness many turned not against the immediate agents of their repression—the army and the Party's *nomenklatura*—but against the forces which imposed those limits: the Russians, the historic enemy. And who could aid them against the Russians? Only the United States, the 'West'. Passion projected absurd irrationalities. In a Third World War somehow 'the missiles will sail over us in both directions, but we will be left unscathed' (Weschler, *op. cit.*, p. 171).* In more rational-seeming terms many Poles accepted the symbolism of NATO weapons as their own 'defence'; in some never-explained way, cruise and Pershing

---

* Among such notions still canvassed in Poland is that of a writer ('We Must Build an Ark before the Flood') in the *Biuletyn Dolnoslaski* (Lower Silesian Bulletin), March 1984. This offers the following scenario for a war between NATO and the Warsaw Pact: day two to four, a front is established near the Elbe, where Soviet and GDR armies engage with NATO: day four, Polish regular forces strike the Soviet army in its rear (Soviet army disintegrates). Meanwhile Polish reservists and irregulars attack Soviet reinforcements moving through Poland to front, and (with the aid of the Polish regulars returning victorious from the front) 'hold back the Soviet drive. . . until the NATO forces arrive.' As for nukes, NATO plans 'envisage a particularly heavy bombardment of Poland. . . aimed at checking the armed Soviet millions proceeding towards the Elbe. . . However, maybe NATO's plans would change if it were known that an uprising would erupt in Poland'. It seems that some Poles will still entertain any crack-brained fantasy, no matter how bloodthirsty and self-centred, rather than pursue the same objectives (greater Polish autonomy and democracy) in alliance with Western peace forces.

missiles (some of which will be targeted on Poland) were visualised as a protective net extending to Poland's eastern borders and keeping the Russians out.

This was scarcely fertile ground for dialogue with peace movements. And some of the intellectual communicators, the internationally-minded circles of KOR (and then of KOS), were throughout 1982 and 1983 in prison where no communication was possible. Moreover, there may have been theoretical reasons why KOR/KOS had not been disposed to enter dialogue. A founding document of what was to become KOR's position was Jacek Kuron and Karel Modzelewski's *An Open Letter to the Party* of 1965.* Although many of their views had been modified by 1980, perhaps this response to nuclear weapons remained un-revised? Nuclear weapons (they then said) were 'a modern addition to the traditional arsenal of anti-revolutionary arguments'.

Today, when the stocks of nuclear weapons are more than enough to destroy the world, the governing elites of the two great blocs which share power in the world decry revolution as a crime against internal peace and humanity. Those who possess the arsenals filled with the means of nuclear annihilation. . . demand obedience from the masses in the name of avoiding a world-wide nuclear war.

But (Kuron and Modzelewski then went on):

A world nuclear conflict would be absurd from the point of view of the goals of both great blocs; it would lead to the destruction, if not of the whole of mankind, at least of the major powers. . . It would be suicide. The two great blocs do not want mutual destruction in any case, but are engaged in an economic, political and diplomatic competition based upon a division into spheres of influence. In their struggle against revolutionary movements, atomic weapons are a means of blackmail.

And a reference to the views of the 'Chinese bureaucracy' suggested that they shared Mao's view that nuclear weapons

---

* First published in English in the American *New Politics*, Vol. 5, nos. 2 & 3. Reproduced in part (without explanation of origin) in Tariq Ali (ed.), *New Revolutionaries* (1969).

were a 'paper tiger'.

The view that nuclear weapons are an instrument of blackmail and of internal discipline, but could never be used since
their use would be plainly irrational and against the interests
of any ruling elite is, of course, widely held also in the West.
It shores up some theories of 'deterrence'. I do not credit
it because I do not consider that history has ever been cut
out of that kind of rational, self-interested cloth. But the
evidence as to an irrational acceleration in the arms race
may have been slow to get through to Poland, where, in any
case, the active circle of KOR was submerged in other preoccupations. It seems to me possible that this old scepticism
as to the threat of nuclear war—and suspicion of it as a form
of Soviet-sponsored blackmail against any popular movements designated as 'destabilising'—may have underscored
KOR's suspicion of the Western peace movement.

A dialogue of a kind is now starting. Poles are not always
easy to understand. Absolutists in argument, in political
practice they arrive at ambiguous compromises. Violent in
mutual recriminations, they respond to real domestic
violence with abhorrence. Even in the worst post-war purges,
the Polish Stalinists did not often shoot their victims. The
murder of Father Jerzy Popieluszko caused a national trauma,
whereas the murder of Pio la Torre was for some North
Italians (but not for Sicilians) just one more example of
Mafia norms.* In no other Communist country whatsoever
could Lech Walesa still be half-free and taking his lunch to
work. For this reason one must learn to endure with good-
humour the furious Polish-centric arguments of the past two
or three years, in which the problems of Europe and the

---

* Pio la Torre, leader of the Sicilian region of the Italian Communist
Party, was murdered by the Mafia in Palermo on April 30th, 1982,
after he had taken a leading part in the campaign against the cruise
missile base at Comiso: see Ben Thompson, *Comiso* (END Special
Report), pp. 12-13. In England more recently there have been
suggestions that an elderly woman in Shropshire, Miss Hilda Murrell,
an active anti-nuclear campaigner, may have been murdered
'accidentally' by intelligence snoopers. All that we can be certain
of, in this democratic country, is that, whatever the truth is, it will
remain an 'official secret'.

world must always be measured against the Polish imperative. It is usual for such arguments to by-pass the stage of attempted reason and to move directly into savage and contemptuous sarcasm or into a polemical lunge at the throat.

There is also a moral stridency to be expected from men and women who walk always within the shadow of prison. This gives them a licence to abuse, in the knowledge that in our safety we will suffer abuse in silence. We are informed that the overriding threat comes from Soviet totalitarianism, and that the Soviet Union menaces West Europe with military blackmail, and that they *know* that this is true since, unlike us, they have suffered this truth in their own persons. We are accused of nourishing 'the spirit of Munich'. (Such accusations, like similar charges of 'appeasement' in a letter to me from the pseudonymous Czech, Václav Racek, are industriously extracted in Conservative Party HQ and sent out with their speaker's notes.) There is even, on occasion, a hint of moral blackmail. They are risking themselves every day (as they are): why will the Western peace movement, in its comfortable freedom, not 'risk' itself in their support? The first common task is to stop the 'expansion of tyranny from the East into the West'—

> And this means paying a certain price. We are fully willing to pay our part of that price and it is a sad fact that, apparently, the free people are not.
>
> ('Letter from KOS', *END Journal*, 11, August–September 1984.)

Dear friends in Solidarity or KOS, if any of you should read these pages! We submit. We do not enter any moral contest. We honour your commitment, and we would not dream of weighing our own in the same scales of 'risk'. It is true that many in the Western peace movements have, as a result of non-violent actions, briefly visited prisons; and for many women these visits are repeating and becoming longer. But for many of us our commitment involves us in few risks, save those of ridicule and of the expense of spirit and life. So let us take your moral case as won.

Yet what 'price' are we failing to pay? What 'risk' would

we take if we endorsed, without examination, every one of
your assertions? Can you really suppose that we are nervous
of incurring the displeasure of Mr Zhukov and the Soviet
authorities? We have incurred this already. Do you suppose
that those who publish, in the pages of *Commentary* or
Encounter, declamations against the overriding threat of
Soviet totalitarianism incur (if they live in the West) any
risk whatsoever? On the contrary, if we were to subscribe our
own names to these declamations we would be rewarded
with the applause of the Western establishment. What we
would place at risk would be rationality, for the sake of
placing our impeccable moral credentials upon exhibition.

Yes, we live in the 'free world', although the air of
freedom becomes more rarified year by year. The flow of
information available to us is greater than can be found in
Warsaw. We have sought—as you would do if you were here—
to put our freedoms to use. It is our measured view that the
cold war cannot be blamed upon one side only, but is a
reciprocal, mutually-reinforcing process. We do not share
your view that Soviet military power is a present menace to
the West; on the contrary, recent experience, not least in
Poland, suggests increasing weakness on the Soviet side. We
regard all measures of militarisation as enhancing our
common dangers, blocking the escape-routes to the future,
and that their 'price' will beggar imagination. We consider
that, together, we should be defining the positions of a third
way, detached from the tug of the cold war's tides.

In this we may be wrong. But we must address the matter
not in hectoring moralisms but in rational terms. Solidarity
encountered, at the end of 1981, the limits of the Communist and cold war 'possible'. It also encountered the limits
of an argument which has recently been presented by Mihailo
Marković, the independent Yugoslav Marxist philosopher:

> The liberation of Eastern Europe can only be the work of Eastern
> Europeans—to be sure with the support of all those who resist every
> kind of oppression. This liberation will take a lot of time, it will
> require enormous moral strength, risk and sacrifice.
>
> (*END Journal*, 12, October–November 1984.)

This argument has my profound assent: not only can liberation not be brought from without, but the attempt to do so
will enforce repression. Yet how can we offer this argument
to a Pole? For the majority of the nation, in most disciplined
and non-provocative ways, attempted non-violent self-
liberation, with a display of 'enormous moral strength, risk
and sacrifice'. And the answer was *nyet*. With their heads
smashed against these stony limits, is it not inevitable that
some Poles should search for dramatic alternatives: perhaps
'a miracle'?

Solidarity's Western admirers have searched in the same
way. Timothy Garton Ash has candidly argued that 'I believe
the United States would be morally justified in using force
to help the Poles defeat General Jaruzelski—if that were
possible without risking a war in Europe and a nuclear
holocaust, which of course it is not.' (*N Y Review of Books*,
November 22, 1984.) No doubt many Poles think the same.
Many Westerners might feel such a cause to be morally just
(as they did fifty years ago in Spain), but I have already
expressed my nausea at the assumption by the United States
of such an imperial 'moral mission'. If President Reagan
wishes to be cast as Lord Byron at Missolonghi, then I hope
that he will go back to Hollywood and play the part in a
silent movie. And, as Ash agrees, this option has been closed
by the realities of modern war. What other options do he and
his friends offer?

Mr Ash, in a tentative counterfactual essay in 'missed
opportunity' (*The Polish Revolution*, pp. 324–330), suggests
that Solidarity's positions might have been held open if 'the
West' (that is, certain Western governments and banks) had
promoted early in 1981 an imaginative 'Marshall Plan' of
some 20 billion dollars, tied to a series of hidden and not-so-
hidden conditions. In return for these credits, 'the West'
would have demanded guarantees of Solidarity's independent
status, would have demanded the full disclosure of information on the Polish economy to 'the West', would have
dictated extensive reorganisation of Polish industry, and
would have explored the possibility of channelling aid in
preference to private agriculture and (if direct aid) through

the Church. In short, 'the West' (or certain Western governments and banks) would have used this 'Marshall Plan' as a
gentle instrument of weakening the Polish authorities and
privatising sectors of the economy.

It is not difficult to see that Mr Ash, bumping his head
against the same limits of the possible, has come up with a
fantasy of his own. There might be circumstances in which
a Polish government would buy its way out of crisis with
Western credits even upon unfavourable conditions. But
these circumstances certainly did not exist in 1981–3, when
the blocs were entering a major contest of 'face' about
intermediate nuclear weapons, and when Pershing IIs were
rising on the West German horizon. Neither Mr Ash nor his
Polish friends can rationally suppose that, in the prevailing
terms of East–West confrontation, the Communist authorities (or 'the Russians') would have tolerated a Western
essay in graduated destabilisation and privatisation.

What might, conceivably, have been tolerated would have
been Solidarity's survival in return for a package of aid
accompanied by some major Western concession. And that
concession could have come only in the most sensitive
area of all: the nuclear and ideological confrontation. 'The
West' might have bought the continued existence of above-
ground Solidarity for the cancellation of Pershing II missiles.
And, then, not only would Poland have been freer but both
Poland and West Germany would have been more secure.
The only rational options open, within the domain of
possibility, lay in some bargain which traded some real
measure of Western disarmament in return for the consolida-
tion of Polish freedoms. Polish self-liberation is only possible
within the larger politics of peace.

Some of us in the peace movement have said this insistent-
ly, before martial law and since. The best place for Western
concession (we have argued) would be in reductions of the
militarisation of West Germany. This leads on to a re-
consideration of Rapacki-type solutions, linking West
Germany with the GDR, Poland and Czechoslovakia, leading
on from a nuclear-free zone to mutual reductions in conventional arms, and the increasing opening of frontiers to

the flow of persons and ideas. Everything has been going
in the opposite direction, and, in consequence, the Polish
situation is getting worse.

A serious dialogue on such a common strategy has scarcely
yet been opened with our Polish friends.* It has been refused,
on occasion, for trivial reasons. Because, some twenty-five
years ago, Rapacki-type solutions were, in very different
circumstances, favoured by Communist governments, they
must for that reason be a Communist trick which cannot be
enlarged into a third way of peace. Or it has been refused,
in terms of an emotional utopian absolutism. Poland must
either be 'free'—to the point that Poland may opt, if it
wishes, to join NATO—or any intermediate station is an
insult to the Polish nation.

Mr Lawrence Weschler has perhaps conveyed to some
Polish friends that I have been offering this kind of insult.
For he quotes 'a well-known British peace activist and
historian' (guess who?) as 'commenting' on the 'unbridled
nationalism of the Poles' and as warning the citizens of
East European nations that 'even following extensive
loosening of their internal totalitarian political systems,
their countries must still remain within the Soviet sphere of
influence—somewhat like Finland'.

I gather that my supposed views (as presented by Weschler)
may have got back to some persons in KOS, who have
taken the greatest offence. So E.P. Thompson—or 'the
Western peace movement'—wish to turn Poland into another
Finland!!! Let me rehearse my published views once more.
I have argued for the perspective of an 'Austrian solution'
for Europe, with the mutually agreed withdrawal of Soviet
and American forces from Europe, East and West. I have
argued also that, in the shorter run, the 'Finlandisation' of
Western Europe is less likely than the 'Finlandisation' of
some nations in Eastern Europe: that is, the Soviet presence

---

* There is a suggestion that such a dialogue may now be beginning:
notably, in Jacek Kuron's *Open Letter to All People in the World
who care about Peace* (June, 1984). But Kuron wishes to enlist the
peace movement in support of his Polish strategies: he does not yet
see it as an equal partner, working towards common strategies.

and hegemony might be loosened, and greater autonomy be
gained, in response to Western concessions. I have argued
that we will not get out of the cold war confrontation in
one sudden flip-over but down a gradient; and that, as
intermediate way-stations, the increasing 'Finlandisation' of
the East and 'Swedenisation' of West Europe, is to be both
worked for and welcomed.

It would be nice if Poland were to be 'free' tomorrow,
although it would be less nice if Poles were to take their
place in NATO's councils. But neither is going to happen,
this side of a 'miracle'. Meanwhile, Finland is not a terrible
place, nor as trussed-up and terrified as *Encounter* polemicists
pretend; and if I suggest that the route to Polish freedom
might be through the Finland station, this ought not to
occasion a lunge at my throat. The mistake is to suppose
that if a nation escapes from one sphere of influence it must
at once join the other: only-two-sides. But the third way of
peace must be working—and working together, East and
West—for the withering away of *both* spheres of influence
and an enlarging space of autonomy in-between. It may be
that Adam Michnik of KOS has glimpsed this possibility
when he writes that it is 'not unthinkable that a spectacular
peaceful solution in Poland will become the starting point
for the resolution of international tensions' (Weschler, *op.
cit.*, p. 248). But to achieve this peaceful solution will require
the common efforts of Solidarity and of the Western peace
movement, with all their associated political forces and
cultural resources. It will not be brought by NATO bluster
nor bought by Western banks. For what some risk-taking
friends in Poland *still* will not understand is that 'the West'
(in this form) is concerned not in the least with the advantage
of the Polish people. It is concerned with exploiting
perceived 'weaknesses' (for the Polish renewal appeared
only in its aspect as Communist 'weakness' to them) and in
furthering NATO's advantage against the Warsaw bloc.

I commenced this digression on the matter of Poland
from a consideration of the question of 'destabilisation'. I
have agreed that there were misrecognitions between the
peace movement and Solidarity, and that an opportunity

was lost. But nothing in this argument lends any support to the view that the strategy of the peace movement is an agent of destabilisation. On the contrary, Polish repression and the consequent and continuing risks of real (and bloody) destabilisation arise precisely because the strategy of the peace movement has *not* been taken. The third way of peace is not just one desirable option. It is the only way out.

There are still those in the Western peace movement who advise keeping all these considerations (which they describe as 'human rights') in a 'pending' file. Yes, they would like to see all these 'human rights'. But realism dictates a two-stage programme, like the lift-off of a space rocket. First must come disarmament (where the onus lies with the West). Second, there will follow, as light follows day, a period of detente, in which ideological hostilities will soften and some democratisation will ensue on the other side.

These arguments are well-intended but they lack the realism to which they aspire. Detente, in the early seventies, did not favour democratisation: least of all in the USSR and Czechoslovakia. And those dreadful people, Soviet citizens or Czechs or Poles, who are suffering their own domestic abuses, will make their own decisions and move in their own ways. They will not wait about compliantly until such moment as a Western committee (perhaps meeting in Boston or in the Friends Meeting House on Euston Road) looks at its watch, and signals to them that the second stage of democratic lift-off may now, with due sobriety, begin.

Those dreadful people will act impulsively and untidily and without consultation, and make trouble for us. But they will not only make trouble. They will see openings towards peace which we, with our western perceptions, can never see. They will contribute new themes to our understanding, as 'dialogue' and 'trust' have done. They will greatly enrich the theoretical content of the 'third way', and stand the theory on two legs instead of one. This now is going forward, in Moscow, in Budapest, and in the circles of Charter 77 in Prague. The most perspicacious essay on the perspective of 'a democratic peace' has come, not from a Western pen, but from a Czech: Dr Jaroslav Šabata in *Voices from Prague*.

The most eloquent plea for the peaceful Europeanisation of Europe has come from a Hungarian: György Konrád in *Antipolitics*.

The two-stage lift-off theory will not work in that form. It is wrong to say that 'human rights' must be a precondition of disarmament: that way we will get neither. It is wrong to say that 'human rights' will be the consequence of disarmament: our friends on the other side have not given us power-of-attorney to make that decision. Both must take place together, as part of one single process, the making of a democratic peace.

This is not to say that this little formula will disperse all complexities. If the forty-year-old knots of the cold war begin to be cut things will fall apart in unpredictable ways. There will be political lurches, in both West and East. Western nations may attempt their own social transitions, or may (Spain, Greece) decide to get out of NATO. In the East there may be new renewals and Springs. As a matter of course, the hard men of NATO and the Warsaw Pact will do all in their power to extract advantage for their own side. We have seen that Mr Zhukov is in the extraction business with the Western peace movement now. And it is clear that the opaque think-tanks of Washington are bubbling with powerful thoughts as to whether or how far independent peace initiatives in the East might be exploited to the advantage of Uncle Sam. A learned Theban, an analyst in the Policy bureau of the US Department of Defense—a man so close to the sweaty armpits of power that he must enter the caveat that 'the views expressed here do not necessarily reflect those of the US government'—has recently surveyed the 'Eastern European Doves' (Robert English in *Foreign Policy*, 56, Fall 1984):

> The United States should keep quiet and allow the East and West European peace movements to support each other as natural allies in their struggle against the military policies of both superpowers. For however unequal it seems and however threatening the West European peace movements appear to NATO, the greater threat is to the Soviets.

It is good to know that the United States will 'keep quiet' for a while, and permit us to do our own thing, although we should remember that there are other agencies, with sweatier armpits, which do not feel bound to follow official governmental briefs. (They are rather active in Nicaragua today.) But I think that the analysis of our learned Theban is wrong. What the growth of an independent peace movement over there will do is 'threaten', not the 'Soviets', but the whole rationale of the cold war. What it will strengthen, immeasurably, is the third way of peace.

Yet that cold involuntary moon will still patrol, tugging the tides of politics this way and that. As we watch new friends appear at our front we must still take care to watch our backs, where the true destabilisers of the Two Sides will seek to exploit to their own advantage the motions for peace in the Other.

In my view we should search together, not from some sudden cancellation of 'Yalta', but for a more gentle gradient in which disarmament and the opening of human communications go together. Western peace movements have no brief to interfere or to 'change the social system' in the East (as Mr Zhukov alleges). That is the business of the East's own citizens, if they so wish, just as political changes in the West are our own. But it is normal for us to welcome such advance, in any part of the world, of those rights of expression, access to information, and self-organisation without which the fluency of citizen communication is not possible.

I have written repeatedly about a 'healing-process' between the blocs. This cannot rest upon a neo-Leninist strategy in which 'vanguards' on both sides lock onto a common programme. While mutual solidarities inevitably will arise, our business should be not to draw this discourse into narrow channels but to throw it outwards to the widest public. Our discourse between the blocs, just as our discourse within our own nations, must be a plural discourse and a discourse of alliance. We must talk candidly with the officials, search out their doves, but break out of the captivity of conducted 'peace rituals and repressive hospitality.* We must talk candidly with the democratic opposition, not only about our agreements but about our disagreements. We should pursue the proposal of Charter 77, in its remarkable letter to the END Convention in Perugia (*END Journal*, 12 October–November 1984), of attempting round-table trialogues, in which officials, independents and Western movements meet together. And if the spaces for independent citizen initiatives in the East began to close in 1983–4, then in the immediate future we must press them open once again.

This is work, not only for those who wear badges and consider themselves to be activists for peace. It is work for all who wish to heal our human culture. It is work for orchestras, for scholars, for writers, for travellers, for young people and for their music. It is perhaps, most of all, work for the younger generations, on both sides, who do not bear the traumas of the past.

For some of us in the past five years it has seemed lonely work, which only a few scores or a few hundreds were doing. But the first openings in that 'iron curtain' have been made. We ask now for others to come and help us, not according to our directions, but finding their own openings in their own way. Fence-cutters of the world, unite!

If the work gathers way, the entire field-of-force of post-war international politics may be transformed. We may find that the dedicated operators of the cold war, despite their substantial resources, are fewer and less powerful than we supposed. But these are the true Iagos whom we may never forgive: those who seek to foul the springs of discourse: those who scurry from the West, in the masks of goodwill, to exposed persons in Prague or in Warsaw or in Moscow, conveying slander and seeking to twist dialogue to the tunes of NATO propaganda: those who, in the name of 'unity', seek to split the peace movement and turn a remnant to

---

* As any anthropologist can tell us, the host-guest relationship can be an unequal one of obligation and control. Communist states have developed the hosting of visiting delegations, with heavy constraints of protocol, to a fine art. The problem of transforming formal and invigilated exchanges into informal and open ones is now on our agenda.

Moscow's service. These operators endanger the future of the world far more than the hapless servitors of nuclear weapons, quietly yawning and rolling their joints, deep in the silos of Grand Forks, North Dakota or the Kola peninsula. It is not these bored young men but the ideologists with 'moral ends' who will send the missiles on their way.

Only one thing is certain: the world cannot go on as it is. We must make a new world, of new inter-nation and inter-bloc relations, or there will be no world at all. And I mean a new *world*, and not just a healed Europe. Today that cold patrolling moon is tugging the tides of cold war across the entire globe. It is the whole world which is threatened and which must be repaired, and the non-aligned peace movement must look for its allies everywhere.

This is not to say that the North–South contradiction, or the imperatives of the hungry half of the world, have displaced for us the political priority of healing the East/ West confrontation. Indeed, a certain kind of flight into sentimental 'Third Worldism' could be an evasion of the responsibilities of the North. It is, precisely, the irrelevant aggressions of the East/West conflict which are now being exported wholesale to the South—quite literally exported in the atrocity of the arms trade, in the export of military infrastructures, in 'aid' given to juntas and debt-ridden tyrannies, in the contest for spheres of influence, and in the consequent screwing-up of political, economic and social life. Our duty to the South still demands that we heal the contradictions of the North. But the third way must become a global way.

I cannot find any sound reason for predicting the outcome. If I have a sense that the world may continue and may be renewed, I can support this by no more than the pricking in my thumbs. My sense, or 'suspicion', is shared by others, 'that the Iron Curtain is but a pile of decaying ideological rubbish, which has to be held upright by the extensive military hardware of the two blocs and by the mutual blackmail of the nuclear threat'. The words are those of Zdena Tomin (*New Statesman*, October 26, 1984), herself a former spokesperson of Charter 77 and now an involuntary exile in

Britain, whose resilience and wise advice have heartened us in our work of putting Europe back together.

I share her hope:

That the human, social, historical, and in a true sense political, conditions for the crumble and fall of the Iron Curtain are here; that it is a workable dream.

▲ 'A SHIELD AGAINST CHAOS' ▲

Early in October, 1979, an 'expert' sort of young man came upon the BBC news, and informed us that we are to have 140 cruise missiles with nuclear warheads stationed on our soil. These are to be called Tomahawks, a reassuring cowboys-and-Indians sort of name. They are to be our 'contribution' to NATO. . .

I find this in an article which I wrote for *New Society* in December 1979. It comes with a sense of shock to realise that, for me and many others, the peace movement in its present form has now been in existence for five years.

An immense amount of life has been poured into that interval. What has that expense of spirit—those innumerable tramping feet, that milliard of public meetings and committees, that tonnage of correspondence and of publications, those frosty benders beneath the shadows of clattering helicopters—what has all this achieved?

If we ask this from the perspective of 'arms control', then the facile answer is 'nothing'. I said, at the CND demonstration in Hyde Park in October 1981: 'We have not yet stopped one missile in its tracks.' And we still have not yet stopped one.

In West Europe we were given a four year time-table to stop cruise and Pershing. The task became obsessional: it polarised the political life of nations, in which the peace movement contested, upon unequal terms, with the resources of established power. And we failed.

In the wake of that failure, the sharks' fins of the successor systems now cleave the waters. In Britain we have not stopped Trident nor the Tornado. America's sea and air-launched cruise missiles are entering deployment, and little pirate armadas (such as the *Iowa* task-force) are being prepared to support the rapid deployment forces. The MX is a-building. The Mediterranean (Sicily, Sardinia, Pantellaria) is being militarised. In the East the GDR and Czechoslovakia have been drawn into the nuclear-basing club, while Soviet cruise missiles are in advanced testing. The Atlantic and Pacific oceans are busy with the sharks' fins of both sides. Japan is under United States' pressure to rebuild its military forces. 'Conventional' armaments are being hyped up in Europe, not as an alternative but as an addition to nukes. And President Reagan's eyes are now set on the stars. . .

It would be easy to conclude that the rival military establishments will go ahead with their procurements despite whatever we can do, and that 'arms control' will only be a code-word for measures to control public opinion: that is, for controlling us. At the best, the peace movement has only forced the armourers to modify their rhetoric. We hear little these days about 'warning shots' or 'limited' nuclear war.

Yet if we ask the same question in political terms, then we get different answers. It is not true, even in immediate political terms, that the record of the past five years is one of unrelieved defeat. In the major heartlands of the Cold War, at the cost of the fierce polarisation of political life, the armourers have triumphed. This was signalled by the return to power in 1983 of Chancellor Kohl and of Mrs Thatcher; by the disciplinary controls imposed on the Warsaw bloc (notably the repression of Solidarnosc); and by the fudged American election—between two variants of cold war advocacy—and by four more years for President Reagan.

But the power of the armourers has been slipping at the edges. Denmark has refused contributions to cruise and Pershing. Holland has gained a muted victory for peace, in postponing the deployment decision, and Belgium is likely to follow. Greece continues to negotiate with her neighbours a

Balkan nuclear-free zone. In Spain the outcome of the long-delayed referendum on NATO still hangs in the balance. Not only Romania but also, it seems clear, Hungary and Bulgaria have been resisting Soviet military pressures. In New Zealand the incoming government has honoured its electoral pledges, proclaimed the islands to be nuclear-free, and is negotiating with neighbours a South Pacific nuclear-free zone. It is not true that 'nothing can be done'.

Yet these are only the visible signs of far deeper political transformations. We have lived with these for so long—we have ourselves *been* that transformation—that we have scarcely noticed what is going on. A first effect, in major Western nations, has been the polarisation of opinion; but a polarisation which at the same time has shattered beyond repair the all-party Atlanticist 'consensus' (excluding only certain Communist Parties) which had for thirty years legitimated not only every measure of armament but also the official management of opinion.

Of critical importance has been the detachment of major Western Social-Democratic Parties (West German, Danish, Dutch, Greek and the British Labour Party) from their automatic Atlanticist complicity. Around this there has been a much wider movement of opinion, ranging through Greens and smaller nationalist parties, churches, trade unions and professions, women's movements, and deeply into Liberal and (in some nations) Christian Democratic opinion.

At the same time the contest against particular weapons-systems (cruise and Pershing) passed by imperceptible stages into a contest by West European nations to regain their autonomy from United States hegemony. This has not been checked by the first deployments. For it is now evident that there are divergent European versus American national political objectives (notably, West German *ostpolitik* which is increasingly endorsed by substantial conservative interests) —divergencies accentuated by increasing competition between United States and West European economies, dramatically expressed by the interest-rates which have lifted the US dollar like a gas-balloon.

This cross-Atlantic tension is an enduring trend, and there

is no way in which the old kind of American military-diplomatic-economic hegemony can be reimposed on Western European nations. Paradoxically, now that NATO Chieftain Reagan (with his Tomahawks) has got his four more years this is bound to accelerate the disintegration of NATO in its old form, since Reagan is C-in-C of exactly those forces (military adventurers, merciless financiers, and illiterate amateur diplomats) who most provoke alarm among cautious West European elites. Lord Carrington, the incoming Secretary-General of NATO, is more flexible than the late, loud and unlamented Dr Joseph Luns. But, not for the first time, Carrington has taken the wrong job for the wrong boss at the wrong time. He will be kept busy as the aristocratic caretaker of a preserved bourgeois monument in a state of decay.

The NATO ruling groups won the great Euromissile contest. But the price of victory was almost as high as the price of defeat. They do not wish to re-enact the traumatic political contest of 1981–3. As Norman Birnbaum has written:

> While the peace movement did not block Euromissile deployment, that will be the last military decision imposed by NATO's technocrats: matters of arms, strategy and tactics are now subject to public scrutiny. The parties of the European centre and right have exhausted nearly all their political credit in enforcing the Euromissile decision, and European governments are increasingly at pains to avoid giving the impression of blind subservience to the United States.
>
> ('Europeanization of Europe', *Bulletin of the Atomic Scientists*, January 1985.)

Kohl, Thatcher and Craxi are aware that alternative governments wait in the wings, which would depart from the forty-year-old Atlanticist norms. In 1984 they altered course from abrasive confrontation to little gestures of 'dialogue', borrowing the peace movement's own lines. Ministers scurry on visits to East European capitals, and (despite denials) a fragile 'second tier' of diplomacy is being erected between the superpowers. Symptoms of confusion and self-doubt are spreading within the European governing parties and the armed services themselves. These tensions have enforced upon the United States a return to the negotiating table. The Geneva talks are not being held because President Reagan has been born again in his second incarnation, and wishes to go down in the history books as a Man of Peace. They are not being held because the United States wishes to reach an agreement with the Russians. The talks are necessary to placate Western public opinion and to hold NATO together.

These tensions need not point in the direction of peace. Indeed, if it were not for the presence of the peace movement and its political allies, they could point to the resurgence of competing West European nationalisms, with the dominant statist and capitalist institutions (West German and French) working to create a new Euro-superpower, armed to the teeth with home-made provisions, both nuclear and conventional: Hades, Exocets, Mirages and Tornados. But the faction-fighting within NATO which will continue for several years will afford a significant political space within which peace forces can press for alternatives. These alternatives might include, but must go far beyond, scenarios for 'alternative defence'. They must be *political* alternatives, which envisage Rapacki-style diplomacies of reconciliation and mutual security between the nations of East and West Europe.

The refraction of the ideas of the peace movement, in their challenge to the premises of the Cold War, has penetrated every area of political and intellectual life. In Britain five years ago public discussion of matters of 'defence' was controlled within a supposed all-party 'consensus' which had endured for thirty years. I wrote in December 1979:

The 'all-party consensus', and *especially* the submission of the Parliamentary Labour Party to the 'consensus', is the lynch-pin of the whole operation. It is this fiction which legitimates all that is done to us—the suppression of information, the manipulation of the media, the exclusion of critical questions from the arena of national political life.

(*Writing by Candlelight*, p. 271.)

That lynch-pin has now been struck out and the matter of 'defence' has been thrown open to the nation's debate. If the debate was not won in the unfavourable terms of the General Election of 1983, yet it is worth recalling that about one-third of the electorate then voted for parties supporting policies which, in the previous seven or eight general elections, had not even been on offer as serious options. That is not a bad beginning.

There are other consequences of this collapse of the fiction of consensus. It is more difficult to manage the broadcasting media in the old 'consensual' ways (although it should be made much more difficult than it is), while civil servants become increasingly resentful at being forced to undertake, in the name of 'national security', partisan party-political tasks of misinforming the public and of concealing information from parliament. The Sarah Tisdall and Clive Ponting cases may be leading us to a crisis of confidence within the public service, which can be resolved in only two ways. Either we must have a repeal of the Official Secrets Acts, new measures for Freedom of Information, and new forms of public accountability over military and security operations. Or Mrs Thatcher will arm the authoritarian security state with even more draconic powers.

Our balance-sheet of the past five years gives unexpected results. The massive international disarmament movement has, in the past years, achieved no measures of disarmament. Nor does it seem likely to achieve any, not even a qualified 'freeze', in the immediate future. But the implosion of the peace movement has achieved extraordinary results in the spheres of politics and of general consciousness. We have stripped the veils of consensus from our nuclear predicament and made it visible to all; our movements have precipitated the crystallisation of new political forms and alliances; they have made visible not only the weapons but also the premises of the Cold War. There is a paradox here. For our movements have acquired a reasonable expertise as disarmers, while we have remained puerile as politicians. Yet our successes have been registered where our expertise is least.

What conclusions should we draw from this? First, we

must accept and welcome this enlarged political agenda. A peace movement must engage with the 'national security' state (in West or East); must attend to its alliances in the Third World; and cannot avoid engagement with the problems of bloc division.

The threat of war does not rest upon weapons-systems alone, as if these were some kind of self-generating automata; it rests also upon political and ideological confrontation. The Cold War stands upon two legs: a permanent war economy and a permanent enemy hypothesis. Of the two, it may turn out that it is the ideological leg which is the more brittle; and the one which the peace movement, as a movement of ideas and popular energies, is best equipped to overthrow.

It is the permanent enemy hypothesis ('What about the Russians?') which has held in check the peace movement. The animating spirit of modern statism—on both sides of the Cold War—exists in this hypothesis: in some worst-case analysis the Other *might* be an enemy, or would be an enemy if it were not for nuclear 'deterrence'. It is normal in times of war for states to acquire emergency powers. What distinguishes the Cold War era is that the hypothesis of 'emergency' is built into the daily routines of the peacetime state. This supplies, for the authority of the modern state, what the hypothesis of Satan supplied for the medieval church. It is the need for 'defence' against a worst-case hypothesis which legitimates the paramountcy of 'national security' in whose name the Moscow Trust Group is harassed, and the employees at GCHQ Cheltenham are despoiled of their trade union rights.

The permanent enemy hypothesis is the most jealously-guarded component of ideology on both sides of the Cold War since it is highly functional for the governing elites. They would not know how to govern without it. It is necessary for there to be an enemy in order to keep client states in control. It is an ever-present means of internal ideological and social control. This keeps the security organs on constant alert, and can be used to lampoon peace movements in the West and civil rights movements in the East as potential traitors or auxiliaries of the Other.

Even more alarming, the permanent enemy hypothesis has come to serve, for the vast and variously-assembled populations of the two superpowers as a surrogate nationalism. Not for the first time, Middle America has been 'walking tall' and chanting 'four more years' in a spurious nationalist fervour whose fiction is that America is not a nation at all but is 'the Future' or 'the Free World'—a nationalism which defines its identity in 'standing up to the Commies' in Grenada, Nicaragua or the Soviet Union.

Reagan has won in the polls because he knows how to massage this enlarged and braggart nationalist ego. And if dismal recent reports are to be trusted, there is now an authentic surge of nationalist feeling in the Soviet Union also, whose citizens are constantly told that they find their identity as custodians of 'the heartland of Socialism' threatened by imperialist warmongers—a mood neither so brash nor so aggressive as the American mood, but nevertheless xenophobic (there are new penalties for hosting foreigners in Soviet homes) and introverted. Not for the first time, Russia is turning in upon herself. As a new succession crisis develops, there is evidence of the old siege mentality in which the entire political and cultural world is viewed in Manichean terms. The battle rages between Soviet light and imperialist darkness, and any intermediate tone or third way is instantly exposed as a cunning NATO trap.

These ideological forces are as threatening to peace as are any nuclear missiles, and there is no way in which a serious peace movement can keep them off the agenda. How, then, is the permanent enemy hypothesis to be confronted, when the ideologists and politicians of both sides are doing their best to confirm their enemy status with every move? It is no good offering a flat denial: 'the Russians (or the Americans) aren't coming.' The Russians are already there, as unwelcome occupants of several East European countries and in the five-year old (and still unending) war in Afghanistan. The Americans are already there, based across the globe, and they may well be coming, to Nicaragua or Cuba or the Middle East. And if we are right to show that the scenarios of Russian hordes sweeping down on the Channel Ports are implausible or absurd, nevertheless it is in the nature of a worst-case hypothesis that it will flicker in the popular imagination and can never finally be disproved.

The only way to contest the worst case is to envisage a better case, and then to summon up all our forces to work to bring that better case about. We cannot 'prove' this better case: it is the business of the peace movement to place it on the agenda, as historical possibility. And this is why the European peace movements occupy a space of peculiar opportunity and responsibility: opportunity because the unique political conditions of Europe, at this sensitive interface between the blocs, present to us a possible better case in which a healing and mediating process might commence on this continent: responsibility, because our duties to the Third World and to peace forces in the USA and USSR will best be met, not by ineffectual moralising about superpower sins, but by resolving our own political problems—that is, by disengaging Europe from the Cold War polarities and by strengthening the political and economic resources of the non-aligned world.

The opportunity is presented to us because those very forces which are exacerbating the tension between the superpowers are making Europe more vulnerable, provoking increasing opposition among the public of both halves, and forcing the question of greater autonomy upon the agenda. And here also the peace movement of the past five years has been a significant precipitate.

This may yet prove to be as important as any part of our work in the past five years. Beneath the carapace of censorship, East and Central Europe are now seething with debate, to which our voices have made some contribution. The dialogue now comes through to us in searching individual voices or from groups which signal a fellowship in our common cause. As discussion develops it becomes evident that there is as wide a plurality of opinions and perspectives in the East as in the West. And it is evident that even at the level of nation-states, there are diverging objectives and pressures for greater autonomy (Romania's truculence, Hungary's quiet and cautious 'westpolitik', Honecker's frustrated attempts at the same) which are analogous to the pressures away from superpower dominance in the West. As the Kremlin's succession-crisis drags on (a crisis which may have a bearing on the same issues), making Soviet policy by turns inert and capricious, the pressures for autonomy will grow.

We should not for a moment undervalue the importance of messages addressed to the Western peace movement from such influential organisations as Charter 77 and KOS. They are the sign that the old ideological compulsions of the Cold War which have at times divided the forces of the future from each other—peace as 'pro-Soviet', human rights as 'pro-American'—are breaking down. 'Peace' and 'liberty' are searching for convergent strategies.

Yet in my own view, at this moment, the growth of this dialogue, drawing in more voices and more sections of the public, is its own sufficient objective. There are thirty years of misrecognitions and suspicions to be worked through. The aim must for the time being be convergence and not identity.

To be effective, the dialogue between East and West must engage widening constituencies of citizens. It must not be co-opted by official diplomatic organs, and it must not be short-circuited into a few advanced intellectual groups. It must involve majority peace movements from the West, must be plural, and it cannot exclude the 'officials' of the East.

The issue here is not whether one talks with the 'officials' but how one talks and what one talks about? It is inevitable that there will be some abrasive exchanges. But we should refuse to be diverted into ideological generalities. We should demand the exchange and circulation among the publics of both sides of our policies and publications; rights and facilities of communication with any citizens on matters of peace; the opportunity for peace activists to visit each others' countries, to hold public and open workshops, seminars and lectures, and to meet with whom they please;

and guarantees that peace workers (whether in good or ill standing with the authorities) will not be harassed. That is an attainable minimum programme for dialogue, which cannot be dismissed as a 'provocation'.

If the ideologues of the World Peace Council have become confrontational, and are seeking to divide the Western peace movements, it does not help if radical sections of the Western movement become confrontational in return. We should not waste efforts investing, with drums and moral dramas, the castles of neo-Stalinist ideology; we should move around these and explore every road of dialogue, leaving their self-righteous custodians to starve in our rear. Forty years of complex interactive history cannot be reduced to a moment at its origin ('Yalta'); to heal that fracture in human polity and culture will require multiple initiatives of a kind far broader than accepted notions of 'politics'. And, in my own understanding, it is not moralistic dramas that the most hard-pressed of our independent friends in the East are asking for. Western radicals, in a half-open society, are accustomed to an abrasive style, to forcing open argument by challenge, confrontation and polemic. We understand too little the more subtle and silent pressures within the closed societies on the other side, which may work towards a similar convergence by less advertised means. For the sake of a self-righteous exercise in confrontation, we in the West may inflict real damage on friends in the East, forcing un-necessary polarisations upon them, and turning back the quiet tides of cultural convergence.

Moreover, if we are serious about the perspective of a historic compromise between the blocs, commencing in Europe—a perspective which would include nuclear-free zones, Rapacki-style diplomacies, bi-lateral agreements between nations East and West, the opening of frontiers to all kinds of travel and communications, mutual security agreements, the progressive 'Finlandisation' of Eastern Europe and 'Swedenisation' of Western Europe, and which might culminate in the mutual withdrawal of all American and Soviet forces from both halves of Europe—if we are serious about this, then these are processes which may be initiated by movements from below but must, in the end, be registered by the institutions of states. At some point in the future, under a new US President and a new First Secretary of the CPSU, there must be Summit meetings and conferences of European nations. Should we not be searching out the doves (or the realists) within the bureaucracies of both blocs now?

In conclusion I must make one matter absolutely clear. I have entered into argument, in these pages, with opponents of the peace movement, and have followed them into their own premises of political 'realism'. I make no apology for this. The peace movement is not just one of moral 'protest'. It exists to act in the real world, and to act with effect. We must propose our own historical agenda, and this must commence from the world as it is. The agenda which I have sketched is not one in which individuals—or single nations—can opt out of that world. It proposes a complex reciprocal process, in which the peace movement is an effective political agent, pressing forward and monitoring the transition to a healed human world.

But if it is to succeed in this, it must arouse everywhere a new kind of peace consciousness, founded upon the human ecological imperative of neighbourly survival. This means that it is right to found its position on an absolute: the refusal of nuclear weapons. It cannot entangle itself in the vocabulary of 'perhaps' or 'if-they-will-we-will' or in the theology of deterrence theory. If this leads us to be accused by our opponents of one-sidedness or moralism, then let us be one-sided moralists. Only an unqualified and implacable refusal of the obscenity of nuclear weapons will be strong enough to break that system at one point or another: and once the system begins to be broken, anywhere, we must summon up an international response. *That* will be the point at which all the politics in these pages will come in.

Nothing enforces this more clearly than the insanity into which the United States is now leading the world. Not even Jonathan Swift could have imagined so savage a satire on human endeavour as Star Wars. For what is the case with this? It is proposed that, in some 25 years, after the expenditure of several trillion dollars, United States technology will emerge with an impenetrable anti-ballistic missile shield. It has even been proposed, by President Reagan in a rhetorical aside, that at this point the United States will reveal all its technology to the USSR, although it is not yet certain that Reagan will still be President in 25 years time. (If he could circumvent the US Constitution he might still have some difficulty with his own.) So that it is proposed that, at astronomic cost, an astral venture will be set in motion (a venture which leading scientists and strategists have stated to be impossible) in order to achieve an end— the blocking of each others' missiles—which could be achieved tomorrow, at no cost at all, by a rational agreement by both to disarm.

When a palpable insanity grips national leaders it is necessary to probe the matter a little further. Nations do not normally lay heavy burdens on their tax-payers and inflate the national debt just to humour the fantasies of a leader— even one just born-again by ballot. We may suppose some hidden agenda or some ideological delirium here. In this case I detect both. The hidden agenda is supplied, of course, by the 'alchemists of the laboratories' and the very powerful arms manufacturing lobby, whose lips are drooling with the prospects of full order-books twenty and thirty years ahead. But even this powerful lobby, which is not yet a majority shareholder in the United States economy, could not trick the state and the public into a manifest insanity if there was not some even more powerful ulterior political drive.

Star Wars is the ultimate decomposition of deterrence theory, and the attempt by United States nuclear ideologists to return to the womb of Hiroshima. Ever since the Soviet Union reached forward to nuclear 'parity' they have become increasingly fretful. They possessed this huge bludgeoning and blackmailing power—which, however, could never be used, and, even worse, the world was beginning to tumble to this fact.* For a decade they have been trying out this

---

* See Alan Wolfe's wise comments, 'American Democracy and Nuclear Weapons', *World Policy Journal*, Fall 1984.

and that trick to regain nuclear 'superiority', but all were implausible. Then they tried scenarios of 'limited' nuclear war, on the territory of allies and other nations, but these have proved implausible also. Delving back in their memories, President Reagan and his friends recalled those blissful five years, from 1945-50, when the United States had the Bomb and the Other did not. It is out of that frustration, and that delirium of ideology, that Star Wars was born. Let us abolish the Other's Bomb! Let us arm the moral ends of America with an impermeable shield! Let us once again be able to threaten a world which cannot threaten us! Once the solution was found (out of pure ideology) then money and know-how *must* be able to bring it about.

It is an ideological delirium which vibrates all the chords of the worst traditions of American right-wing populism. With astonishing simplicity it combines isolationism (they can't get us) with external menace. It combines the citizen's faith that whatever America does must be moral—and that the Bomb is God's gift to protect the 'Free World'—with the old American preference for 'fixing things' by technological means rather than by political resolutions. It massages the American ego by intoning homilies about 'saving humanity', while drawing humanity within new dimensions of danger.

We should not dismiss this as mere politician-talk, as cynical rhetoric to cover more limited objectives. Star Wars, with its space-fic glitter, encodes ideological forces which act in their own right. The President may himself be a true believer.

To find the most powerful nation on the earth to be crawling back into an ideological womb is a sign that the whole era of deterrence theory has at length come to an end. But it is a terrifying signal of our human predicament. This combination of material avarice (the arms lobby) and of ideological self-delusion is the apt terminus to my essay on 'Exterminism', written five years ago.

It is because the minds of our rulers are unhinged, and chaos has moved closer to us so that it chills the future's breath, that I affirm once again the imperative of refusal. The much-abused 'unilateralists', the campers at Greenham or Comiso, the demonstrators at the Livermore Laboratories, the harassed Moscow Trust Group, the 'Swords into Plough-share' youth—they may not have got every argument right, but they affirm the one essential argument upon which our survival depends. There can be no technological shield against nuclear evil. There is—and there has been for forty years—only one shield against chaos: that pitifully weak and yet somehow indestructable shield, the human conscience. In the past five years that shield has become international. It is the peace movement.   I salute its work.

ABOUT THE AUTHOR

Edward Palmer Thompson was born in England, served in Africa and Italy during the war, and returned to England to graduate from Cambridge University. In 1957, he helped found the magazine *The New Reasoner;* he later served on the editorial board of *The New Left Review.* Since 1972 he has been working full-time at writing, with some spells of teaching in the United States (at Pittsburgh, Rutgers, and Brown universities) and in India.

In early 1980, E.P. Thompson drafted the Appeal for European Nuclear Disarmament, which, after much revision, was signed by many thousands of Europeans and became one of the platforms of the new peace movements. In Britain, he works actively with the Campaign for Nuclear Disarmament (CND) and with the Committee for European Nuclear Disarmamemt (END). He has been a guest speaker to the peace movements in Finland, Denmark, Norway, West Germany, Belgium, France, Ireland, and Iceland. While acting as visiting professors at Brown University, Thompson and his wife, Dorothy, were welcomed at peace-movement rallies in several parts of the United States.

E.P. Thompson is also the author of *Beyond the Cold War, The Making of the English Working Class, Whigs and Hunters,* and *William Morris,* and a coauthor of *Albion's Fatal Tree.* He is author of the historic pamphlet and a coeditor of the book *Protest and Survive.*